D0830896

1 9 2600260 5

FIVE DAYS THAT SHOCKED THE WORLD

OSPREY
PUBLISHING

FIVE DAYS THAT SHOCKED THE WORLD

Eyewitness Accounts from Europe
at the End of World War II

NICHOLAS BEST

First published in Great Britain in 2012 by Osprey Publishing,
Midland House, West Way, Botley, Oxford, OX2 0PH, UK
44-02 23rd Street, Suite 219, Long Island City, NY 11101, USA
E-mail: info@ospreypublishing.com

OSPREY PUBLISHING IS PART OF THE OSPREY GROUP

This title is published in the United States as *Five Days that Shocked the World* (St Martins Press)

A CIP catalogue record for this book is available from the British Library

ISBN: 978 1 84908 946 3

Page layout by: bounford.com, Cambridge, UK
Index by Sharon Redmayne
Typeset in Bembo
Originated by United Graphics Pte., Singapore
Printed in China through Worldprint Ltd.

12 13 14 15 16   10 9 8 7 6 5 4 3 2 1

Osprey Publishing is supporting the Woodland Trust, the UK's leading woodland conservation charity, by funding the dedication of trees.

www.ospreypublishing.com

Front Cover: Top: The Red Army storms the Reichstag, 30 April 1945. (akg-images); Bottom: Berlin lies in ruins as civilians try to return to normality. (Corbis)

CONTENTS

PART FOUR: TUESDAY, 1 MAY

PART FIVE: WEDNESDAY, 2 MAY

PART SIX

INTRODUCTION

Few episodes in history can have shocked the world more than the five days at the end of April 1945 that began with the murder of Mussolini and ended with the news that Hitler had killed himself at his bunker in Berlin. The departure of both dictators had long been expected, but the manner of their going was no less awful for that: Mussolini and his mistress dangling upside down in front of a jeering mob, Hitler's body reduced to a Wagnerian pile of ashes while Magda Göbbels poisoned her children and demented staff at the Chancellery enjoyed group sex before going to their own deaths. Not even the most operatic of novelists could have made it up.

Equally horrifying were the atrocities being committed by the Russians at the same time as they stormed across Germany. The atrocities were at their worst in Berlin, where mass rape on an unprecedented scale was taking place as the Russians surrounded the capital. That their own menfolk had behaved just as badly in Russia was no consolation to the women of all ages who fled in terror, often committing suicide to avoid gang-rape by troops from the Soviet republics with little experience of such Western niceties as electricity or indoor plumbing.

Horrifying too were the revelations from the concentration camps that were beginning to emerge as Hitler and Mussolini died. Dachau was captured by the Americans on the same day as the Duce was strung up in Milan. Ravensbrück fell a day later, just as Hitler was taking his own life. The first photographs from Belsen and Buchenwald had been released that week and were being shown to an incredulous public. Most were too awful to be published in newspapers. They were exhibited in towns and cities instead, so that people across the free world could see the evidence with their own eyes and understand exactly what had been going on in Nazi Germany.

They had all read the newspapers and heard the rumours about the camps, but they didn't necessarily believe them. Radio reporter Richard Dimbleby, a man of unimpeachable integrity, had great difficulty persuading a dubious BBC to broadcast his first eyewitness report from Belsen. Others too had been disbelieved as they spelled out what they had seen. During World War One, it had been widely rumoured that the Germans on the Western Front were melting down human bodies for fat. The rumours had later turned out to be false, almost certainly the work of British propaganda. Now the rumours had surfaced again, with additional tales of mass gassings, living skeletons, shrunken heads and lampshades made of tattooed skin. Small wonder that people were sceptical.

Indeed, the London cinema showing the first film from the camps was picketed that week by an angry crowd, outraged that their own government was lying to them again. Their anger was shared by millions of Germans, well aware that bad things had happened in the camps, yet convinced that the atrocities had been grossly exaggerated by Allied propaganda in order to justify the war.

But the photographs didn't lie. 'SEEING IS BELIEVING' was the title of the exhibition sponsored by the *Daily Express* in London that week. People queued in their thousands to see the Buchenwald pictures and came away speechless. Later, they saw the Belsen film in the cinema: skeletons bulldozed into burial pits and German civilians standing beside the SS at the graveside, all of them filmed in one take so that there could be no accusations of trick photography. The photos didn't lie. There were too many of them, from too many different places, supported by too many eyewitness accounts for the stories to be false. It simply wasn't possible.

Yet is there any need for another book on an already well-documented week, no matter how shocking it was? The answer has to be yes if the material is new or intriguingly unfamiliar. Everyone knows, for instance, that Hitler was in Berlin when he died, but how many know that his sister was at Berchtesgaden, living anonymously as Frau Wolff and keeping her own counsel as the other guests in her boarding house discussed her brother's death? Or that Leni Riefenstahl, Hitler's favourite film director, was in an Austrian ski resort, unable to find a bed for the night when people learned who she was? Or that the future Pope Benedict had deserted from the Wehrmacht and was walking home, terrified that he might still be shot or hanged from a tree for dereliction of duty?

Audrey Hepburn was in Holland, delighted to avoid conscription into a Wehrmacht brothel, but so malnourished that her ambition to become a ballet dancer was looking increasingly unrealistic. Eleven-year-old Roman

Polanski was living virtually feral on the streets of Krakow. Bob Dole, badly wounded by a German shell, was lying paralysed in an Italian hospital, listening to the cheers for the end of the war in Italy and wondering if he would ever be able to move his toes again. All sorts of people, some famous at the time, others to become famous later, remembered exactly where they were and what they were doing as the events of those extraordinary five days unfolded around them.

I have told their stories in their own words wherever possible, concentrating on well known or interesting people not normally associated with the events being described. I have covered all the core events of that week as Hitler killed himself and the Nazis scattered, but I have also wondered where Marlene Dietrich was at the time, and Günter Grass, Henry Kissinger, Jack Kennedy and a host of others. I hope it makes for an interesting mix, an unusual picture of Europe at the end of one of the most painful few weeks in its history.

A word of warning. The definitive truth has not always been easy to discover. Quite a few eyewitnesses, particularly in Hitler's bunker, changed their stories in later years and gave differing and often contradictory accounts of the same events. Others kept silent for decades and then had trouble remembering dates and facts correctly. I have always envied authors who feel able to state with certainty that a particular eyewitness was either wrong or lying. For myself, I prefer to report what the witnesses said, putting it in context where necessary, and then leave it to readers to make up their own minds. But I can say with certainty that what follows, or something very like it, definitely happened!

—

Warm thanks to Senator Bob Dole and Lord Carrington for their contributions to the book. Also to Peter Devitt, assistant curator of the RAF museum at Hendon, who helped me find out more about Operation *Manna*, Katharine Thomson of the Churchill Archives Centre at Churchill College, Cambridge, and Alec Holmes, whose surgical knowledge enabled me to make sense of Mussolini's autopsy. Thanks too to Andrew Lownie, my agent, and Kate Moore and Emily Holmes at Osprey Publishing.

And finally, an apology to President Jimmy Carter for my failure to find an appropriate context for his generous contribution. For the record, he says he was at sea with the US Navy when Hitler died, wishing he could be in Times Square in time to join the celebrations when the war ended. To my great regret, I couldn't find a suitable place to mention it in the book.

PART ONE:
SATURDAY, 28 APRIL

'Our uniforms are grey and so are our forebodings about a future that gives us not a glimmer of hope. I just want to sleep, sleep and suddenly wake up to discover that it was all nothing but a bad dream...'

Helmut Altner

CHAPTER 1: THE DEATH OF MUSSOLINI

Time was running out for Mussolini. Fleeing the Allied advance near Lake Como, he had been captured by Italian partisans on the afternoon of 27 April 1945 and taken to a safe house in the mountains where even his few remaining friends couldn't find him. He and his mistress Clara Petacci had arrived at Azzano in the early hours of 28 April and had spent the rest of the night under guard in a peasant's house high above the village. They had been watched over by two young partisans who had stayed awake all night outside their door. One of the young men, spying on Clara as she washed in the outhouse before bed, had reported back to the other that Mussolini's girlfriend had magnificent breasts. He could quite understand why the Duce kept her for his mistress.

Now it was morning again, late morning, and Mussolini had just woken from a deep sleep. Clara had cried during the night, her mascara staining the pillow, but Mussolini had slept very heavily. His eyes were bloodshot when he awoke, his face pale and grey beneath the stubble. It was obvious to his captors that Italy's former dictator was in the depths of despair as he braced himself for whatever the new day would bring.

He ate little for breakfast, toying with a plate of bread and salami in the bedroom while the partisans stood guard over him. He asked them if the Americans had taken Como during the night, nodding resignedly when they said they had. Afterwards, Clara went back to bed, pulling up the covers and trying to catch up on her sleep while Mussolini sat on the edge of the mattress looking out of the window towards the snow-covered mountains across the lake.

He was still there when the executioners came for him at four that afternoon. They came upstairs in a hurry, led by a tall man in a fawn raincoat who called himself Colonel Valerio. In reality, the man was Walter Audisio, a Communist veteran of the Spanish Civil War who had remained a committed anti-Fascist ever since.

Audisio was carrying a sten gun as he burst into the room.

'Quick!' he told Mussolini. 'I've come to rescue you.'

'Really?' Mussolini didn't conceal his scepticism. 'How very kind of you.'

'Are you armed?'

Mussolini had stolen a knife from the kitchen the night before and hidden it in the bed. But he assured Audisio he wasn't armed.

Audisio turned to Clara. She was still in bed, her face against the wall. 'You too,' he told her. 'Come on. Get up.'

Mussolini put his coat on while Clara rummaged frantically among the bedclothes.

'What are you looking for?' Audisio demanded.

'My knickers.'

'Don't worry about them. Just get a move on.'[1]

Clara was forced to leave her handbag behind as well as her underwear. She clattered reluctantly down the stairs and was escorted out of the house while her lover trailed along in the rear. Lia De Maria, whose house it was, watched from a side window and crossed herself nervously as they disappeared. She liked what little she had seen of Clara. She hoped nothing unpleasant was about to happen to her.

They stumbled down the mountain path, Clara in her high heels clinging desperately to Mussolini, who had no strength left to support her. He almost fell at one point, steadying himself against a wall. Clara tried to help him, but was pushed roughly away. Mussolini had nothing to say to her as they continued past a trio of women washing clothes in a stone trough and made their way towards the main road. They were spotted by an old man coming down the hill with a bale of hay on his back and by a woman strolling with a child. Nobody recognised Mussolini, although they all wondered why the smartly dressed woman with him was crying.

A car was waiting for them on the road, a black Fiat saloon with a Rome number plate. Rosita Barbarita was walking her dogs nearby as the party appeared. Audisio waved his gun and told her to go away. Rosita did so, hastily beating a retreat as Mussolini and his mistress were shoved into the back of the Fiat.

Audisio found a seat on the mudguard as the car started off. His companions stood on the running boards with their weapons at the ready.

The two young partisans who had guarded Mussolini during the night followed at a brisk trot, hurrying along behind the car as it headed along the mountain road towards the little village of Mezzegra and the lake beyond.

It hadn't gone more than a few hundred yards when it stopped again at a bend in the road out of sight from either direction. The driver pulled up at the gates of the Villa Belmonte. Mussolini and Clara were ordered out and told to stand against the wall. Clara threw her arms around her lover and stared in disbelief as Audisio mumbled a few words about a sentence of death and justice for the Italian people.

'You can't do that!' Clara protested. 'You can't shoot Mussolini!'

'Get away from him!' Audisio replied. 'Get away or you'll die too!'

But Clara Petacci wasn't listening. She refused to let go of Mussolini. She was still clinging to him, still protesting, when Audisio pulled the trigger.

——

While Mussolini went to his death, his wife Rachele was in hiding a few miles away, at the southern end of the lake. With nowhere else to go, she and their two youngest children had been taken to Cernobbio, just outside Como, where a friendly Blackshirt had given them shelter in his own home. The house wasn't safe, but it was better than being on the streets, where Fascists and anyone else associated with Mussolini were being hunted down and killed without compunction.

Rachele Mussolini was in despair as she listened to the gunfire all around. The imminent arrival of the American Army had been the signal for a mass uprising against the remaining Fascists in the north of Italy. Mussolini himself had fled a few days earlier, with a vague idea of making a last stand in the Alps, only to find his supporters melting away as the Americans advanced. In panic, he had written to his wife, telling her to save herself and the children, and had joined a column of German soldiers heading back to Germany. He might have got away with it if an Italian partisan hadn't recognised his face under a German helmet. Instead, he had been arrested and taken to the mountains to await his fate.

His letter to Rachele had been written when he was still contemplating a last stand in the Alps:

Dear Rachele,

Here I am at the last stage of my life, the last page of my book. We two may never meet again, and that is why I am writing and sending you this letter. I ask your forgiveness for all the harm I have unwittingly done you. But you know that you are the only woman I have ever really loved. I swear it before God, I swear it before our Bruno, in this supreme moment. You know that we must make for the Valtellina. Take the children with you and try to get to the Swiss frontier. There you can build up a new life. I do not think they will refuse to let you in, for I have always been helpful to them and you have had nothing to do with politics. If they do refuse, surrender to the Allies who may be more generous than the Italians. Take care of Anna and Romano, especially Anna who needs it so badly. You know how I love them. Bruno in heaven will help you.

My dearest love to you and the children.

Your Benito.'[2]

Taking Mussolini at his word, Rachele had left for Switzerland in the middle of the night with fifteen-year-old Anna Maria and seventeen-year-old Romano in tow. The border was only three miles from Como, easily identified by the bright lights twinkling peacefully beyond Italy's blackout. They had joined a queue of cars at the frontier, where an Italian officer sent by Mussolini was waiting to help them across. They had been within five yards of safety when the Swiss border guards, after a study of their papers and some discreet telephoning, had shaken their heads regretfully and told them they would not be allowed in. It was 'absolutely impossible' for the Mussolinis to enter Switzerland.

Rachele had been disappointed but not downhearted as they turned away from the frontier. In fact, she had felt rather relieved at the thought of not having to leave Italy. They had driven back to Como in the dark, along a road clogged with Germans and Italians fleeing in every direction. Anti-Fascist partisans were already streaming back from Switzerland and pouring down from the mountains to seize control of the country. There had been outbreaks of shooting from time to time, although Como itself had been quiet when they returned.

They had driven straight to the Fascist headquarters, only to discover that no one there had any idea what to do with them. Seeing that they were wasting their time, Rachele and her children had left again, Anna Maria sitting disconsolately on the steps outside as they wondered where to go and what to do next. It wasn't until dawn that help had arrived in the form of a Mussolini supporter who had taken pity on them, as Rachele gratefully recalled:

One of our faithful Blackshirts insisted that it was too dangerous to hang about in the streets. We held a conference and he advised us to take refuge in a house some way away, where he lived. We made for it. Our arrival caused something of an upheaval in the small, poorly furnished cottage. They had no food to spare, and I ended up making breakfast for everyone with what remained of the provisions I had brought with me.

The Blackshirts went off to find news of the Duce and when they came back said they were going to take us to join the column in which my husband was travelling. They also told me that our car had been stolen.

The sound of shooting came nearer. We looked down the road through the tiny window and witnessed scenes of panic. Our hosts were terrified and I spent all my time encouraging them. Helping others made my own distress more bearable. A young boy, recognised to be a Fascist, was murdered before our eyes. A single denunciation was enough for immediate execution. Every now and then we listened to the radio broadcasting orders to hunt the Fascists down without mercy. From a nearby hospital badly wounded soldiers, wearing whatever they could find, came flying out to scatter all over the town. The whole world seemed to have turned into a living hell. The children were panic-stricken.[3]

In the circumstances, it had proved impossible for Rachele and her children to rejoin Mussolini. And now it was too late, although they didn't know it yet. They had been hiding in the Blackshirt's house for the past two days, too scared to show their faces outside while civil war raged all around. Rachele knew, though, that they would have to leave soon because they were putting the Blackshirt in grave danger by staying. He and his whole family might be dragged out and shot if they were caught with the Mussolinis under their roof. The decent thing to do was to hide somewhere else until the killing had stopped. But where? With chaos in the streets and everybody against them, Rachele Mussolini was uncomfortably aware that she and her children had nowhere else to go.

———

The execution of Mussolini did not go as planned. The sten gun jammed when Audisio fired. Cursing, he grabbed his revolver, only for that to jam as well. Seeing what was about to happen, Mussolini threw open his coat, according to one eyewitness, and faced Audisio squarely, defying him to do his worst. 'Shoot me in the chest,' he said.

One of Audisio's men hurriedly gave him his own weapon. This time there was no mistake. Clara Petacci was hit first and died at once. Mussolini fell back against the wall next to her and slid to the ground, still alive. Walking over, Audisio shot him again at close range. Mussolini jerked convulsively and then lay still, his body just touching Clara's by the wall. Everyone else watched in horror, aghast at what they had just seen. It had happened so fast that they all remembered it differently when they talked about it afterwards.

Audisio needed a cigarette when it was all over. The driver had one too, although he didn't smoke. No one said anything as they stooped to pick up the spent cartridge cases. Behind the wall, the people at the villa had heard the gun shots but were waiting a while before coming to investigate. They didn't want to get mixed up in anything that didn't concern them.

The time was still only a quarter past four. The rain that had been threatening all afternoon was beginning to fall as the partisans finished their cigarettes. Leaving the two young men to guard the bodies in the drizzle, Audisio and the others got back in the car and set off for the town of Dongo, where they carried out a number of further executions, among them several of Mussolini's ministers and Clara Petacci's brother. Then they returned to the Villa Belmonte.

Clara and Mussolini were taken down to the main road and thrown into a removal van, on top of the other bodies. The van was then driven through the darkness to Milan. The plan was to put the bodies on display in the Piazzale Loreto the next day, where fifteen hostages had been shot by Fascists the previous August. It would be justice, of a sort, now that the war was coming to an end. Audisio's only serious worry, as the van set off, was that American patrols might intercept them on the way and prevent them from reaching their destination.

CHAPTER 2:
IN BERLIN

While Mussolini met his end, Adolf Hitler sat shaking in Berlin, so debilitated in mind and body that he could barely understand what was happening as the ceiling reverberated above his head. The bunker at the Chancellery was solidly constructed, concrete piled on concrete to withstand the heaviest bombardment, but Berlin is built on sand and the walls rattled whenever a Russian shell came close, dislodging lumps of plaster that fell in dusty showers all over the floor. The shelling had begun several days before and was drawing nearer all the time as the Russian Army closed in. It was obvious to everyone in the bunker, even Adolf Hitler, that it would only be another day or two at most before the Russians were knocking on the door.

Hitler had a map in front of him as the shelling continued, an ordinary civilian map showing the approach roads to the city. He was using it to plot the advance of General Walther Wenck, who had been ordered to relieve Berlin with his troops. Hitler had no idea how far Wenck had got, or how many soldiers he had left, or even where the Russians were any more. But he was going through the motions anyway, constantly arranging and rearranging a set of buttons across the map, moving them here and there with quivering fingers as if disposing his forces in a game of chess. Every now and again he shouted orders as well, barking out commands to no one in particular. In his mind, if nowhere else, Hitler was still winning this war against the Bolsheviks.

The Russian Army had completed the encirclement of Berlin three days before. Its troops could see the Reichstag through their field glasses, the big, domed Parliament building that stood at the very heart of the city. Elsewhere in Germany, the Russians had linked up with the Americans on the Elbe and the British were pushing towards the Danish border, encountering increasingly feeble resistance as they went. In another few days, no matter what happened in Berlin, the war would be over and Germany would be defeated for the second time in a generation.

The defeat had always been inevitable. Hitler's generals had always warned him that it would come to this, right from before the war, when they had examined the British, French and Russian armies in their war games and had concluded that however they fought it, Germany was bound to lose in the end. The economists had agreed, pointing out that Germany's soil was thin, reminding Hitler that the country lacked the mineral resources to fight a sustained campaign. Hitler had accepted their view initially, arguing in *Mein Kampf* that fighting the British was a mistake to be avoided, that a war on two fronts was never a good idea. But he had ignored his own assessment in the summer of 1939 and now the whole country was paying for his folly.

Yet there was still hope, in Hitler's mind at least. He had long since lost confidence in his other generals, but he still had some faith in General Wenck. If anybody could get to Berlin, Wenck could. Once he was there, pushing the Russians back, a corridor could be opened out of the city, a lifeline to the American Army in the West. The Americans were the key now. Hitler had persuaded himself that they would never allow a cultured country like Germany to fall into Bolshevik hands if they could prevent it. The Americans would come to Germany's aid first, if that was what they had to do to keep the Communists out of Europe.

But they couldn't do it without Wenck. His troops were said to be near Potsdam somewhere, still struggling towards the capital. Until they arrived, there was nothing for Hitler to do except sit and wait, obsessively pushing buttons around the map while shells rained down and the bunker continued to reverberate. From time to time he dictated increasingly frantic telegrams to his staff – 'Where is Wenck? What is happening to the Ninth Army? When will Wenck and the Ninth Army join?'[1] – but without receiving any answer. Nobody in the bunker had any real idea of what was happening in Germany any more.

Up above, on the streets of Berlin, the fighting was fast and furious as the Russians advanced towards the city centre. Every available German was struggling to hold them back. The outskirts had already fallen, and most of the suburbs, but the Germans were still clinging to the central area around the Tiergarten and the Brandenburg Gate, stubbornly refusing to capitulate. Hitler had promised them that help was on the way, the tanks and guns of Wenck's army hurrying to save them from the Red menace. The Germans in the centre were hanging on by their fingertips, desperate not to give in before Wenck arrived.

They were fighting like men possessed, even the ones who no longer believed a word Hitler said. They fought because they had no realistic alternative. They knew only too well what would happen if they surrendered to the Russians. The men would be taken for slave labour, transported to the Soviet Union for the rest of their natural lives. The women would be mass-raped, as they already had been wherever the Russians had found them. There was nothing for the Germans in surrender. Even if they did want to give up, their own side wouldn't let them. Fanatics from the SS and the Hitler Youth were hanging men from lamp posts or shooting them on the spot if they showed any sign of wavering. The Germans in Berlin were trapped between a rock and a very hard place.

For Helmut Altner, it was the fear of capture that kept him fighting. Still only seventeen, he did not want to spend the rest of his life in a Soviet prison camp. He had been conscripted at the end of March and given only four days' training before being sent to the front. A girl had offered to hide him as he advanced, but he had been too scared to accept. Instead, he had gone into battle with his comrades, most of whom had long since been killed. Altner was a veteran now, after the hard fighting of the past two weeks.

It seemed an age ago, but was actually only a few days, that he had heard the battalion commander promising his troops victory within twenty four hours. The man had come forward to address them at a position just behind the line:

Hitler has issued an order: 'Hold on another twenty four hours and the great change in the war will come! Reinforcements are rolling forward. Wonder weapons are coming. Guns and tanks are being unloaded in their thousands. Hold on another twenty four hours, comrades! Peace with the British. Peace with the Americans. The guns are silent on the West Front. The Western Army is marching to the support of you brave East Front warriors. Thousands of British and Americans are volunteering to join our ranks to drive out the Bolsheviks. Hundreds of British and American aircraft stand ready to take part in the battle for Europe. Hold on another twenty four hours, my comrades. Churchill is in Berlin negotiating with me.'[2]

It was wishful thinking. Winston Churchill wasn't in Berlin and no one was coming to their rescue. Hitler might not be in Berlin either, for all Altner knew. The only reality for him was the constant shelling from the Russians in the western suburbs, the rattle of machine guns that had begun before dawn that day as the Russians advanced across the Reichssportfeld towards the barracks at Ruhleben. Altner had woken in the dark to the sound of incoming fire and had gone into action at once, grabbing his rifle and a few belts of ammunition and rushing outside to find out what was happening. It had been impossible to say for sure in the dark. The only certainty was that they were being attacked from several different directions at once and that chaos reigned all around.

The Germans had managed to halt the Russians after a while, although not before they had captured the Reichssportfeld. The fighting had died down towards dawn as both sides consolidated their positions. A Russian tank had appeared shortly after first light, filling Altner with dread as it rumbled to a halt in front of his trench. He had failed to spot the white flag it was carrying and thought his last moment had come. Instead, a head had emerged and a Russian with a loud hailer had exhorted the Germans to surrender: 'You will be well treated, and you will be able to go home as soon as hostilities are over. Soldiers, there is no point any more. Do you really want to lose your lives in the last hours of a war already lost?'[3]

Several Germans had taken the Russians at their word, quietly making a break for the enemy lines as soon as they thought no one was looking. Ordered to shoot them down from behind, Altner had fired over their heads instead. He had no quarrel with anyone who wanted to desert. He would have deserted too if he hadn't been so terrified of capture.

Fighting had resumed later as hundreds of Hitler Youths arrived from their homes in a desperate attempt to recapture the sports complex and the Olympic stadium. By mid-afternoon they had succeeded in pushing the Russians back, but only at a dreadful cost in killed and wounded. Altner found himself now with a handful of unfamiliar soldiers, ordered down to the subway station to try to reach the city centre along one of the U-Bahn tunnels and then attack the Russians from the rear. With much of the line already in enemy hands, it seemed like a suicide mission to Altner as he followed the rest of his squad into the tunnel:

> Our uniforms are grey and so are our forebodings about a future that gives us not a glimmer of hope. I just want to sleep, sleep and suddenly wake up to discover that it was all nothing but a bad dream, that there was no war, that there are no ruins, no dead and

ripped apart bodies, but that there is peace and that the sun shines and life pulses without the threat of coming to an end at any moment. But this is only wishful thinking. We are condemned to death and do not know why, nor do we know why we are not allowed to live![4]

———

While Altner disappeared into the gloom, actress Hildegard Knef and her lover were a couple of miles south, on their way to fight the Russians at Schmargendorf. Film producer Ewald von Demandowsky had been called up into the Volkssturm – the German home guard – and sent straight into the front line. Hildegard had insisted on accompanying him, rather than stay behind on her own. Just nineteen, ravishingly pretty, she had no illusions about what would happen if the Russians got hold of her. She preferred to remain with her boyfriend and take her chances in the fighting.

She had tried to disguise herself as a man for the purpose, but despite her deep voice had been rapidly unmasked when they reported for duty. Nevertheless, she had been given a helmet, a machine gun and a handful of grenades and shown how to use them. She had acquired a jackknife as well and tucked it into her boot, reminding herself to cut upwards if she ever had to use it, upwards from the wrist rather than across.

Now she was on her way to Schmargendorf's freight yard with Demandowsky and a few others. There were ten of them in all, a ragbag assortment of Russia veterans, Hitler Youth, SS and old men spaced at twenty-yard intervals as they made their way across the rubble. They were crawling some of the way, running and jumping the rest to avoid becoming a target. They managed to reach the freight yard unharmed, but were spotted by Russian snipers when they tried to cross. Hopping over the rails like a kangaroo, Hildegard sprinted for an abandoned train and dived underneath a freight car as the snipers opened up. She made it in time, but one of the Hitler Youths with her wasn't so lucky. Hildegard could still hear the sound of him calling for his mother as he died.

The German front line lay across the yard, a row of foxholes hastily dug beside the tennis courts. Hildegard and Demandowsky found shelter in a garden shed, next to a lieutenant who was surveying the tennis courts through his field glasses. He had camouflaged his helmet and shoulders with foliage, looking to Hildegard as if he was about to go on stage in *A Midsummer Night's Dream*.

There was a dead SS man outside. Hildegard and Demandowsky were trying to move his body when the Russians launched an attack:

> Orrraaaay! It's coming from behind us, behind the tennis courts. The lieutenant looks up. They screech like monkeys, he says, when they attack they always screech like monkeys. He raises his fist and slams it down in the mud, twenty machine guns start rattling and chattering, we pull ours up and stick an ammunition belt into it. It starts heaving and bucking, wants to go it alone, resents our meddling, starts throwing itself from side to side, gets hot, jams, dies. EvD picks it up, crawls out and runs for the shed. The houses behind us are on fire.[5]

The Russians were beaten off and did not attack again before dark. Hildegard was grateful for the respite, if only because it gave her the chance to have a pee at last. She volunteered for the first turn on guard duty that night, occupying a foxhole all to herself while Demandowsky got some rest in the shed. Early evening was the best time to be on guard, because the Russians rarely attacked in the early evening. That was their time for getting drunk and raping women, as Hildegard soon discovered:

> I stand there in my hole, in the water, keep a firm hold on the machine gun and the pistol, peer through the glasses over the yard, see shadows, chew the rest of the cheese, hear something crack and rustle, hear screams, dreadful heartrending screams, high thin shrill. I call out softly to the next hole: 'Are you there?'
> 'Yes.'
> 'What's that screaming?'
> Russians are in that house over there started on the women shitshitohshitohshit.[6]

Hildegard was terrified, acutely aware of the horrors the Russian Army inflicted upon helpless women. She had heard it first-hand from East Prussian refugees at Dahlem. The Russians had raped the women of East Prussia repeatedly before beating their brains out. One woman had told Hildegard that her sister's breasts had been cut off and her husband crucified against a door. Crouching miserably in her foxhole as the screaming continued, with a gun in one hand and her knife in the other, Hildegard Knef was determined that nothing of the sort would ever happen to her if she could avoid it.

CHAPTER 3: HIMMLER SUES FOR PEACE

While the fighting raged in Berlin, Heinrich Himmler was on his way to Lübeck, returning to his Baltic headquarters after a Wehrmacht conference at Neuroofen. With so many refugees on the road, the journey was taking him most of the day, although normally it would only have been a couple of hours.

Himmler was not a happy man as he drove. With Berlin about to fall and the German Army in full retreat, he was uncomfortably aware that a day of reckoning was fast approaching for the Nazi leadership, a calling to account for all the atrocities committed over the past five years. As head of the SS, he knew the Allies would show no mercy when they caught up with him. His only real chance of survival was to have something to offer them in return for his own life, a bargaining chip to get him off the hook.

Himmler had been careful not to mention it at the conference, but he had made a clandestine approach to the Americans on 23 April, requesting peace negotiations through the good offices of Sweden's Count Folke Bernadotte. At Bernadotte's suggestion, he had written a letter offering to surrender all German forces in the West to the Anglo-Americans, but without saying anything about the troops still fighting the Russians in the East. Bernadotte had undertaken to deliver the letter in secret to the Western Allies, with the caveat that in his view they would be very unlikely to consider any German surrender that did not include the Russians as well.

The Allies' reply was waiting for Himmler when he got back to Lübeck. It was not what he had been hoping for. As Bernadotte had anticipated, the British and Americans were not prepared to contemplate a separate peace without the Soviet Union:

A German offer of surrender will only be accepted on condition that it is complete on all fronts as regards Great Britain, the Soviet Union as well as USA. When these conditions have been fulfilled, the German forces must immediately on all fronts lay down their arms to the local Allied commanders. Should resistance continue anywhere, the Allied attacks will be ruthlessly carried on until complete victory has been gained.[1]

That was not all. Himmler was appalled to hear that the Allies had released the details of his approach to the press. He had made the approach in strictest confidence, without Hitler's knowledge, intending to negotiate a surrender package behind the Führer's back that would ensure his own survival unpunished, perhaps even as head of a post-war German government. But the Allies had betrayed him. They had deliberately leaked the story to the newspapers that morning and it had been picked up by foreign radio. Himmler's treachery would be all over Germany by the next day.

As if on cue, there was a phone call for him soon after he got back to Lübeck. It was from Grand Admiral Dönitz, who had heard the news from Wehrmacht headquarters and wanted to know if it was true. Himmler hastily assured him it wasn't. He assured the Wehrmacht as well, ringing army headquarters of his own accord to deny the radio reports and insist that he had had no contact with the Allies. Then he sent for SS Brigadeführer Walter Schellenberg, his go-between in the negotiations with Count Bernadotte in Denmark. He wanted to hear from Schellenberg why the negotiations had failed, and why his name was all over the news when Schellenberg had been under strict instructions to conduct the whole business in secret.

Schellenberg went to meet Himmler with deep reluctance. He was under no illusions about the summons. Himmler had a bad habit of blaming others for his own miscalculations and leaving them to face the consequences. As he drove to Lübeck late that afternoon, it seemed distinctly possible to Schellenberg that he might be taken out and shot as soon as he had made his report to Himmler.

Schellenberg had been hoping that Count Bernadotte would accompany him to the meeting for moral support, but Lübeck was now too close to the front line for that. Instead, rather than face Himmler alone, Schellenberg telephoned ahead and arranged for someone else to go with him. 'I realised that my position with Himmler would now be so difficult that I should have to face the fact that I might be liquidated. I therefore arranged for an astrologer from Hamburg to accompany me. Himmler knew this man personally and thought very highly of him. He could never resist having his horoscope read, and I felt this would soften his reaction to the disappointment.'[2]

The astrologer was Wilhelm Wulff, a self-appointed seer who by his own account had been one of hundreds of German astrologers arrested after Rudolph Hess's flight to Scotland in 1941, interrogated by the Gestapo as they sought an explanation for Hess's behaviour. Wulff had been released after a while but remained under observation, threatened with severe punishment if his horoscopes proved to be inaccurate. He was almost as nervous as Schellenberg as an SS car collected him from Hamburg and drove him to Lübeck, where he was to meet Schellenberg before reporting to Himmler later that evening.

'Make sure that Himmler sends me to Stockholm,' were Schellenberg's first words when they met.[3] Wulff asked to be left alone for an hour while he consulted his charts and prepared some horoscopes. Then the two of them set off for the police barracks in the suburbs that housed Himmler's headquarters.

It was getting on for midnight by the time they arrived. They were taken down a dimly lit corridor and shown into a room containing beds, a table and wooden benches around the walls. They sat down to wait, but Himmler did not appear. Midnight came and went, heralded by an air raid siren sounding the all clear, but there was still no sign of the SS leader. Schellenberg and Wulff were evidently in for a long night. Settling down on one of the benches along the wall, they ran once more through the points they were going to raise with Himmler when he arrived, and then resigned themselves to a lengthy wait.

—

While Schellenberg went to meet Himmler, Count Bernadotte had remained in Denmark, horrified to learn from the radio that his discussions with the Allies had gone public. He was staying with a Danish official when he heard his own name on the news, followed by an announcement that he had been conducting negotiations with Himmler for a German surrender.

Bernadotte's first reaction was one of despair. As a cousin of the King of Sweden, his main object in agreeing to act as a go-between was to ensure a peaceful German withdrawal from Norway and Denmark, one that left his fellow Scandinavians unscathed as the Wehrmacht pulled out. He had negotiated mainly with Schellenberg, but he had seen Himmler too, meeting him secretly at the Swedish consulate in Lübeck on 23 April. They had had a long talk by candlelight in the aftermath of an air raid. Himmler had admitted that Germany was beaten and had told Bernadotte that if Hitler was not already dead, he soon would be. He had asked Bernadotte to approach the Anglo-Americans about a possible surrender, adding privately that if his overtures were rejected he himself would go to the Russian front and seek an honourable death in battle.

Himmler had spoken in strictest confidence, as had Bernadotte when he relayed Himmler's message to the British and American ambassadors in Stockholm. It was frustrating, therefore, to hear their names on the radio and know that they had been exposed. But was it a disaster? Bernadotte certainly thought so at first. 'My initial reaction was that this had spoilt everything, and that there was no further possibility of negotiations.'[4] Thinking it over, however, he wasn't so sure. It certainly meant that Himmler was out of the picture, but was that really so bad, when the Allies were refusing to deal with him anyway?

It might actually be good, if Hitler was forced to appoint someone else to succeed him instead, as he would surely have to. Whoever Hitler appointed would not be as distasteful to the Allies. Either way, Bernadotte's main concern was still to ensure a peaceful capitulation of the German forces in Norway and Denmark. He had told Schellenberg so that morning, before the SS man set off back to Lübeck to explain himself to Himmler.

—

Himmler, Schellenberg and Bernadotte all assumed that they had been deliberately let down by the Allies, who had leaked the news of their negotiations to the press. In fact, the Allies had done nothing of the kind – not officially, anyway. The decision to leak the story had been taken by a lowly British official at the United Nations conference in San Francisco. He had acted on his own initiative, without telling anyone else what he was doing.

Jack Winocour, a press officer for the British delegation, had first learned of Himmler's approach on 27 April, when Anthony Eden, Britain's Foreign Secretary, had mentioned it casually at a briefing. Winocour had assumed that the story was being released to the newspapers, but had seen no mention of it anywhere. As the afternoon of the 27th wore on, and the wire services still hadn't run the story, he had wondered if it was being deliberately kept secret, and if so, why?

It was Himmler who still controlled the ghastly administrative apparatus of the Nazi state. It was he who would surely be Hitler's heir, and who would attempt to perpetuate the legend. Surely Hitler now knew of Himmler's treachery? Or if he did not know why had we not begun to tell the world with every means at our command that Hitler's comrade-in-arms had betrayed him?

There had been a long silence throughout the day. I had earlier been convinced that Eden was merely announcing to us what must soon be a matter of common knowledge in the nerve centres of war in Washington and London. The Foreign Secretary would not have taken thirty people into his confidence on a matter of this kind, if it was intended that secrecy should be maintained.[5]

But the silence had continued into the evening. Winocour was preparing for bed when Paul Scott Rankine of Reuters news agency rang after midnight to ask if he had anything for the afternoon papers in Europe. Winocour hesitated for only a moment. Speaking strictly off the record, he gave Rankine the story. Half an hour later, every paper in Europe was remaking its front page and the BBC was broadcasting the news of Himmler's treachery across the world.

Winocour woke later that morning to find the San Francisco correspondents in an uproar as they hurried to find out more. At the ten am briefing at the Palace Hotel, it was reported that Himmler had said that Hitler had suffered a brain haemorrhage and only had a few more hours to live. For mischief, Winocour added quite untruthfully that Himmler had offered to deliver Hitler's body to the Allies as proof of his good intentions. Winocour knew he wasn't telling the truth, but he knew too that Hitler would be outraged if the story reached him. The power of black propaganda was not to be underestimated in war.

By late afternoon on the 28th the story had spun completely out of control. Assured that it was about to happen, the Associated Press took a gamble and put out a news flash announcing Germany's unconditional surrender. There was no truth in the rumour, but the UN meeting in San Francisco's opera house almost broke up in disarray as the delegates flooded outside to learn more, leaving Russia's Foreign Minister Vyacheslav Molotov vainly trying to restore order with his gavel. President Harry Truman was consulted in Washington, but could shed no light on the matter. He knew about Himmler's approach to the Allies, because he had discussed it with Winston Churchill on the transatlantic telephone, but he had heard nothing of surrender. Truman got Admiral William Leahy to telephone General Eisenhower in Europe to ask if it was true. Eisenhower's people in turn rang

Churchill's in the middle of the night, but no one had heard anything. If the Germans had surrendered, it was news to anyone in Europe.

Accordingly, Truman decided to scotch the rumour. Just after half past nine that evening, he summoned the White House correspondents to the Oval Office. Refusing point blank to discuss Himmler's approach, he confined himself instead to a short statement about the so-called surrender. 'I just got in touch with Admiral Leahy and had him call our headquarters' commander-in-chief in Europe,' he told the correspondents. 'There is no foundation for the rumour. That is all I have to say.'[6]

—

In Berlin, Adolf Hitler learned of Himmler's treachery at about nine o'clock that evening. The news was brought to the bunker by Heinz Lorenz, head of the German Information Office, who came hurrying over from the Propaganda Ministry with a radio transcript of the Reuters report, apparently confirming an earlier report by Radio Stockholm. Telephone operator Rochus Misch saw him arrive:

> Hitler was sitting on the bench outside my switchboard room with a puppy in his lap when Lorenz, whom I had heard arrive at a run, handed him the paper on which he had jotted down the radio dispatch. Hitler's face went completely white, almost ashen. 'My God,' I thought, 'he's going to faint.' He slumped forward holding his head with his hands. The puppy plumped to the ground – silly how one remembers such trifles, but I can still hear that soft sound.[7]

By other accounts, Hitler clutched the transcript to his chest and yelled that he had been betrayed again – and by *der treue Heinrich* this time, the only Nazi he could trust, the one leader whose loyalty had never been in question. Heinrich Himmler was the nearest Hitler had in the party to a friend. If Himmler had betrayed him, then nobody could be trusted any more, nobody. Rudolph Hess was mad and Hermann Göring had always been corrupt, but Himmler? Hitler couldn't believe it.

He calmed down after a while, turning deathly white in the process, so pale that he looked like a corpse. What remained of his mind was working overtime, swiftly assessing the implications of Himmler's treachery. Was Himmler planning to assassinate him? Deliver him alive to the enemy? Was there anybody left in the bunker whom he could trust? Or were they all just waiting for a chance to offer him as a hostage in return for their own miserable lives? It was impossible to know.

But at least there was a scapegoat to hand, someone on whom Hitler could take revenge for Himmler's disloyalty. SS Gruppenführer Hermann Fegelein was Himmler's liaison officer in the bunker, a widely disliked opportunist whose wartime career had been devoted solely to his own advancement. Himmler might be beyond Hitler's reach, but Himmler's creature was still in the bunker. Fegelein was in close arrest after being caught trying to desert.

Fegelein was an unpleasant man, a corrupt womaniser who bullied people below him and flattered those above if he thought they might be useful to him. He had been Hitler's unofficial brother–in–law since June 1944, when he had married Eva Braun's sister Margarete. Since then, he had never been afraid to throw his weight around or butt in on senior generals' conversations if it suited him. He had made full use of connections that went right to the top.

But Fegelein's loyalty had always been to himself rather than anyone else. Seeing no future in the bunker, he had slipped away on 26 April, quietly returning to his apartment off the Kurfürstendamm, where he had a suitcase packed with money and jewellery, ready for a quick getaway. Blind drunk, he had rung Eva Braun from his flat, urging her to abandon Hitler and come away with him while she still could. Eva Braun had refused, so Fegelein had planned to escape with a redhead instead. His own wife was already out of Berlin, heavily pregnant with a child that probably wasn't his.

Hitler had noticed Fegelein's absence on 27 April. His staff had telephoned the apartment, ordering Fegelein to return to the Chancellery at once. When Fegelein failed to comply, he had been arrested, still drunk, and brought back under guard. He was being interrogated, prior to an impromptu court martial, when the news of Himmler's treachery arrived.

Enraged, Hitler decided to have Fegelein shot at once, without waiting for a trial. Eva Braun tried to intercede on her brother-in-law's behalf. Red-eyed with weeping, she went to Hitler and begged him on her knees, telling him that her sister was about to give birth, telling him that the child couldn't possibly grow up without a father. But Hitler wouldn't listen. A search of Fegelein's office had revealed documents indicating that he knew about Himmler's contacts with Count Bernadotte. If Hitler couldn't call Himmler to account for his treachery, then he could at least have Fegelein shot instead. Brushing Eva aside, he gave the order without hesitation.

By most accounts, the execution was carried out immediately in the Chancellery garden. Hitler was so angry that he called for the execution report after only a few minutes and exulted like a schoolboy when it came. Even Eva Braun was reportedly forced to concede, through her tears: 'Poor, poor Adolf. They have all deserted you. They have all betrayed you!'

But there was no more time to think about betrayal. Hitler had a busy night ahead. Test pilot Hanna Reitsch was about to leave the bunker, flying the newly promoted Field-Marshal Robert von Greim out of Berlin after his appointment as the commander of a now non-existent Luftwaffe. They were planning to take off in a light aircraft from the road leading to the Brandenburg Gate. Hitler had given them both a cyanide capsule as a leaving present, in case the attempt failed and they were captured by the Russians.

Once Greim had gone, Hitler intended to dictate his last will and testament to Traudl Junge, his young secretary. After that, if there were no more surprises, he was going to get married. With so little time left, he had decided to wed Eva Braun at last, his mistress of many years. The Führer was going to make an honest woman of his most loyal companion, just hours after ordering the execution of her sister's husband.

CHAPTER 4:
NAZIS ON THE RUN

Hitler intended to take his own life when the time came, rather than suffer the humiliation of capture by the Russians. Propaganda Minister Josef Göbbels intended to do the same with his wife and children. The only other Nazi leader in the bunker was Martin Bormann, who had no intention of dying and was planning to make his escape at the earliest opportunity. The rest of the leadership was scattered far and wide across the country. Like Himmler, most were still desperately hoping that they could somehow find a way out of the disaster that they had brought down on their own heads.

Grand Admiral Karl Dönitz had spent much of the day on the road, returning from the same Wehrmacht conference as Himmler to his own headquarters at Plön, near Kiel. Setting off soon after dawn, he had driven 150 miles westwards along roads crowded with refugees and strafed continually by Allied aircraft. Dönitz had watched in despair as the farmers in the fields abandoned their ploughs and ran for cover every time an aircraft appeared. It was obvious to him that the war was lost and could not last more than a few days longer at most.

That being so, Dönitz's primary concern now was to help as many Germans as possible to escape from the East and flee westwards before the Russians arrived. The German Navy was doing its best to help, but Dönitz was bitterly aware that its few remaining vessels were desperately short of fuel and very vulnerable to attack. His job, as he saw it, was to keep the fight going and hold a corridor open until all the refugees had escaped to the West, either by land or sea, where they could safely surrender to the Anglo-Americans rather than the Russians. But he knew that it was a formidable task, with the countryside in chaos and the Wehrmacht visibly disintegrating with every hour that passed.

Dönitz had worked himself into a state of despair by the time he got back to Plön. He called immediately for his son-in-law, Günther Hessler, a U-boat ace who had once sunk fourteen Allied ships on a single patrol. Taking Hessler aside, Dönitz told him in strictest confidence that he had come to a momentous decision. With the war lost and no hope of a negotiated peace, he intended to surrender the German Navy as soon as further resistance became impossible and then seek his own death in battle. He wanted Hessler to know in advance because he would have to take care of Dönitz's wife and daughter after he was gone.

Hessler was shocked. Seeking death in battle was a very German idea, but a very foolish one too, in his opinion. He tried to talk Dönitz out of it, arguing that the country was going to need him in the difficult times that lay ahead, pointing out that a leader of Dönitz's stature would be far more use to his country alive than dead.

But Dönitz refused to listen. Mulling it over on the way back from the Wehrmacht conference, he had decided that he much preferred death to dishonour. In his view, it was far better to fall in battle than live with the shame of surrendering his beloved navy to the enemy. If nothing else, Dönitz would be following his own sons, both of whom had already fallen for the Fatherland at sea.

—

Dönitz's headquarters were at Plön because it was one of the few remaining places in the north of Germany not immediately threatened by British or Russian troops. It was also very close to the Baltic coast, just a short ferry ride to the safety of neutral Sweden. As such, the town was full of high-ranking Nazis who were converging on it in ever-increasing numbers as their enemies advanced, much as men on a sinking ship converge on the highest point because they have nowhere else to go.

Albert Speer, the Minister of Armaments and War Production, had been in Plön since 25 April. He was camping in the woods overlooking Lake Eutin, living in a pair of construction trailers that had been set up for him among the trees. He was protected by troops from a tank regiment who stood guard around the clock while Speer kept a low profile and waited for events to unfold elsewhere.

Speer had been one of the last Nazi leaders to leave Berlin before the Russians completed their encirclement of the city. He had had a long meeting with Hitler on the evening of 23 April, an awkward farewell in the bunker with an abstracted Führer who had treated his once favourite architect with an indifference bordering on contempt. Afterwards, Speer had been summoned to Eva Braun's room to say goodbye to her too. They had sat up until the small hours, two old friends speaking with the candour of people who knew they would never see each other again:

> We were able to talk honestly, for Hitler had withdrawn. She was the only prominent candidate for death in this bunker who displayed an admirable and superior composure. While all the others were abnormal – exaltedly heroic like Göbbels, bent on saving his skin like Bormann, exhausted like Hitler, or in total collapse like Frau Göbbels – Eva Braun radiated an almost gay serenity. 'How about a bottle of champagne for our farewell? And some sweets? I'm sure you haven't eaten in a long time.'[1]

Speer had been touched by Eva Braun's concern. In his view, she had been the only person in the bunker capable of any humanity, complaining to him about all the killing, asking why so many more people had to die unnecessarily. He had been sorry to leave her when the time had come to go.

He had spent a few minutes in the Chancellery before he left, admiring the remnants of the building that he himself had designed. The electricity had gone, so it had been impossible to see much in the dark. Speer had stood in the Court of Honour for a while, trying to picture the splendid architecture above his head. He knew that it lay in ruins, like so much else in Germany. He was worried that there would be very little of the country left, if Hitler in his madness ordered the destruction of the remaining infrastructure before the war's end in order to deny it to the enemy.

Unknown to Hitler, Speer had secretly made a radio recording in Hamburg a few days earlier. The recording urged the German people to ignore any order from Hitler requiring them to destroy everything before surrendering. Speer considered that enough damage had been done to Germany already. Any more would simply increase the German people's misery without achieving anything useful. He had decided that Hitler would have to be overruled if he ordered further destruction as a last act of defiance before killing himself:

> I wanted to issue a call for resistance, to bluntly forbid any damage
> to factories, bridges, waterways, railways and communications,

and to instruct the soldiers of the Wehrmacht and the home guard to prevent demolitions 'with all possible means, using firearms if necessary.' My speech also called for the surrender of political prisoners, including the Jews, unharmed to the occupying troops, and stipulated that prisoners of war and foreign workers should not be prevented from making their way home. It prohibited Werewolf activity and called on villages and cities to surrender without a fight.[2]

The speech had been recorded at Hamburg radio station in conditions of utmost secrecy. Two radio engineers had made a gramophone record of it, worrying Speer with their non-committal expressions as they listened to the treasonable content. The speech had not yet been broadcast and was not going to be until the last possible moment. The dilemma for Speer was to decide when that moment should be.

Hamburg's Gauleiter, the local Nazi leader and a personal friend of Speer's, had offered to have the speech broadcast at once. After seeing Hitler for the last time, however, Speer could not bring himself to give his assent. Still mentally in thrall to the Führer, he had come to the conclusion that there was nothing to be done for Germany and the drama across the country would just have to run its course. Rather than make speeches to the nation, Speer had taken himself off to Plön instead, where he sat now, waiting in his caravan for the announcement of Hitler's death that must surely come in the next day or two.

Joachim von Ribbentrop's movements were uncertain, but he too was somewhere on the way to Plön, travelling by road from Berlin. Like Speer, he had left the city on 24 April, just before the Russians arrived. Unlike Speer, though, Ribbentrop had left reluctantly, because he would have much preferred to stay behind and share the Führer's fate in the bunker. But Hitler had refused to allow it. He had no further use for his Foreign Minister, a man whose advice over the years had rarely been less than disastrous.

The other Nazis had no use for Ribbentrop either. All the important party members had forsaken him long ago. Dim and pompous, insufferably overbearing, he had made few friends as German Foreign Minister and had no one to turn to as he headed for Plön. He was so desperate not to be cast out that he had tried to return to Berlin at one point, urgently seeking an aircraft to fly him back to the capital. But his request had been refused and

Ribbentrop had been abandoned to his own devices, no longer the central figure he had once been in the affairs of state.

He had little idea of what to do next as he travelled north. Hitler had told him to make contact with the British and propose an alliance against the Bolsheviks, but his chances of success were almost non-existent. Indeed, Hitler had probably only suggested the idea to get rid of him.

Ribbentrop's immediate plan was to join Dönitz at Plön and wait there until he could contact the British. If all else failed, he was thinking of going to ground in Hamburg after the fighting had stopped, living anonymously in a rented flat for a few months until the dust had settled and he could show his face again. The British were talking of hanging Nazi leaders after the war, but Ribbentrop couldn't believe they were serious. Hanging was not for people like him. It was for criminals and murderers, not the leaders of the nation. Ribbentrop had never done anything wrong, by his own reckoning. All he had ever done was carry out his orders, and his orders had been given to him by Adolf Hitler.

———

Hermann Göring had just arrived in Austria, a prisoner at his family castle in Mauterndorf. He was being watched over by the SS, who had orders to shoot him as soon as Berlin fell to the Russians.

Unlike the other Nazi leaders, Göring had gone south after leaving Berlin, heading initially for Berchtesgaden, Hitler's mountain retreat in Bavaria. He had been expecting Hitler to join him there, only to discover later that the Führer intended to die in Berlin instead. Disconcerted, Göring had wondered if this meant that he was supposed to succeed Hitler as Führer in accordance with the decree of 1941 that required him to take over if Hitler's freedom of action was restricted or he was in any other way incapacitated.

Unsure of his ground, Göring had telegraphed Hitler on 23 April to find out:

> My Führer! Following your decision to remain in the Berlin fortress, do you agree that I should take command of the Reich, as stipulated in the decree of 29 June 1941, with full powers, both internal and external?
>
> If I receive no reply before 2200 hours, I shall assume that you no longer enjoy freedom of action and I shall act on my own initiative.[3]

Unfortunately for Göring, his telegram had been intercepted in the bunker by Martin Bormann, perhaps his bitterest enemy among the other Nazis. Bormann had wasted no time in persuading Hitler that Göring was plotting to overthrow him and seize power. He had urged Hitler to have Göring shot at once. But Hitler had demurred, responding instead with a telegram to Göring insisting that he remained in full control: 'Decree of 29 June 1941 is rescinded by my special instruction. My freedom of action remains total. I forbid any move by you of the kind you have indicated.'[4]

Hitler's telegram had been followed by another, drafted by Bormann, who had ambitions to become Führer himself if anything happened to Hitler: 'Hermann Göring. Your action represents high treason against the Führer and National Socialism. The penalty for treason is death. But in view of your earlier services to the party, the Führer will not inflict this supreme penalty if you resign all your offices. Answer yes or no.'[5]

Göring had not had time to reply before the SS arrived to arrest him. More than a hundred soldiers had surrounded his house at Berchtesgaden, confining Göring to his room at gunpoint and refusing to let him see his wife and daughter. The men almost certainly had orders from Bormann to shoot Göring out of hand, but were reluctant to comply. Instead, they had contented themselves with keeping him under close arrest, as his wife bitterly recalled:

> Armed SS men invaded the house and I had to go to my room.
> I sat down, almost paralysed, unable to collect my thoughts. For
> the second time that day I had the impression of dreaming and
> of having left reality behind me. Some twenty minutes went by.
> Unable to bear it any longer, I tried to rejoin my husband but a
> guard was standing in front of the door of his study and prevented
> me from entering. After about an hour, Hermann came out to
> dine with us, under the watchful eyes of the SS. It hardly needs
> to be said that none of us were able to swallow a mouthful. But
> at least we were still together. From my seat at the table I could
> see the photograph of Adolf Hitler hanging on the wall. I had a
> sudden desire to tear it down and throw it out![6]

A day later, Berchtesgaden had been bombed by the Allies. Escorted by US Mustangs, Lancasters of the Royal Air Force had appeared shortly after first light, targeting Hitler's house at the Berghof. They had flown so low that Flight Sergeant Cutting, a rear gunner on one of the Lancasters, had seen the flash of the bombs as they hit the Berghof and Flying Officer

Coster had watched the neighbouring SS barracks going up in smoke. Göring's house had been damaged too, the roof collapsing and the stairs giving way as he and his family huddled together in the cellar. Emmy Göring had prayed without success for a direct hit to kill them all and put them out of their misery.

The damage had been so extensive that it had proved impossible to remain in Berchtesgaden after the raid. Göring had persuaded the SS to move them to Mauterndorf instead, fifty miles away in Austria. He owned the castle there, which he had inherited from his Jewish stepfather. Formerly the summer palace of the Archbishops of Salzburg, it stood on a promontory high above the town, heavily restored in medieval style by his stepfather.

The move had been traumatic. One of the SS had discreetly advised Emmy Göring to insist on travelling in the same car as her husband for the journey, to prevent him from being executed on the way. A chauffeur had taken charge of her jewel case, only to abscond with it en route. Other people had deserted too, quietly abandoning the Görings to their fate. The castle itself had been cold and forbidding when they arrived, a cheerless place that Emmy Göring had never liked. It was said to have a secret passage that led underground to the market square in Mauterndorf, but that was little comfort to the Görings with an SS guard gazing unblinkingly at them from every corner.

The Görings were waiting on events now, in common with everyone else. The SS had orders to shoot Göring in due course, but their orders might easily be overridden by developments in Berlin. The SS were in several different minds about what to do. The Luftwaffe was a factor as well, outraged at the idea of its erstwhile commander being murdered by a gang of thugs. The Luftwaffe had little time for Göring, but even less for the SS. There was talk, some of it encouraged by sympathisers in the SS, of the Luftwaffe making an attack on the castle to rescue Göring and protect him from his captors if the worst should come to the worst. But that was a bridge that they would only cross when they came to it.

—

For Rudolf Hess, far away in South Wales, there were no bridges to cross any more. Following his dramatic flight to Scotland in 1941, he had been a prisoner at Maindiff Court, an outpost of Abergavenny's mental hospital, since June 1942. Hess had spent the day in his room, as usual, hard at work on his memoirs. He had been writing all afternoon, covering sheet after sheet with his ramblings, pausing only at half past six to call for a hot water bottle to ease the stomach pains, perhaps imaginary, that caused him so much distress.

It was a race against time for Hess. He knew the war was almost over. He had known it ever since the American Army crossed the Rhine at Remagen. In Hess's mind, they must have used specially trained Jews to hypnotise the Germans and prevent them from defending the bridge. He was determined to get his memoirs down on paper before the end came. It was most important that he did:

> I had been imprisoned for four years now with lunatics; I had been at the mercy of their torture without being able to inform anybody of this, and without being able to convince the Swiss Minister that this was so; nor of course was I able to enlighten the lunatics about their own condition…
>
> Outside my garden lunatics walked up and down with loaded rifles! Lunatics surrounded me in the house! When I went for a walk, lunatics walked in front of and behind me – all in the uniform of the British Army.[7]

Hess kept scribbling until it was time for dinner. He ate a hearty meal and then began writing again immediately afterwards. He continued writing far into the night. It was the only agreeable occupation that remained to him, now that the 'lunatics' had taken over the asylum.

PART TWO:
SUNDAY, 29 APRIL

'Seeing it for myself, I really understood the appalling viciousness of war. Inanimate bombs dropping from the sky, wounded people lying in the streets, the lack of food and water were awful, but not as bad as a human being, dressed in a soldier's uniform, committing an atrocity against another, defenceless human being...'

Sophia Villani

CHAPTER 5:
CHAOS IN ITALY

Blood was oozing from the back of the removal van as Audisio's partisans drove the bodies of Mussolini and the others to Milan in the dark. They were stopped several times on the way by American troops who flagged them down at road blocks and examined Audisio's credentials by flashlight. Trusting to luck that the Americans wouldn't notice the blood, Audisio produced a pass from partisan headquarters signed by a US intelligence officer and told them he was travelling on the orders of the Committee of National Liberation.

They reached Milan just before eleven pm on 28 April. Audisio stopped to make a telephone call at the Pirelli works on the Via Fabio Filzi and was surprised to find himself arrested by another band of partisans as he returned to the van. He and his men were accused of being Fascists and lined up against the factory wall with their faces to the brickwork. Audisio could hardly credit what was happening as he tried to protest, only to be told that he would be shot out of hand if he opened his mouth again. The corpses in the van and a list of Fascists in his possession had convinced his captors that he too was a Fascist, removing Mussolini's body to a place of safety. It wasn't until after two am on 29 April that a partisan officer arrived from headquarters to identify Audisio and his men and order their immediate release.

The van continued on its way, heading for the Piazzale Loreto in the centre of Milan. It drove along the Viale Padova, waking a man named Giuseppe Marchi, who rushed to the window to see what was happening. By-passed by the American Army en route to the north, Milan had been seized by the partisans four days earlier. An orgy of killing had followed as Fascists were arrested en masse and old scores settled. Hundreds of people had died and the fight was still continuing as rival groups struggled for control. A heavy motor vehicle driving through the deserted streets in the middle of the night was an obvious cause for concern at a very nervous time. Marchi watched discreetly through the gap in the shutters and did not return to bed until he had seen the removal van disappear safely in the direction of the Piazzale Loreto.

It arrived some time after three am. The Piazzale was a vast open space at the junction of five main roads. The partisans had just renamed it the Square of the Fifteen Martyrs in memory of the hostages shot at the filling station there in August 1944. The van drew up at the same spot and the bodies of Mussolini and the others were thrown out, dumped in a heap beside the now derelict garage to show that the martyrs had been avenged and justice, after a fashion, had been done.

The bodies remained where they had fallen until daybreak. They were guarded by eight of Audisio's men, too exhausted after forty eight hours without sleep to do anything except slump wearily against the girders of the building as dawn came up over the city. The news of Mussolini's execution had already leaked out and was spreading rapidly as passers-by came to see for themselves. By eight am a large crowd had gathered and was growing larger by the minute as more and more people came hurrying in from all over Milan. Some wore partisan armbands and carried rifles and shotguns with them. Others were in their Sunday best, on their way to mass until their attention had been caught by all the commotion.

Somebody hauled the bodies apart and tried to lay them out in order. Clara Petacci was placed against the legs of her brother Marcello, with Mussolini's head on her breast. Two young men emerged from the crowd and began to mutilate Mussolini's body, stamping repeatedly on his head and kicking his jaw until his face had been completely disfigured. Somebody else shoved a stick into his hand and closed his fingers around it while the crowd cheered. Then a woman appeared with a gun and emptied five shots into his chest, one for each of the sons she had lost in the war.

The crowd quickly became hysterical at that, determined to have its revenge on Mussolini. Audisio's men lost control as the mob surged forward. Warning shots were fired, but no one took any notice. The mob fell on the bodies, spitting and snarling, lashing out with their boots and fists, yelling obscenities at the corpses. Audisio's men sprayed them with a hose, but to little effect. The people were determined to have their pound of flesh, venting their frustration on Mussolini and his cronies for all the miseries they had suffered in the long years of war.

'Who do you want to see?' yelled a man in shirt sleeves, his bare arms covered in blood as he held up a corpse.[1]

The crowd roared out one name, then another. The man held them up in turn, one after the other, all the Fascist leaders who had been Mussolini's accomplices in the war. He held up Mussolini too, his eyes wide open as his head lolled forward, and Clara Petacci, her face bruised and her thighs caked with blood as she flopped in the man's arms. The crowd was delighted. It bayed for more.

'Higher!' people yelled. 'Higher! We can't see.'

Somebody produced a rope. One end was thrown over a girder. Mussolini's body was hauled up by the ankles until everyone could catch a glimpse of him, dangling upside down above the crowd. Clara followed, her nakedness in full view as her skirt fell over her face. A woman was jeered as she stood on a stepladder to tie the skirt back between Clara's legs. Her features were relatively serene, despite the battering she had taken. She remained a beautiful woman, even in death. But Mussolini looked ghastly, his face a swollen mess, his lips drawn back from his teeth like a baboon's.

The crowd exulted at the sight. Thousands hooted in derision as the man they had so recently applauded in life hung limp and forlorn beside his mistress, part of his skull missing from a bullet wound in the head. Their bodies were swiftly joined by two others, strung up alongside them like a row of carcasses in a butcher's shop. Jim Roper, one of the first war correspondents to reach Milan with the advancing Americans, arrived just in time to see the bodies twisting in the wind:

> Mussolini's face was ashen grey. His dark jowls hung loosely. He wore a nondescript military jacket and grey riding breeches of the Italian militia, which had a tiny red stripe down the sides. But the air of splendour which once surrounded the blacksmith's son who rose to become the world's first dictator was gone. His body, which had been manhandled many times, was covered with grime. He wore high black boots, but there was no lustre left in their polish.'[2]

The bodies had been hanging for some time when a truck arrived, bringing another of Mussolini's henchmen for execution. Achille Starace had been a Fascist since 1920, a fanatical supporter of the Duce from the first. As party secretary, he had persecuted Jews and identified himself very closely with Mussolini's cult of personality. Now, he was forced to pay the price as the partisans took their revenge. The *New Yorker's* Philip Hamburger joined Roper in time to see it:

> The fanatical killer who was once secretary of the Fascist party was brought into the square in an open truck at about ten thirty in the morning. The bodies of Mussolini and the others had just been hanging for several hours. I had reached the square just before the truck arrived. As it moved slowly ahead, the crowd fell back and became silent. Surrounded by armed guards, Starace stood in the middle of the truck, hands in the air, a lithe, square-jawed, surly figure in a black shirt.
>
> The truck stopped for an instant close to the grotesque corpse of his old boss. Starace took one look and started to fall forward, perhaps in a faint, but was pushed back to standing position by his guards. The truck drove ahead a few feet and stopped. Starace was taken out and placed near a white wall at the rear of the gas station. Beside him were baskets of spring flowers – pink, yellow, purple and blue – placed there in honour of fifteen anti-Fascists who had been murdered in the same square six months before.
>
> A firing squad of partisans shot Starace in the back, and another partisan, perched on a beam some twenty feet above the ground, turned towards the crowd in the square and made a broad gesture of finality, much like a dramatic umpire calling a man out at the home plate.
>
> There were no roars or bloodcurdling yells; there was only silence, and then, suddenly, a sigh – a deep, moaning sound, seemingly expressive of release from something dark and fetid. The people in the square seemed to understand that this was a moment of both ending and beginning. Two minutes later, Starace had been strung up alongside Mussolini and the others. 'Look at them now', an old man beside me kept saying. 'Just look at them now.'[3]

~

After dumping Mussolini's body in the square, Audisio drove on to partisan headquarters at the Palazzo Brera to make his report and announce the dictator's death on the radio. The first bulletins stated simply that Mussolini had been executed, but later reports carried graphic accounts of the scene in the Piazzale as he and his mistress hung side by side while the mob pelted them with abuse. Winston Churchill was horrified when he heard, delighted to see the back of Mussolini but appalled at the outrages inflicted on Clara. Adolf Hitler made no comment when he was handed the news on a slip of paper, but the section about Mussolini hanging upside down was later heavily underlined in pencil, almost certainly by the Führer. He had already announced that he had no intention of being taken alive by the Russians, put on display in a monkey cage for the amusement of the rabble. He did not intend to share Mussolini's fate in death either.

Rachele Mussolini was still at Cernobbio when she learned of her husband's fate, listening to the radio in the Blackshirt's house:

> 'Justice has been done!' the voice proclaimed. I found myself thinking that Benito was now beyond the reach of human ingratitude and beastliness. He had given everything for Italy – even his own life.
>
> The men who died with him I had known for years, in fair days and foul, as his colleagues. Some were better than others and some I had liked more than others, but they all remained steadfast and loyal to the end, despite the risk.
>
> And that woman too, the woman whom they put alongside Benito at the very last moment so as to increase the scandal which she paid for with her life.[4]

That was the worst of it for Rachele, the ultimate betrayal. Her husband had been with another woman when he died. She couldn't believe it, couldn't accept that Mussolini had chosen to share his final moments with someone other than the mother of his children. Rachele still had the last letter he had written her, the one in which he had sworn that she was the only woman he had ever really loved.

But there was no time to brood about that now. Too much was happening outside:

> I was prostrated by the news of the murders and barely noticed the shooting going on all around the house. Civil war was in full swing. My children never left me and their sobbing added to my grief, though I did my best to keep back my tears. The hours dragged on until it occurred to me that our presence in the

house might involve our hosts in serious trouble. I talked it over with the children and we agreed that we had better put an end to all this uncertainty. So we sent someone to tell the Committee of Liberation at Como where we were.[5]

Before long, three partisans arrived and began to search the house. A policeman went through Rachele's suitcases while a young partisan found a miniature of her dead son Bruno in a valuable frame. 'This belongs to the people,' he told her, quietly pocketing it for himself. Rachele complained to the policeman, who made him give it back.

That afternoon, at her own request, she and her two children were taken to the police station at Como. Rachele had begged the Bishop of Como to take Romano and Anna Maria into his care, but he had judged it wiser to refuse. Instead, she asked for her children to be placed in police custody, where they would be much safer than on the street. With so much killing going on, there was no knowing what might happen to them if they were left on the street.

They were separated at the police station, the children hustled away while Rachele was transferred to the women's section of the prison. She was supposed to sign the register on arrival, but the prison governor apparently insisted that it was unnecessary and scratched her name out to protect her identity. She was put in a small cell with several other new arrivals. The women were so upset at finding themselves in custody that only one of them recognised Rachele, who quickly swore her to secrecy.

Newcomers of both sexes continued to arrive during the afternoon and early evening as Como's Fascists were rounded up. Revenge was not long in coming, as Rachele soon discovered:

> We could hear something of what was happening outside. Someone in the courtyard read out a list of names, and this was followed by a burst of machine gun fire and, after an interval, the rumbling of cart wheels. The process was endlessly repeated and it went on like that all night. It was a ghastly business. The young woman who had recognised me was frantic about her husband. He was one of those in the courtyard, and every time the names were given out she clung to the window bars and screamed hysterically. Another woman was swearing she was a Communist who had been imprisoned for infanticide and yelling to be let out.[6]

Alone among the women, Rachele remained comparatively calm. Still unrecognised, she was a puzzle to her cellmates, who kept asking why she wasn't crying. 'Haven't you left anyone behind?' they demanded. But Rachele was past all that. With her husband gone, she had no tears any more. She had lost her fear of death too. It was only a matter of time before her turn came to face the firing squad, but Rachele Mussolini really didn't care what happened to her now. All that mattered was that it didn't happen to her children as well.

———

Further south, in an 18th-century palace overlooking the Bay of Naples, the German Army in Italy was about to surrender. The Germans still had half a million men under arms, but with most of Italy in Allied hands and their escape routes to the north blocked by partisans, they had little option but to raise the white flag. A delegation had arrived at Caserta the previous day to negotiate the terms.

The delegation comprised two middle-ranking officers – Lieutenant-Colonel Viktor von Schweinitz of the Wehrmacht and Major Eugen Wenner of the SS – and an interpreter. They had been horrified to learn on arrival that there were no terms to negotiate. Mindful of the mistake made in November 1918, when the German Army had been allowed to march home with all its weapons as if it had never been defeated, the Allies were insisting on unconditional surrender this time around. They had given the Germans a two-page surrender document to sign, accompanied by eighteen pages of supplementary details. The Germans had sat up most of the night studying it.

The document presented them with a host of problems, not least that they lacked the power to agree to it. They were under instructions from their commanders not to accept the internment of the German Army after its surrender. They had been ordered to negotiate its return home instead. But the Allies were adamant that there would be no going home for the German Army after it had laid down its weapons. Its men were to be imprisoned behind the wire until the Allies were ready to release them.

Wenner and Schweinitz couldn't agree on a response. In a military bungalow in the grounds of Caserta's Bourbon palace, they discussed it into the small hours of 29 April. Wenner was for capitulating, but Schweinitz was worried that the Wehrmacht had forbidden him to accept internment and would repudiate the agreement if he did. There seemed no way out of the impasse until Gero Gävernitz, their interpreter, pointed out that German soldiers were being killed as they spoke and more were dying every minute. Schweinitz relented at that, reluctantly agreeing to accept the surrender terms if he could get them past his chief, General Heinrich von Vietinghoff, at Bolzano.

A telegram was quickly drafted to German HQ. It was past four in the morning as Gävernitz took it to General Lyman Lemnitzer, the American representative at the talks:

> With the draft of the telegram in my pocket, I drove in the early dawn alongside the cascades of the Royal Park, which reflected the waning moonlight, to General Lemnitzer's office in the huge building of the Royal Palace.
>
> I found him still at work at his desk. He was greatly encouraged when I showed him the draft of the message and ordered it to be encoded at once. As Wally, our OSS radio operator, had not yet taken up his post at Wolff's headquarters in Bolzano, the message was sent to our office in Bern, Switzerland, from which point we requested that it be taken by courier to Vietinghoff's headquarters at Bolzano. This lengthy method of transmission made it unlikely that an answer would be received before two or three days at the earliest.[7]

But that was too long for the Allies. Allowing seventy two hours for the news to reach all German units in the field, they wanted the agreement signed that same day to prevent any further loss of life. They calculated that Wenner and Schweinitz would have to leave Caserta with the agreement by three pm at the latest, if they were to be safely back on their own side of the line by nightfall. There was no more time to lose.

Bowing to the inevitable, the two Germans agreed to the surrender. It was signed at two that afternoon, in the ballroom of the royal palace. The room was crowded when they arrived for the ceremony: eleven British and American generals and admirals, a Russian general and his interpreter, several other officers and a battery of newspapermen and radio journalists flown in from Rome for the day. The Germans were disconcerted to see film cameras as well and a row of klieg lights and microphones. They had been expecting to sign the surrender in private, not least because they were afraid of being murdered if their identities became known, killed as traitors by their own people when they got home.

Yet there was nothing they could do about it. Schweinitz repeated his claim that he was exceeding his powers in agreeing to the internment of the Wehrmacht, but was told to sign anyway. Wenner signed too, sitting in a sports jacket at the end of a long table. The ceremony was over by 2.17 pm. The Germans were airborne by three o'clock, taking off in an Allied aircraft from Marcianese airfield, en route for Annecy in the Haute Savoie. From there, they were due to travel in plain clothes to Switzerland and then through the night to Bolzano. The surrender was still a secret, not to be revealed until it came into effect at two pm on 2 May. It remained to be seen what General von Vietinghoff would make of the agreement when he met the two envoys and learned the severity of the terms.

———

Naples had been in Allied hands since October 1943, but the city was still not back to normal. It had been heavily bombed before the Allies arrived, the docks and factories pounded repeatedly in the run-up to the invasion. Food remained scarce and the black market was rife. Prostitution was still rampant, not just among local women, but among others from all over southern Italy who had flocked to Naples to sell themselves to the Allied soldiers, particularly the coloured troops of the American Army, who were the kindest to them and paid the most.

In the port of Pozzuoli, a few miles around the bay from Naples, Romilda Villani had been struggling for years to bring up two illegitimate children without any help from their father. A good-looking woman, she had won a cinema competition at seventeen to discover 'The Girl who is Garbo's Double'. The prize had been a trip to Hollywood and a screen test with Metro-Goldwyn-Mayer. Her father had forbidden her to take it up, so Romilda had gone to Rome instead, where a man claiming to be a film producer had swiftly seduced her, leaving her pregnant with her eldest daughter Sophia, and later also Maria.

Now they were back in Pozzuoli, living in squalor on the Via Solfatara, so named for the sulphur which steamed from the nearby volcano. Their house had been damaged in an air raid, the windows blown out, the walls cracked and the roof sagging, but they had patched it up as best they could and were making do, struggling every day to find enough to eat. Romilda had opened their top floor apartment to American servicemen, giving them an Italian home to relax in for a few hours during the day, somewhere to sing around the piano and forget about the war for a while. The Americans brought food, fantasised about Romilda and smiled at Sophia, so ugly and skinny at the age of ten that she looked as if she had never had a square meal in her life.

Sophia had been only five when Italy entered the war. German soldiers had arrived in Pozzuoli soon afterwards, as she later recalled:

> They were our allies then, and friendly, and my earliest memories are of delightedly watching the young, handsome soldiers in their beautiful uniforms, playing war games in the back yards of the houses on our street. I don't think I had ever seen a blond, blue-eyed man before the German soldiers arrived. It was exciting to stand in front of our house and watch the troops march by, and it was especially exciting when long columns of tanks rumbled down the street.[8]

But the honeymoon hadn't lasted long. As the war came closer, the Germans had turned on their allies, taking out their frustrations on Jewish Italians first, then the rest of the population as well:

> Seeing it for myself, I really understood the appalling viciousness of war. Inanimate bombs dropping from the sky, wounded people lying in the streets, the lack of food and water, were awful, but not as bad as a human being, dressed in a soldier's uniform, committing an atrocity against another, defenceless human being. Now that I actually observed these mounting atrocities from my balcony, I finally understood the full terribleness of war. I saw men grabbed on the streets below me, beaten, thrown into German Army trucks and hauled away. People were shot in the streets without warning. My young eyes saw one appalling, gruesome spectacle after another.[9]

Sophia herself had been a casualty, injured in the air raid that damaged her house. Her chin had been lacerated by shrapnel as she ran for cover. She still carried the scar, as GI Charles Dial had noticed. Sitting with Romilda one afternoon, neither of them able to speak a word of the other's language, he had invited her to bring Sophia to his camp seven miles away, where he would scrounge some food for them and ask the medics to take a look at Sophia's chin. Mother and daughter had duly presented themselves at the gate, only to be arrested as potential looters. Dial had been preparing for guard duty when he heard:

> A guy from C Company comes up to the tent and tells me they've got a blonde and her kid locked up. She told them she'd been

asked out to visit me – and so she had. I went down and got them out of jail and brought them back to our area. Romilda had walked all the way from Pozzuoli with the little girl. She's a cute little kid. Mom has her all dressed up in a navy blue coat and little brown kid gloves – a real effort these days. She's about nine years old – very quiet and serious with very dark eyes. Unfortunately, she'll never have her mother's looks. She's probably scared to death of all us dirty, smelly GIs. I took them over to the medics to see what they could do about the little girl's chin.[10]

The Americans had been good to Romilda and her daughters. So had the Scots, strange men in skirts, fighting off attempts by the street urchins to discover what they wore underneath. The only Allied troops they didn't trust were the Moroccans, who had reportedly been recruited to the war on the promise of all the women they wanted whenever there was no fighting. Some thought nothing of rape, or sex with child prostitutes, thousands of whom were willing to oblige them for nothing more than a blanket or a tin of Spam.

A number of Moroccan soldiers had been billeted on the ground floor of Romilda's house. They were commanded by a French officer who did little to control them, or stop them drinking. With rape a distinct possibility, and child prostitution never far from her thoughts, Sophia had regarded the troops with trepidation:

To get to our flat on the top floor, we had to pass by the Moroccans and it was always frightening. They would talk to us in a language we didn't understand, and with their gestures tease us and pretend that they were going to go after us. Actually they never molested us. A couple of times in the dead of night, though, when they had had much too much to drink, they did come pounding on our door, to frighten us.[11]

But the Moroccans would be gone soon, now that Mussolini was dead and the war all but over. The Americans would be gone too, with their cheerful friendliness and their bars of chocolate. Whatever the future held for Sophia, later Sophia Loren, and her younger sister, later Mrs Romano Mussolini, they knew that it could hardly be more traumatic for them than the immediate past.

—

Harold Macmillan was in Assisi when he learned of Mussolini's death, making a quick visit to the monastery on Mount Subasio where St Francis had lived. As political adviser to Field-Marshal Alexander, the supreme Allied commander in the Mediterranean theatre, Macmillan had done much of the groundwork for the German surrender in Italy, but had decided to absent himself from the actual signing ceremony in Caserta in order to allay the suspicions of the Russians, who did not trust political advisors. Macmillan had spent the day in Assisi instead, visiting the monastery in the morning and going round Assisi's great churches in the afternoon.

It was a very busy time for him. He had been in Bologna on 23 April, a few hours after the town's liberation, inspecting the corpses of local dignitaries shot by the Fascists before they fled. The Fascists' leader had been shot in turn, captured by the partisans before he could escape and executed against the same wall. Macmillan had been shown the blood on the ground and the man's brains spattered against the brickwork.

From Bologna, he had driven by jeep to Modena under desultory sniper fire. The town had been in the process of liberating itself when he arrived. German troops and Italian Fascists had been defending themselves from windows along the main street while partisans advanced from house to house. As the first of the Allies to appear in the town, Macmillan and his British and American companions had swiftly found themselves recruited to the cause:

> Our arrival at the Municipio (or Town Hall) caused some excitement. There was a lot of shouting and embracing. The leader of the partisans kissed me on both cheeks on being told that I was the famous Haroldo Macmillano – said by the BBC to be the ruler and father of the Italian people. I was presented with an armlet and taken into the Town Hall to be formally enrolled.[12]

As a civilian, albeit with a partisan armband, Macmillan had tried to do as little fighting as honour would allow:

> But naturally one had to pretend to do something. It was really quite an exciting little action while it lasted and quite spirited. Of course a lot of partisans fired off their pieces quite aimlessly and threw grenades just for fun. Indeed, these gentlemen and their curious assortment of rifles, grenades, tommy-guns etc caused me more alarm than our opponents.[13]

Afterwards, Macmillan's jeep had come under sniper fire again as he tried to return to Bologna. He and his companions had had to abandon their vehicles and run for cover while the partisans tackled the sniper from a neighbouring house. They had reached Bologna eventually, where girls with Fascist sympathies were having their heads forcibly shaved, and from there had continued to Rome. After a few more days at his desk, Macmillan had slipped away to Assisi with Robert Cecil, a wounded British officer who had been seconded to him as an aide-de-camp.

It was evening when they learned that Mussolini had been hanged, as the first broadcasts had it. As night fell, they also received a message from Field-Marshal Alexander, saying that the Germans had signed the surrender on the terms agreed. Afterwards, Macmillan and Cecil switched the wireless off and went out for a walk, still unable to believe that the war was actually coming to an end. The night was lovely and the whole valley of Assisi was bathed in moonlight as they strolled. In his mind, Macmillan compared Adolf Hitler unfavourably to St Francis and was quietly thankful that he found himself in such a beautiful place as the carnage of the past few years drew to a close at last.

———

In the hilltop town of Sant' Ambrogio, overlooking Rapallo and the Gulf of Genoa, American poet Ezra Pound was in a very different frame of mind as he contemplated Mussolini's death and the advance of the Allied armies. As a US citizen and a long time supporter of Fascism, he was terrified of what the future would hold for him once the Allies were in control. Pound had made no secret of his opinions during the war, signing his name to Fascist manifestos and making pro-Mussolini, anti-Semitic broadcasts on Italian radio. The United States government had indicted him for treason in 1943. The penalty for treason was death.

Pound had lived in Rapallo since 1925. He had spent most of the war in the flat on the Via Marsala that he shared with his English wife Dorothy. But the flat was on the seafront, in the way of the German coastal defences. Ordered out in 1943, Pound and his wife had moved in with his mistress Olga Rudge, who lived at nearby Sant' Ambrogio. The two women knew each other well, although relations were never easy. Olga had a daughter by Pound, who had been fostered out to parents in the Italian Tyrol.

Pound was undecided about what to do as the Fascists fled from Rapallo and the partisans moved in ahead of the Americans. Like many others, he did not regret his Fascist leanings and remained convinced that time would prove him right in the end. He was aware, though, that Fascists were being hunted down and shot all over Italy. He knew too that he was wanted by the Americans, who had circulated his photograph and description. The problem for him was whether to run and hide – and, if so, where? – or whether to stay put and bluff it out.

Pound had already fled once, abandoning Rome hours before the city's capitulation to the Allies in 1944. Heading north on foot, he had slept rough for several nights, travelling a total of 450 miles, some of it by train, to join his daughter's foster family in the Tyrol. From there, he had made his way several weeks later to Sant' Ambrogio, where his wife and mistress had been waiting for him.

He had also tried to give himself up when the Americans reached Rapallo. Presenting himself at their headquarters in the town, he had offered his services 'as having lots of information about Italy which could be of use'. But the Americans had been far too busy when they first arrived to worry about Pound, whoever he might be. Failing to make any impression, he had been sent away again, left to his own devices to do as he pleased. Pound was pretty sure, though, that that would not be the end of the matter. Either the Americans or the partisans would come for him, sooner or later. They surely had his name on a list somewhere.

Until they came, however, Pound could only sit and wait. He kept busy by translating Chinese philosophy from the *Book of Mencius*. He knew that he risked being shot for treason, but he was convinced that the American sense of justice would never allow that to happen. All he had ever done was exercise his right to free speech on the radio, ranting against the Jews on the day of Pearl Harbor, claiming that they had President Roosevelt in their pocket. The Americans surely wouldn't execute him for anything as stupid as that.

—

On the other side of Italy, the US Air Force's 488th Squadron had just arrived in Rimini, its new posting on the Adriatic. Until mid-April, the bombers had been at Alesan in Corsica, their base for repeated operations against German-occupied France and Italy. The squadron had spent most of 1944 in Corsica, taking heavy casualties as the war intensified on the mainland. So many aircrew had been lost that the number of missions they had to fly to qualify for rotation back to the United States had been raised again and again, from twenty five initially to eighty by the end of the campaign. No matter how many sorties they flew, it seemed to the airmen that the bar was always raised just before they reached it, always removed just out of their reach. There was invariably a catch of some kind to prevent them from going home.

Lieutenant Joseph Heller had joined the squadron as a bombardier in May 1944. For the rest of that year he and his friend Francis Yohannon had flown repeated sorties against the enemy, risking their lives in broad daylight as the flak came up at them over the target. The Germans had long since run out of fighter aircraft, but they had a bad habit of sending up a single plane to fly alongside the Americans, radio their exact height and speed back to the anti-aircraft batteries below. The flak that burst around the 488th's B25 bombers was often far too close for comfort.

Heller had been inclined to take the anti-aircraft fire personally. He knew the Germans weren't aiming at him in particular, but that had meant little when the end remained the same: 'They were trying to kill me, and I wanted to go home. That they were trying to kill all of us each time we went up was no consolation. They were trying to kill *me*.'[14]

Heller's worst moment had come on his 37th mission, a more than usually dangerous raid over Avignon in the south of France. From his position in the bombardier's compartment he had seen a plane in front hit by flak, bursting into flames and losing a wing as it fell out of the sky with no possibility of any parachutes. His own aircraft had then gone into a seemingly terminal dive of its own as the pilot panicked. After the aircraft had levelled out, Heller had crawled back to help the top gunner, whose thigh had been shattered by flak. Swallowing his nausea, Heller had poured sulphanilamide into the gaping hole before covering it with a sterile compress. He had administered a shot of morphine in addition after the gunner had complained of the pain. The man had survived, but Heller had never forgotten the horror of that mission. He had remained terrified of flying ever since.

Yet that was all in the past now. Magically, unbelievably, Heller had completed his tour of duty in December 1944. He had filled his quota of sixty combat missions just before it rose to seventy and had qualified for an immediate return to the United States. Heller had spent the days until his departure in a tent with a couple of newcomers, one of whom had brought a typewriter on which Heller had practised his writing skills while he waited. He was thinking of becoming a writer after the war was over.

Heller had been given the choice of returning to America by land or sea. He had plumped unequivocally for the sea, preferring to sail from

Naples and risk being torpedoed, rather than take a flight that he didn't have to. Back in the States, he had immediately asked to be taken off flying status, even though it meant a considerable cut in pay. While the rest of the 488th remained in Corsica, Heller had seen out the war as an air force public relations officer in Texas. He was in San Angelo when the Italian campaign ended, promising himself that for as long as he lived he would never fly in an aeroplane again.

CHAPTER 6:
HIMMLER LOOKS TO
THE STARS

Back in Germany, Heinrich Himmler was about to have his fortune told. In the dimly lit police barracks at Lübeck, he had arrived just after midnight to keep his appointment with SS Brigadeführer Schellenberg and the astrologer Wilhelm Wulff.

The two men shot to their feet as Himmler burst through the door. It was obvious at once that he had been drinking. The smell of alcohol followed him across the room as he ordered the two men to resume their seats and took his own place at the head of the table.

If Himmler was surprised to see that Schellenberg had brought the astrologer with him, he gave little sign of it. The meeting began with Schellenberg's report on Count Bernadotte's failure to negotiate a surrender to the Western Allies. Schellenberg had been terrified earlier in the evening, fearful of imminent execution, but it seemed to Wulff that he recovered his confidence as he began to speak, explaining in detail the reasoning behind the Allies' refusal to negotiate. Himmler listened carefully to every word, chewing on a cigar that he kept picking up and putting down again with a hand that trembled almost uncontrollably.

Himmler was sweating too, his body quivering with barely suppressed emotion as he fought back tears. He had been badly shaken by the Reuters report of his treachery in approaching the Allies. He knew that it could have disastrous consequences for him if Hitler was still alive and got to hear of it. Himmler was convinced that he was about to be arrested at the very least, if not shot out of hand. As soon as Schellenberg had finished speaking, he turned to Wulff and asked him what the stars had to say about his future.

Wulff had brought his astrological charts with him and a stellar chronometer. Spreading the charts out on the table, he divined from them that Himmler might still just survive if he sent Schellenberg to Sweden at once to conduct a fresh round of talks with Count Bernadotte and the Swedish Foreign Minister. Wulff happened to know that Schellenberg was most anxious to visit Sweden in the near future, with no intention of coming back. Once safely on neutral territory, he could arrange for Himmler to follow, slipping across the Baltic to Stockholm before anyone in Germany realised he was gone. It was a better idea than Himmler disguising himself as a farm worker and hiding on an estate in Oldenburg, as one of his subordinates had suggested.

But the SS leader was not impressed. 'Is that all?' he demanded, when Wulff had completed his forecast. He had been hoping for some encouragement from the stars, not just an admission that all was lost and it was time to run.

Yet there was nothing for him in the heavens. Himmler was doomed, if the sky was to be believed. He seemed to lose all control as he yelled at Wulff: 'What's going to happen? It's all over, nothing can be saved now. I'll have to kill myself! Take my own life! Or what else do you think I can do?'

Wulff did not reply. After a spell in a Nazi gaol, at the mercy of the Gestapo, he had little sympathy for Himmler now that the tables had been turned.

'Why don't you tell me?' Himmler begged. 'Tell me. What am I supposed to do?'

'Flee the country,' Wulff advised him, with a shrug. 'I presume you have the necessary documents?'

Himmler did. But they were little comfort to him, as Wulff quickly realised:

'Tell me what to do, please tell me what to do!' Himmler repeated, as he stood in front of me like a frightened schoolboy about to be caned, alternately chewing his fingernails and raising his cigar to his lips with trembling hands. 'What am I to do, what am I to do?' he went on. And then, in answer to his own question: 'I'll have to kill myself; there's nothing else for it!'[1]

Looking at this dreadful little man, Wulff saw that the leader of the SS really did have no idea what to do. With ample time to prepare for his own escape, he had remained paralysed instead, doing nothing to save himself when anybody with any sense would already have fled: 'Himmler had actually made no plans. He had simply come to grief. And in this desperate situation from which there was no way out, an astrologer who had been persecuted by the Nazis and forced to live in their prisons and dark cells as a detainee was expected to advise his torturer.'[2]

The discussion continued for another hour, Himmler poring over the charts as Wulff explained the configurations of Jupiter and Saturn to him. Himmler was desperate to know what the stars had in store for his children and his mistress, Liesel Potthas. He seemed a pathetic figure to Wulff, a minor bureaucrat risen far above his station, only too happy to persecute Jews and political opponents when the going was good, but terrified for his own skin as soon as events took a turn for the worse.

It was decided at length that Schellenberg should go to Denmark, rather than his choice of Stockholm, to negotiate the effective surrender of the German forces in Norway and Denmark. He went back to his hotel at once to begin packing. Himmler himself still hadn't decided what to do next. He had thought of flying to Czechoslovakia, where the German Army was still in control, but Wulff had poured cold water on the idea, telling him that the stars for Czechoslovakia did not look good. Himmler had no idea what to do instead.

Everything depended on Hitler. Once the Führer was dead, beyond any shadow of doubt, Himmler could step into the breach and replace him as Germany's new leader, the man the Allies would have to deal with if they wanted peace. He would be in a much stronger negotiating position once he knew for sure that Hitler was dead. But the Führer wasn't dead, so far as anyone in Lübeck knew. He was still alive, still in charge, and the time for negotiation was fast running out.

The Führer was indeed still alive. Not only that, but he had just got married. In the small hours of the morning, with the Russian front line no more than a few hundred yards away, he had finally married Eva Braun in the conference room at the bunker.

The ceremony had been a civil one, with Göbbels and Bormann as witnesses. It had been conducted by Walter Wagner, a magistrate fighting with a Volkssturm unit nearby. He had been collected in the darkness and driven to the bunker in an armoured vehicle. There, he had been introduced to the Führer and ordered to perform an abbreviated version of the ceremony without any formal publication of the banns.

Like most Germans, Wagner had had no idea until then that the Führer even had a girlfriend. Thunderstruck, not believing that this was happening, he had asked Hitler and the woman by his side if they were both of Aryan descent and free of hereditary diseases. Assured that they were, he had married them at once, citing the special circumstances permissible under wartime regulations.

Eva Braun had been so flustered afterwards that she had begun to sign her maiden name on the marriage certificate, before crossing out the B in favour of *Eva Hitler, née Braun.* Then she and her new husband had held a small drinks party in their private quarters, reminiscing over old times with Generals Krebs, Burgdorf and a few other chosen guests. Hitler himself hadn't stayed long. He kept slipping away to the waiting room outside Göbbels' office, where Traudl Junge, his young secretary, was busily transcribing his last political testament from shorthand.

Hitler had dictated it to her earlier, a long, rambling diatribe about the Jews, Germany, his place in history, all the usual stuff that Traudl had heard many times before. She had expected something different when she began to take it down: an explanation of what had gone wrong, perhaps, or a confession of guilt. Something, at any rate, to justify all the destruction he had brought down on Germany over the past six years. But Hitler had had nothing new to say. He had stood opposite her with his hands on the table, speaking almost mechanically above the din as the concrete walls reverberated endlessly to the sound of shells and bombs exploding overhead:

It is untrue that I or anybody else in Germany wanted war in 1939. It was wanted and provoked exclusively by those international statesmen who either were of Jewish origin or worked for Jewish interests… After six years of war, which in spite of all setbacks will one day go down in history as the most glorious and heroic manifestation of the struggle for existence of a nation, I cannot forsake the city that is the capital of this state.

I wish to share my fate with that which millions of others have also taken upon themselves by remaining in this town. Furthermore, I do not intend to fall into the hands of the enemy, who require a new spectacle, presented by the Jews, as a diversion for their hysterical masses.

I have therefore decided to remain in Berlin and there choose death voluntarily at the moment when I believe that the position of the Führer and the Chancellery itself can no longer be maintained. I die with a joyful heart in the knowledge of the immeasurable deeds and achievements of our peasants and workers and of a contribution unique in history of our youth which bears my name.[3]

And so on. Traudl Junge had heard the bulk of it countless times before, as had millions of Germans on the radio. She felt curiously betrayed as she took it all down again in her immaculate shorthand: 'Here we were. All of us doomed, I thought – the whole country doomed – and here, in what he was dictating to me there was not one word of compassion or regret, only awful, awful anger. I remember thinking "My God. He hasn't learned anything. It's all just the same."'[4]

The only surprise had come when Hitler named the members of the government that was to take over after his death. Traudl had looked up in astonishment when he announced that Admiral Dönitz was to become Germany's new leader, now that Himmler had been expelled from the party. Leader of what, she had wondered, with the country in ruins and the enemy already in the streets of Berlin?

But Hitler was past caring. After dictating his political testament he had continued with his private will, leaving his possessions to the Nazi party, if it still existed, or else to the German state. Then he had gone to the conference room to get married, telling Traudl to type up both documents in triplicate and bring them to him as soon as she had finished.

She had begun at once, typing up her notes in the waiting room while Hitler celebrated his marriage in his private quarters. She typed furiously into the small hours, surprising herself with how few mistakes she was making as her fingers clattered across the keys. Hitler emerged from time to time to see how she was getting on, standing over her and staring unhappily at her shorthand before returning to his party. Göbbels came to see her too. He was in a state of high emotion, as Traudl never afterwards forgot:

> Suddenly Göbbels bursts in. I look at his agitated face, which is white as chalk. Tears are running down his cheeks. He speaks to me because there's no one else around to whom he can pour out his heart. His usually clear voice is stifled by tears and shaking. 'The Führer wants me to leave Berlin, Frau Junge! I am to take up a leading post in the new government. But I can't leave Berlin, I can't leave the Führer's side! I am Gauleiter of Berlin, and my place is here. If the Führer is dead my life is pointless.'[5]

Göbbels too dictated a testament to Traudl, as an appendix to the Führer's:

For the first time in my life I must categorically refuse to obey an order of the Führer's. My wife and children join me in this refusal. Apart from the fact that feelings of humanity and personal loyalty forbid us to abandon the Führer in his hour of greatest need, I would otherwise appear for the rest of my life as a dishonourable traitor…

Together with my wife, and on behalf of my children, who are too young to speak for themselves and who, if they were older, would unreservedly agree with me, I express my unalterable resolution not to leave the Reich capital even if it falls, but rather, at the Führer's side, to end a life that for me personally would have no further value if I couldn't spend it in the Führer's service.[6]

Hitler, Göbbels and Martin Bormann were all standing over Traudl as she completed her work, adding to her nervousness as she struggled with the last page of Hitler's testament. It was virtually torn from the typewriter when it was finished, taken to the conference room to be signed and witnessed at once. The three copies were then handed to three different couriers to be smuggled out of Berlin in different directions. One was to go to Nazi party headquarters in Munich, one to the new Wehrmacht commander Field-Marshal Ferdinand Schörner, and the third to Admiral Dönitz, the man who was to replace the Führer after he was gone.

Hitler went to bed soon after signing his testament. It was getting on for dawn by then, the harbinger of another disastrous day for the German defenders of Berlin. Watching him as he retired to his quarters, Traudl thought that Hitler's life was effectively over now. He would be ready to die as soon as he knew that at least one copy of his testament had reached its destination through Russian lines.

Göbbels was ready to die too, along with his wife and six small children. They would probably die by poison, since everybody in the bunker was being issued with cyanide capsules. Traudl had watched the poison being tested on Hitler's dog Blondi. There had been a smell of bitter almonds as Hitler and a doctor bent over the animal, which had died at once. Hitler's face had been like a death mask as he straightened up afterwards and hurried wordlessly to his room.

But it was Göbbels' children who worried Traudl the most. They were delightful kids, nice-looking and very well-behaved, entirely innocent of the evil that was their father's stock in trade. Playing happily in their room, they had no idea of what was about to happen to them. Their mother had told them that they might have to be inoculated, as a precaution against disease, but that was all they knew. Magda Göbbels hadn't had the courage to tell them anything more. Nor had anyone else.

———

Outside, as dawn came up over the ruins of Berlin, the battle was beginning for the Reichstag, the great Parliament building that dominated the centre of the city. The Reichstag's shattered dome had long been the aiming point for the Russian advance, a highly visible marker for their troops as they pushed forward through the rubble. It had become a symbol for both sides in an increasingly desperate struggle for control of the city. Neither side was prepared to give an inch of ground in the fight. The German defenders understood as well as the Russians that once the Red flag flew over the Reichstag, their capital would be lost forever and the war would all have been for nothing.

The Reichstag stood on the banks of the River Spree. The Russians had crossed the river during the night, forcing their way over the Moltke Bridge 500 yards to the west. The fighting had been long and bloody, with heavy casualties on both sides, but the Russians had managed to establish a bridgehead on the German bank by early morning. As the sky began to lighten, they held one side of the street leading to the open ground in front of the Reichstag. The Germans held the other. The fighting remained relentless, with no quarter given and none expected as they grappled with each other from house to house and building to building across the street.

The German defence was savage. Many of the defenders were SS, hard-faced young fanatics who had come up through the Hitler Youth and had never known anything except Nazism in their young lives. They thought nothing of storming into any building displaying a white flag and massacring the occupants. They hanged cowards from lamp posts and shot deserters out of hand. They fought with the courage of young men who were not afraid to die, who had been taught no higher calling in the service of Führer and Fatherland. As the German defenders saw it, they were fighting to hold the Russians back until Wenck's army arrived, and the Americans with him who were racing to Berlin to protect their capital and save German culture from the Red menace. It was simply a question of hanging on until help arrived from the West.

The Russian attack was equally determined. The Russian generals were in a barely concealed competition to be the first to reach the Reichstag. Whoever commanded the unit that captured the building and raised the Red flag over the city would be a Hero of the Soviet Union for the rest of his life. Habitually cavalier with the lives of their men, the Russian generals didn't seem to care how many were killed as they drove them forward towards the gaunt, grey building that now stood in plain view of them, only a few hundred yards away along the street.

But ordinary Russian soldiers were increasingly reluctant to die this close to the end of the war. So many had been killed in the past few days that their numbers had had to be made up with prisoners of war newly released from German camps. Instead of going home, the prisoners had been sent straight to the front line with guns in their hands, given a chance to atone in battle for the shame of having been a prisoner. Some welcomed the opportunity for another crack at the Germans after all they had suffered in prison camp. Most wanted no further part in the fighting. Their ranks had been stiffened by hard-line Komsomol and Communist Party members, the Bolshevik equivalent of the SS, tough young men who brooked no resistance and insisted on carrying the war to the enemy. To the watching Germans, it sometimes seemed as if the Russians killed as many of their own men with friendly fire as they did the enemy.

The battle for the Reichstag began at half past eight that morning with a preliminary bombardment to soften the defences for the ensuing attack. The bombardment was massive: all the field artillery, rocket launchers, tanks and self-propelled guns that the Russians could bring to bear on the Parliament building. It lasted for an hour and a half, after which the Russians intended to begin their assault against the dazed defenders.

As the fighting continued, however, it quickly became clear that the assault would have to be postponed, perhaps for the rest of the day, because the buildings along the way were still being held by the enemy. The Ministry of the Interior, a massive office complex beside the river, was defended in strength by Germans who stubbornly refused to surrender. The Russians were forced to take the building floor by floor and staircase by staircase, clearing each room of the enemy before advancing cautiously to the next. Progress was so slow that it would be evening, at the earliest, before they could turn their attention to the Reichstag, far too late to launch an assault that day.

But the assault had to come next morning, the generals knew, because next morning was the last day of April. No matter how many people were killed in the process, the Russian commanders were determined to see the Red flag flying over the Reichstag by nightfall on the last day of April. The timing was vital. Any later and Stalin wouldn't be able to claim the credit for it when he took the salute from the Kremlin at the following morning's May Day parade in Moscow.

—

Across the rest of Berlin it was the same story, the Russians closing in on all sides while the Germans struggled to hold them back. There was no fixed front line as the battle raged to and fro. Berlin's canals formed a natural barrier, but the Russians were advancing underneath them along the U-Bahn lines to attack the Germans in the rear. The Germans were doing the same, leading to clashes in pitch darkness as the two sides fought it out in train tunnels far beneath the earth.

Helmut Altner had spent much of the previous day underground, stepping nervously forward with the rest of his patrol along one tunnel after another. They had been attacked by their own people at one point, shot at by Hitler Youth and Waffen-SS as they arrived at a U-Bahn station. Four men had been killed or wounded before the defenders had realised their mistake. The two patrols had then joined forces in an attempt to force a passage past the enemy. Fighting had been furious as the Russians fired at them from an adjacent tunnel, bullets flying in all directions as both sides opened up with Panzerfausts and machine guns. Altner had lost all sense of time as he stumbled for hour after hour through the blackness, often crawling forward on all fours in a desperate attempt to avoid being hit and dying unnoticed in the dark.

He had been enormously relieved when they had emerged at last into the open air, parading for roll call in the ticket hall of a U-Bahn station. He had had enough of fighting underground. If he was going to be killed, he would far prefer it to happen in the open air rather than down a tunnel, like a rat in a drainpipe.

Altner had spent the rest of the night creeping through the no man's land west of the Zoological Gardens, trailing after the man in front as they advanced through the rubble, expecting to be attacked at any moment. They had come under fire once or twice, but had pressed on regardless, heading back to their base at Ruhleben. They had passed a lost child at one stage, crying in the darkness as it called for its mother. They had seen two men furtively cutting the flesh from a dead horse still harnessed to a wagon, and had stepped over dead soldiers from both sides: a Hitler Youth with his head smashed to a pulp, a Russian woman in a brown uniform, her hair in disarray as she lay beside a burned out tank. Mostly, however, the streets had been deserted as they passed, the barricades abandoned and the buildings empty on either side. Everything had been eerily quiet in their immediate vicinity, while the din of battle continued unabated elsewhere.

As dawn approached, and the Russians prepared for their attack on the Reichstag, Altner found himself back at Ruhleben, looking forward to some sleep at last after more than twenty four hours on his feet. The place was full of rumours as he searched for somewhere to lie down. Some Germans still had faith in Wenck's relieving army; others had heard of a new secret weapon that could yet turn the war in their favour: a gas or a bomb or something that could be launched against America with a destructive power never seen before. Altner himself had heard a story earlier that seemed even more unlikely. It was about the Führer in his bunker:

One soldier says that Hitler got married in the bunker under the Reichs Chancellery yesterday. A latrine rumour? That would have been a jolly wedding night under the thunder of the guns! And we still have to go on fighting for this man, to whom Germany no longer belongs! Because of the oath we swore to him, soldiers and civilians have to go on dying. Someone says that Hitler has married an actress and that she will appear as a milkmaid on the new twenty mark note.[7]

Too exhausted to care much, Altner didn't know what to make of the rumour:

Depression has set in. Most people do not want to believe it, and even I find it unbelievable. I think that, as a result of the shock of the news of Hitler's marriage, many of them have started thinking for themselves. Someone says that, once the capital has fallen, he is to be flown out with the whole government from Ruhleben to Brazil to continue the fight from there, in any case as far as possible from the firing, so as to be out of immediate danger. A soldier claims to have seen Hitler climb into an armoured personnel carrier on the 27th, demanding to be taken to the scene of the fighting in the Tiergarten. However, I think this just another fairy story, like so many others.[8]

—

While Altner searched for a place to sleep, Hildegard Knef and Ewald von Demandowsky were thinking of following Hitler's example and getting married. In the freight yard at Schmargendorf, under sniper fire so intense that a water container had just been shot out of Hildegard's hands, Demandowsky had asked her to be his wife. He wanted to marry her while they still had the chance, before one or other of them was killed in the fighting.

Hildegard could think of several objections to getting married, not least that Demandowsky already had a wife. But he argued that no one knew that at Schmargendorf. He saw no reason why the lieutenant shouldn't marry the two of them at once, like the captain on a ship.

They were still discussing it when they heard a rumble from the tennis courts. Peering out of their hut, they saw a tank weaving through the craters, flattening bushes, fences and anything else that stood in its way. Looking closer, they were very relieved to see that the tank was German. 'That's the relief force,' Demandowsky shouted to Hildegard. 'I knew it. I knew it. I always told you they wouldn't let us down.'

As he spoke, a small boy in a Hitler Youth jacket sprinted past them towards the tank. The boy was carrying a Panzerfaust. Before anyone could stop him, he fired it and the tank disappeared in a sheet of flame.

The blast knocked everyone off their feet. Covered in blood, the lieutenant was the first to pick himself up. Rising groggily to his feet, he began to curse the Hitler Youth furiously. Demandowsky chose that moment to announce his wedding plans.

'We want to get married,' he told the lieutenant. 'We'd like you to marry us.'

Still dazed, the lieutenant stood stock still in the glare of the burning tank. With so much else on his mind, he could hardly believe what he was hearing.

'I don't have the authority,' he snapped at Demandowsky, after a moment. He was about to say more when he took a sniper's bullet full in the face. Hildegard watched in horror as the lieutenant slumped wordlessly to the ground, his face a bloody mess, just a lump of red meat under his helmet where his features had just been.

Hildegard didn't linger. She and Demandowsky ran for cover at once, zigzagging hastily across the freight yard while bullets flew all around them. Some soldiers gave them covering fire as they sprinted for the embankment and were pulled up over a wall. Hildegard was glad to see that these were real soldiers, not old men or Hitler Youths or SS. There were fifteen or twenty of them and they clearly knew their business.

The Russians attacked later, giving their usual screech as they charged across the freight yard. Crouching down, the Germans held their fire until the last possible moment, Hildegard gripping the ammunition belt while Demandowsky aimed the machine gun. They managed to beat the Russians off, but they knew it would only be a matter of time before they tried again. The Germans retreated as soon as night fell, quietly abandoning their position and slipping back through the ruins towards Hohenzollerndamm under cover of darkness.

They found a cellar full of civilians and tried to join them, hoping for some shelter from the constant fire in the streets. The civilians were mostly women and children, sitting on kitchen chairs around a single candle stub, waiting passively for the Russians to arrive. They weren't pleased to see Hildegard and the others.

'Go away!' they yelled. 'We don't want any soldiers here. They'll kill us if they find you here. Go away!'

'We just need some water,' said one of the soldiers.

'Have a heart.' A fat woman was indignant. 'We've got children here.'

Another woman, a toothless old hag, took pity on them. Emerging from a corner, she shoved a bottle of water into the soldier's hands. 'God have mercy on us,' she mumbled, as she turned away. Like everyone else in the room, she was under no illusions about what was going to happen when the Russians arrived.

They all seemed mad to Hildegard, like sheep in a slaughterhouse patiently waiting to be killed. Leaving them to it, she was glad to rejoin the others outside. The whole street appeared to be in flames as she emerged. There was no more talk of marriage as she and Demandowsky linked up with some other soldiers and set off at a run for Hohenzollerndamm, where they had orders to dig in at the cemetery and be ready to hold the Russians again when they attacked at dawn.

———

The women in the cellar had every reason to fear the Russians. Thousands of women were being raped every day as the fight for Berlin intensified. It was often the first thing the Russians did when they arrived, after disarming everyone and pocketing their wrist watches.

Some said that the front line troops were well disciplined and that it was the ones who came after who could not be trusted. Others said that the rapists were recently liberated prisoners of war or soldiers avenging similar assaults on their own womenfolk during the German advance. Whatever their motives, the result was always the same for the women. Young and old alike, they were all in danger as the Russians advanced. Some were raped again and again, so often that they lost count after a while. Others were assaulted so brutally that they couldn't walk afterwards and could only crawl away, hoping not to be attacked any further. After all it had endured on the Eastern Front, the Russian Army was not inclined to show any mercy to the German women of Berlin.

Ursula Köster was hiding in a Zehlendorf cellar with her parents and three children when the Russians came for her. She was raped by four soldiers that night and another two next morning. Staggering outside afterwards, she found an upturned bathtub lying in the rubble of the communal gardens. She crawled underneath and hid in it with her six-year-old twins and her seven-month-old son.

Hannelore von Cmuda, aged only seventeen, was raped repeatedly by drunken troops, then shot three times and left for dead. Anneliese Antz was dragged from her mother's bed just before dawn and taken screaming to an apartment, where a Soviet officer roughly assaulted her. Her sister Ilse was stripped naked by another soldier who mistook her half-starved body for a man's before realising his mistake and raping her. 'That's what the Germans did in Russia,' he told her, after he had finished.

Eighteen-year-old Juliane Brochnik hid behind the sofa in her father's cellar when the Russians came. She was safe until two elderly Germans in the adjoining cellar told the Russians where she was. Margarete Probst concealed her blonde hair under a cap, dirtying her face and putting a large sticking plaster on her cheek to make herself unattractive. She succeeded, but other women in the shelter with her at Kreuzberg were less fortunate: 'The girls were simply rounded up and taken to the apartments upstairs,' she remembered. 'We could hear their screams all night. The sound even penetrated down to the cellars.'[9] One of the women was eighty, raped repeatedly by the Russians despite her advanced age.

In another shelter, Margarete Promeist too was raped, despite telling her assailant that she was far too old for him. Margarete was supposed to be in charge of the shelter, but there was nothing she could do against the Russians: 'For two days and two nights, wave after wave of Russians came into my shelter raping and looting. Women were killed if they refused. Some were shot and killed anyway. In one room alone I found the bodies of six or seven women, all lying in the position in which they were raped, their heads battered in.'[10]

Actress Magda Wieland hid herself in a cupboard, only to be hauled out by an Asiatic soldier who then suffered premature ejaculation at the sight of a beautiful blonde. His companion raped her instead. Downstairs, Magda's Jewish friend Ellen Götz was dragged out and raped too, despite the protests of the Germans who were sheltering her. Ellen had hidden in the cellar after escaping from the prison in Lehrterstrasse, but her Jewishness did not save her from the Russians. They raped Jewish women and Communists as well, party members who had concealed their membership from the Nazis for twelve long years and had initially welcomed the Soviets with open arms.

And children too, young girls of eleven or twelve with torn ligaments, bleeding to death from punctured bowels after what the Russians had done to them. Few females were too young or too old for the Russians' attention. Their officers sometimes tried to stop them, but more often than not just laughed instead or attempted to join in. Women soldiers laughed too, amused at the sight of their comrades openly violating German women on the street. Individual Russian soldiers were occasionally kind and gentle, but as an army they showed no mercy as they fell on Berlin. Their country had suffered too much in the past four years for them to show any mercy. And the people of Germany hadn't suffered enough.

CHAPTER 7: BELSEN

In Belsen, the British had just finished burying the bodies. There had been ten thousand bodies when they liberated the camp on 15 April, the vast majority dead from typhus or starvation. The guards had refused to dispose of them for fear of infection, and the remaining prisoners had lacked the strength, so the bodies had been abandoned instead, dumped in great piles around the camp and left to rot.

The British had been shocked beyond belief at the sight of so many corpses. The first soldiers to reach the wire had retched at once, overcome by the smell of death before they had even entered the camp. The living had seemed almost as terrible as the dead, skeletal figures fighting over scraps of food or lying uncaring in their own excrement. The British were hardened troops who thought they had seen it all in the fight across Europe. But Belsen had made them cry like babies.

The worst of it was that Belsen was not even an extermination camp. It had no purpose-built gas chambers or execution sheds. It was simply a holding camp that had gone wrong, overflowing with prisoners from elsewhere who had been moved to Belsen to escape the Russians advancing from the East. The Germans had never fed the prisoners well, but they had found it difficult to feed them at all when the food supply was disrupted by the British advance. The Germans had left the prisoners to starve instead, while remaining perfectly well nourished themselves.

Richard Dimbleby had been the first to reveal Belsen to the outside world. Reporting for the BBC, he had spoken of living skeletons and cannibalism, corpses with their liver and kidneys cut out, men and women clubbed senseless by the SS and then thrown alive into the crematorium.

His report had been measured and calm, but it had been received with frank incredulity by the BBC. They had refused to broadcast it until the story had been verified by independent sources. Dimbleby had telephoned London in a blind rage, swearing that he would never make another broadcast as long as he lived if this one wasn't transmitted. The BBC had reluctantly complied, while insisting on a few cuts nevertheless for their own peace of mind.

Yet Dimbleby had only told the half of it. He hadn't mentioned the children forced to stand and watch as their parents were murdered; the man torn apart by dogs for calling out to his wife; the suspected cannibals made to sit with a dead man's eyeball between their lips and their arms above their heads, beaten to death as soon as they wavered and couldn't hold the position any longer. He had said nothing of excrement inches deep in every hut; children throwing stones at corpses; women who hadn't menstruated since their arrival at the camp; women co-opted into prostitution – fourteen German soldiers a day for five days a week – in return for enough food to keep body and soul together. Nor had he spoken of the prisoners praying for the British to arrive before a planned gas chamber was completed; of guards continuing to kill prisoners even after the British had appeared; of invalids screaming with fear whenever anyone came near them with a needle; of others in a blind panic as they were carried on stretchers towards a building with chimneys, which for Auschwitz survivors could have only one meaning. Dimbleby hadn't mentioned any of these things in his broadcast. There had been only so much his listeners could take at a single hearing.

The British had hardly known where to begin after the initial shock had worn off. Feeding the prisoners and nursing the sick had been the most urgent priorities, followed by burying the dead. Unprepared for the complexity of the task, and with the front line still only a few miles away, the British had made mistakes at first, pressing their own rations on prisoners too far gone to digest food properly, killing unknown numbers with kindness instead of saving them as they had intended.

Michael Bentine, an intelligence officer with the RAF, had been at Celle nearby when a British doctor appeared in a jeep, demanding K rations and chocolate. 'I've never seen anything so awful in my life,' he had told Bentine. 'You just won't believe it till you see it – for God's sake come and help them!'[1] Others had helped too. Lieutenant Robert Runcie and Major Willie Whitelaw of the Scots Guards had delivered a jeepload of sweets and chocolate from their battalion's own rations for the children in the camp. But British Army rations had often proved too rich for stomachs unused to such fare. Prisoners had continued to die at the rate of several hundred a day for weeks after the British arrived.

The bodies had all had to be buried. The prison guards had been made to do the work at first, Germans and Hungarians lugging corpses so putrid that the arms sometimes came away in their hands. The guards had complained that they would catch typhus, but had received scant sympathy from the British. SS guards demanding a few minutes' rest had been made to lie face down in a burial pit, where they had cowered in fear, expecting to be killed at any moment. One guard had committed suicide after a few hours of burial work. Others had begged to be shot. Progress had been so slow that the British had been forced to take over after a while, putting aside their scruples and using bulldozers to finish the job before the bodies decomposed altogether.

The work had been interrupted on 20 April, when a flight of Focke-Wulfs had attacked the camp, machine-gunning the inmates at dawn and killing several non-combatants in a field full of Red Cross vehicles. Four days later, a delegation of German officials had been summoned to the main compound. The mayor of Celle and other local burgomasters had been forced to stand on the brink of an open grave containing a thousand emaciated corpses while a camera filmed them in one take, panning upwards from the bodies to the faces of the burgomasters and the surrounding camp to avoid any accusations of trick photography. The SS guards had been summoned as well. All had listened stony-faced as a speech was broadcast in German from a loudspeaker mounted on a jeep:

> What you will see here is the final and utter condemnation of the Nazi party. It justifies every measure which the United Nations will take to exterminate that party. What you will see here is such a disgrace to the German people that their name must be erased from the list of civilised nations.
>
> You who represent the fathers and brothers of German youth see before your eyes a few of the sons and daughters who bear a small part of the direct responsibility for this crime. Only a small part, yet too heavy a burden for the human soul to bear. But who bears the real responsibility? You who have allowed your Führer to carry out his terrible whims. You who have proved incapable of doing anything to check his perverted triumphs. You who had heard about these camps, or had at least a slight conception of what happened in them. You did not rise up spontaneously to cleanse the name of Germany, not fearing the personal consequences. You stand here judged through what you will see in this camp.[2]

But the burgomasters had proved reluctant to take any of the blame. Leslie Hardman, a rabbi with the British Army, had watched with contempt as the officials listened sullenly:

> They looked down into the pit of human wreckage and saw something of the outcome of the brutality, sadism and perversion committed in their name. They saw the heaped mounds of earth crouching like huge, patient sheep-dogs waiting to enclose their charges in their final pen. They saw the khaki of the British soldier, the hideous striped garb of the inmate, the white collar of the padre. But they had known nothing, seen nothing, heard nothing.
>
> Stolid, unmoving, they listened to the officer's words; then one of them, a woman, began to cry. Her sobs broke against their solidity, fell into the vast grave and were lost. The groans of the dead beat against our ears. But the burgomasters had seen, heard and known nothing.[3]

Chaim Herzog, a Haganah activist before the war, but now a British officer, shared Hardman's contempt. Herzog had visited several camps as the British advanced, including Belsen. He had never seen the slightest flicker of embarrassment on the faces of ordinary Germans forced to contemplate their countrymen's handiwork:

> When the villagers arrived to confront their nation's atrocities, neither I nor anyone else I knew saw any expression of horror or remorse at the brutalities done in their name. For Germans to say, then or today, that they knew nothing of what had transpired – as nearly every German claimed – was a desperate lie. I was there. I saw the faces of the ordinary citizens. I saw the close proximity of the towns to the camps. I smelled the rotting corpses of the Jews and gypsies and Poles. Believe me, the German people had to have known – the truth was omnipresent and inescapable.'[4]

Sixteen-year-old Esther Brunstein, transported to Belsen in January but now happily liberated by the British, told them of trudging from Celle station towards the camp:

> On the way I remember seeing neat little red-roofed houses. It seemed another world, one in which we had played no part for so long and I was surprised to find it still existed. We could see

children and adults peeping through the curtained windows, looking on at the throng of skeletal creatures in striped concentration camp garb. I wondered then and still wonder today what thoughts went through the minds of these onlookers. Were they really unaware, as so many later claimed, of what did go on in their Fatherland?[5]

Some war correspondents had asked the same question of the local population. A few Germans had admitted to hearing rumours, but had attributed them to Allied propaganda. Only one man, a farmer, had confessed to being aware of Belsen's reputation. He had turned a blind eye rather than find out more:

I didn't know very much about it. Each morning I had to drive up there with a cart full of vegetables, swedes and turnips mostly, and one of the SS guards took the horse and cart from me at the gate. After a bit the cart and horse were returned and I drove away. I was never allowed inside and I didn't want to go in anyway. I knew something horrible was going on, but I didn't ask about it lest I should find myself inside.[6]

The farmer did not impress the correspondents, but he found an unlikely ally in Willie Whitelaw. He and Runcie had driven over from Bad Bevensen, where the Scots Guards were resting for a few days before continuing the advance. They had been as shocked as anyone by Belsen and never forgot what they had seen. Yet Whitelaw was prepared to give local Germans the benefit of the doubt when they claimed they hadn't realised the extent of what was going on: 'The countryside around it gave no clue to the horrors inside the compound. I can readily believe that many Germans in the neighbourhood had little appreciation of what was happening.'[7]

The only good news was that the dead had finally been buried – among them Anne Frank from Amsterdam, who had recorded in her diary as early as October 1942 that Jews were being taken away and gassed. The last of the bodies had been bulldozed into a mass grave on 28 April. Inmates were continuing to die in hundreds every day, but they weren't being left to rot any more. They were being taken away instead and buried at once, not just abandoned where they lay. There were no more corpses in Belsen. They had all been cleared away and the effect on camp morale was palpable.

The delousing was almost complete too. One more day and everybody in the camp would have been squirted with DDT powder, their clothes fumigated and their bodies scrubbed clean. The first of the contaminated huts had already been destroyed, its occupants removed to more sanitary quarters and the huts incinerated with a flamethrower. Adding to the good news, some genius had introduced lipstick to the camp. A large consignment had just arrived, enough for every woman at Belsen to paint her lips if she wished. Huge numbers had done so, happily recalling that they had been feminine once and might be so again one day. Lipstick had turned out to be an enormous morale booster, making all the difference between life and death for some of the women in the camp.

But the Union Jack still didn't fly over Belsen. The British had been there for two weeks, yet they refused to fly their flag over so much evil. They intended to raise it once, symbolically, when the inmates had been restored to health and the camp had been cleansed of all shame. Until then, the Union Jack remained firmly in its locker. No British symbol of any kind flew over the horror of Bergen-Belsen.

—

While rank and file German guards assisted in the clearing up at Belsen, the camp's commandant was being interrogated by the British. Josef Kramer had been taken in irons to the nearby prison camp at Celle, where dumbfounded British officers had been interviewing him for days, trying to fathom the mind of a man so blind to the realities of what had happened at Belsen.

The only consensus they could reach was that Kramer was a man of ox-like stupidity. Because of the typhus, Belsen had been handed over to the British under flag of truce. Ordered to supervise the handover, Kramer had done exactly what he was told, remaining at his post to meet the British instead of escaping while he had the chance, as the worst of the SS had done. It had never crossed his mind that the British might not be happy about what they found at Belsen.

Kramer had been unemployed before the war, an electrician looking for work. The SS had made him an officer and given him a good job in camp administration. He had risen rapidly through the system, working at Auschwitz and other places before transferring to Belsen. He was a member of the Nazi party, but only because it was necessary for his job. He had no interest in politics, nor any great animosity towards the Jews, although he had gassed plenty. It was all just a job to Kramer. He did what he was told and got his meal ticket in return.

The British had been outraged at his indifference to the suffering in the camp. Under the terms of the truce, Kramer had expected to return to his own lines after the handover, but the British had clapped him in irons instead, shackling his legs and beating him with rifle butts. They had imprisoned him in the cooler at first, the cold storage room at the officers' mess. Then they had sent him to the prison camp at Celle, assisted on his way by a shower of stones from Wehrmacht troops as outraged as the British at what they had seen in Belsen. Kramer wasn't going to rejoin his own side, now that the camp had been handed over. He was going to stand trial for war crimes instead.

So was Irma Grese, his erstwhile lover. They had met at Auschwitz, where she had been known for her striking blonde looks and her cruelty. Irma Grese had apparently derived sexual satisfaction from the beatings, arbitrary shootings and random selections for the gas chamber that she had administered at Auschwitz. Her mother had committed suicide when she was a child and her father had beaten her repeatedly. He had refused to allow her to join the Bund Deutscher Mädchen, the female equivalent of the Hitler Youth, and had beaten her again when she joined the concentration camp service. He wouldn't have the uniform in the house.

Irma Grese had wanted to be a nurse, originally. Bullied at school for her lack of intelligence, she had embraced Nazism instead. Some of the Jewish women at Belsen had been doctors in their previous lives, making a good living out of medicine while an Aryan girl like Irma couldn't even get a job as a nurse. But she had shown them who was boss in Belsen. She had had the power of life or death over them, and she had exercised it at will.

So had Juana Bormann and Elisabeth Volkenrath, a hairdresser in her previous life but a monster at Belsen. So had other female guards, former secretaries and typists who had turned into strutting sadists in German uniform. The word at Celle was that they too would be put on trial after the war, held to account for what they had done instead of going free. There was talk of the death penalty for some of them, although they found it hard to believe. They had broken no German laws and the Allies were civilised people. The British didn't hang young girls. Whatever penalties they imposed, they would surely never hang the female guards at Belsen for something that had happened in wartime.

—

While the guards awaited their fate, other Germans were still working at Belsen – mostly nurses or civilians who had had nothing to do with the atrocities in the camp and were continuing with their duties under the British. Among them was Georg Will, a professional cinema manager from Berlin.

Will had moved to Belsen the previous year after cinemas in the capital had been forced to close. He had run the camp cinema for the guards while his wife Liesel ran the canteen. The two of them had quickly become part of the Belsen machine, supplying comforts for the SS and keeping them entertained when they were off duty. The Wills had lived well as a result, with a pleasant flat above the cinema and a private supply of tinned food that they had kept carefully to themselves at a time when thousands were starving to death only a few hundred yards away.

Now that the British had arrived, however, the Wills were wondering if they too might have to pay a price for their involvement with Belsen. They had seen Josef Kramer taken away in shackles, terrified out of his wits as the Wehrmacht stoned him and the prisoners bayed for his blood. They had seen guards manhandled and Fritz Klein, the camp doctor, thrown into a burial pit by furious British soldiers. The Wills had committed no atrocities themselves, but they remained uneasy, nevertheless. They were worried that they had been on the wrong side at a time when the Allies were evidently in no mood to forgive and forget.

There was, however, a redeeming factor that they hoped would work in their favour. Liesel Will's younger sister was an officer in the United States Army. Appalled by the anti-Semitism of the Nazis, Captain Marlene Dietrich had renounced her German citizenship before the war and become a naturalised American instead. She had spent the war years singing to the troops of her adopted country, supporting them in their struggle against the land of her forefathers. She had done so with mixed feelings, aware that the Americans had right on their side, but aware too that every bomb or shell that fell on Berlin posed a threat to her widowed mother, particularly now that the Russians were closing in on the capital.

Marlene Dietrich was with the American Army as it advanced into Bavaria. She had been with the army since the previous September, so close to the front line that she had sometimes been shelled by German 88s and had to be evacuated in a hurry from the Battle of the Bulge. She had cheerfully traded her movie-star status for the life of a soldier, sheltering in stables and bombed-out houses, sharing her sleeping bag with lice and rats, washing in a bucket. She had made a point of never grumbling or complaining.

The troops had loved her for it, Germans as well as Americans. Surprised to find herself a Wehrmacht pin-up, she had sung *Lili Marlene* to wounded German prisoners and had encountered little hostility on the streets as she advanced into her native land. Instead of reviling her as a traitor, many ordinary Germans had come to her with their problems, asking her to put in a good word for them with the Americans.

Marlene Dietrich knew her sister was in Belsen. As she liked to imagine it, the Wills had been taken there as hostages to discourage her from entertaining Allied troops. The truth was rather more complicated. Like millions of other Germans, the Wills were just trying to survive. They had been part of the regime at Belsen when the Nazis were in command. Now that the Allies had arrived, though, they wanted to make the most of their American connection. They were expecting Marlene to visit them in the next few days, just as soon as she could get hold of a jeep. They were hoping she would take care of them when she appeared, see them right with the British. The Wills were going to need all the help they could get with the British, now that awkward questions were beginning to be asked about exactly who had done what at Belsen.

—

In London, it was Sunday afternoon. Crowds were flocking to see the first pictures from the camps, the ones that had been too dreadful to print in a newspaper. Photographs from Belsen, Buchenwald and Nordhausen had just been put on display instead, publicly exhibited at various places around the capital so that people could see for themselves that Dimbleby and others had not been exaggerating their reports from Germany.

Mollie Panter-Downes was one of those who travelled to London that day to see the pictures. Like millions of others over the next few days, at exhibitions all over Britain and the United States, she saw the bodies on the wire, the ovens and the living skeletons and understood at once just why the war against Germany had been so necessary:

> It has taken the camera to bring home to the slow, good-natured, sceptical British what, as various liberal journals have tartly pointed out, the pens of their correspondents have been unsuccessfully trying to bring home to them since as far back as 1933. Millions of comfortable families, too kind and too lazy in those days to make the effort to believe what they conveniently looked upon as a newspaper propaganda stunt, now believe the horrifying, irrefutable evidence that even blurred printing on poor wartime paper has made all too clear. There are long queues of people waiting silently wherever the photographs are on exhibition. The shock to the public has been enormous.[8]

That wasn't all. Britain was full of well-fed Germans, prisoners of war who received the same rations as British servicemen, under the Geneva Convention. The British themselves were half–starved after five years of war, but the enemy in their midst were getting twice as much, sleek SS men shovelling away the calories while British civilians could only stand and watch. After seeing the photographs from the concentration camps, the British wanted to know why the Germans were being fed so well, and how long it ought to continue, when they had treated their own prisoners with such inhumanity and contempt.

CHAPTER 8:
OPERATION *MANNA*

Food was short in Britain, but in some parts of occupied Europe it was almost non-existent as the war entered its final stages. In the skies above Holland, an air drop had begun that afternoon, a mass delivery of supplies to the people of the Netherlands. Over the next few days, Allied bombers were scheduled to drop hundreds of tons of food supplies and more than fourteen million individual ration packs to the famished Dutch, enough to keep them going until the war ended and the roads could be reopened to normal transport.

It was not before time. After months of disruption as the fighting came closer, Holland had finally run out of food. Thousands had already died of hunger and tens of thousands more would follow within a week or two, if the situation was not urgently addressed. The occupying Germans had just cut the ration for Dutch civilians from 400 calories a day to 230, not nearly enough to sustain life. The many Dutch who could find no food at all had long since eaten their family pets and were subsisting on grass, sugar beet and tulip bulbs. In Amsterdam, one church alone housed 1,500 bodies in mouldering piles, urgently awaiting burial.

The German starvation of the Dutch had been deliberate at first, a sharp reduction in the food supply to punish them for the help they had given the Allies at Arnhem in 1944, when a mass rail strike had prevented German reinforcements from hurrying to the battlefield. But the policy was no longer deliberate. Cut off from home by the Allied advance, the German forces in Holland had recently developed a keen interest in the welfare of the civilians under their control. They had secretly approached the Allies for help in feeding them.

Mindful of what had happened in Buchenwald and Belsen, the Allies had agreed to a meeting to discuss the problem. General Eisenhower had sent Major-General Sir Francis de Guingand to consult representatives of Arthur Seyss-Inquart, the Nazi Reichskommissar of Holland, at a school in Achterveld on the Allied side of the line. The Germans had not had the authority to agree to a ceasefire, but both sides had accepted that the problem was urgent and something had to be done. They had arranged to meet again on 30 April to finalise the details.

Yet time was of the essence, with the Dutch so short of food. Although the truce was not yet in place, the Allies had decided to begin the food drop anyway, hoping for the best and trusting to luck that the Germans would not oppose them. The weather had been bad on 28 April, but it improved slightly on the 29th. The air bases of East Anglia remained shrouded in fog, which prevented the Americans from taking part in the first day of the drop, but bases elsewhere were less badly affected. The RAF rose to the challenge.

They made a test run first, a preliminary drop by two Lancasters flying along a corridor prescribed by the Germans to see if they would be allowed to drop food over the designated area without being shot at. The two Lancasters had been chosen because they had not yet been fitted with secret new radio equipment and were therefore expendable if they fell into enemy hands. One Lancaster had a Canadian pilot, the other Australian. It was a tense time for both crews as they took off early on the morning of 29 April and headed through a squall of bad weather towards the Dutch coast. Visibility was so poor that Canadian Bob Upcott was forced to fly on his instruments through the murk. It wasn't until they reached Holland that the weather suddenly cleared up, giving him a bird's eye view of the German defences only a few hundred feet below:

> When we passed the Dutch coast we saw anti-aircraft guns that pointed their muzzles in our direction. We even saw tanks that tried to keep their gun barrels on us. We were looking right down a number of barrels. All the guns were still manned and they didn't have any reason to do otherwise since the war was still going on.[1]

There were very few Dutch about. They had been warned to expect a food drop at some point, but they weren't expecting it so soon. The two Lancasters flew straight on towards the drop zone at Duindigt, a race track near The Hague. Upcott found the target without difficulty and commenced his approach run:

The Australian pilot was on my port side, flying echelon port. I dropped first when we were over the race track, while the Australian dropped almost that same moment. I had waited a little bit too long with the drop, because I partly overshot the drop zone. Half of the load slammed into the bleachers at the end of the race course.[2]

But the drop had been made, one way or another. The Lancasters flew safely back to Britain, unmolested by the Germans except for a hole in Upcott's fuselage that had probably come from a pistol shot. As soon as they were over the North Sea, they radioed back to base that the mission had been successful. The BBC thereupon announced the commencement of Operation *Manna* on the lunchtime news. Shortly afterwards, an armada of 200 Lancasters set off for Holland, scheduled to arrive over their respective drop zones just before two that afternoon.

Pathfinder aircraft led the way: Mosquitoes flying ahead to mark the drop zones with red target indicators. Alerted by the BBC, the Dutch on the ground had also marked the centre of each zone with a red light in the middle of a white cross or T. There were four zones across Holland initially, each near a major city. The Lancasters rumbled towards them, hoping that the reports were accurate and they would not be fired at when they crossed the Dutch coast.

It was a mission of mercy for the RAF crews. They had been greatly looking forward to it. Some of the men were due for leave, but had volunteered to fly anyway rather than miss the operation altogether. After months and sometimes years of raining down bombs on Europe, knowing that innocent civilians were being killed along with the guilty, they all wanted to be part of Operation *Manna*. Dropping food to starving people was much more to their taste than bombing them into oblivion.

Some aircraft flew with a full complement, but others took only a skeleton crew, leaving more room for food. Some carried a full armament, while others lightened the aircraft by ditching their guns. The crew had all received rudimentary training in a mercy drop, learning to release their load from a very low altitude and at a slow speed so that the bags wouldn't burst on impact. It was quite the opposite of what they had been used to in their war against the Germans.

Flight-Sergeant Pat Russell piloted one of the Lancasters in the first wave. Their drop zone was an airfield south of Rotterdam. With five panniers of food in the bomb bay, Russell wasn't sure what to expect as they approached the Dutch coast:

We flew across Holland at an altitude of about two hundred feet and could see the crowds out in the streets waving anything they could lay their hands on. Here and there, the green uniforms of the Wehrmacht stood out; needless to say, they weren't waving. In fact, several aircraft came back with bullet holes in them.

After our previous operations, when we had been dropping nasties on Germany from 21,000 feet, the Manna flights were a joy for all sorts of reasons. We now had official instructions to fly low, which was normally not allowed but was highly enjoyable. We no longer expected to be shot either by fighters or flak. And we were caught up in the obvious excitement of the crowds below.[3]

Dutch reporter George Franks shared the excitement. He had hitched a lift on a Lancaster to witness the relief of his countrymen from the air:

From the moment we crossed the Dutch coast, people in the fields and roads and in the gardens of the sad little houses, waved frantically. But it was not until we were actually flying over The Hague that we saw what this manna from heaven really meant to the Dutch. Every road seemed full of people waving flags, sheets, or anything they could grab. The roofs of tall buildings were black with Dutch citizens welcoming us. On a barge we saw the Dutch tricolour bravely hoisted; across a large flat roof an Orange flag was colourfully stretched.

The people were certainly overjoyed to see these huge bombers emptying their bomb bays one after another on the target area, as thousands of food bombs fluttered out like confetti from a giant hand. And along the roads leading into The Hague were carts, prams and bicycles as the populace seemed to race to join in the great share-out. Unfortunately, owing to the recent spell of bad weather, we were just too late to give them their Sunday dinner, but with amazing enthusiasm the RAF aerial grocers certainly delivered the goods.[4]

Flour, yeast, sugar, margarine. Dried egg, peas, beans, cheese. Bars of chocolate. Cans of meat and bacon, dehydrated potato. Some airmen dropped cigarettes as well, tins of Players from their own rations. Others made parachutes out of handkerchiefs and dropped a personal gift of sweets and chocolate. It all fell to earth in a great shower, while the Dutch cheered and the aircrew waved. The Germans watched from a distance, still manning their defences in case the Allies dropped paratroops instead of food. First aid workers watched too, ready to assist if anybody was hit by a falling sack. The Dutch had been warned to keep away from the zones until the drop was over, but some couldn't help themselves and ran out into the open as soon as the Lancasters arrived, laughing and shrieking with the excitement of it all. For the people of Holland, most of whom were thirty or forty pounds underweight after the worst winter any of them had ever known, the arrival of the RAF that rainy afternoon really did seem like manna from heaven.

—

It was more than food, for the Dutch. It was the realisation that the war was nearly over and they had not been forgotten. The Dutch saw the Allied planes flying to their aid and knew that people were thinking of them in London, that plans were being made and help was on its way. The Germans would be gone soon and they would be among friends again, free at last after so long under Nazi occupation. The Dutch were not an emotional people, but it was easy to forget that as the Lancasters swept overhead and the emaciated figures below ran out of their houses and waved their national colours in the street. Another few days and they would all be properly looked after again. The whole ghastly nightmare would be over.

Journalist J. G. Raatgever was having a meagre lunch with his family at The Hague when the RAF arrived:

> We stared at each other. Bombers on Sunday? I looked outside and there I suddenly saw over the roofs two bombers, which roared like heavy cockchafers to the west. My youngest daughter began to cry and asked anxiously: 'They won't do us any harm?' But we understood suddenly: those are the Allied planes that bring us food. We left our meal, raced outside, waved with hats, shawls, flags, sheets, with anything, to the planes which by now were thundering over our streets in an interminable stream. In a flash our whole quiet street was filled with a cheering, waving crowd and the elated people were even dancing on the roofs. Many had tears in their eyes, others could not utter more than a few inarticulate cries.[5]

Seventeen-year-old Arie de Jong was there too: 'One could see the gunners waving in their turrets. A marvellous sight. Everywhere we looked, bombers could be seen. No one stayed inside and everybody dared to wave cloths and flags. What a feast! Everyone is so excited with joy. The war must be over soon now.'[6]

A ten-year-old boy was playing in his family's third floor apartment when he heard the familiar sound of Lancaster engines. The bombers came over every night, but he had never heard them in daylight before:

> On a bright, sunny morning, when I was playing or reading in my attic room, I heard the usual nightly sound approaching. But this time it was very unusual, it was broad daylight! The sound quickly grew louder and louder, the attic trembled and a moment later a dark shadow flashed past the window. I rushed to the window and must have been stunned.
>
> There they were, Lancasters, the first time we could see them. I thought they would fly straight into the room, they were at such low altitude, and one after another they roared over the houses. In the distance, there were many more. Coming from the east, the Lancasters flew in loose formation over The Hague. They were over the whole town. I could not count them. It was one broad, mighty stream of aircraft, many more than a hundred.
>
> Far away, in the direction of the Malieveld (an ancient tournament field) one could see clouds of dark specks falling from some of the aircraft. I did not understand what that could be and at that moment it did not matter at all.

The boy climbed up to the roof for a better view as the Lancasters flew overhead:

> They were black and brown giants, had four engines and a double rudder, guns poking out everywhere. One could easily look into the glass turrets and cockpit, could clearly see the airmen. They waved to us, made the V-sign, some of them had Dutch or British flags fixed inside the front gun turret.
>
> Some of the aircraft roaring over had their bomb doors still open. Sometimes an aircraft rolled slightly to and fro, meant as a greeting. The coloured roundels on the fuselage and wings were clearly visible, as were their registrations. Some of the airmen will have seen the little boy on the flat roof, but of course they raced past. And I was not the only one waving. There were many people waving from windows. Some were even waving the Dutch red–white–blue flags, though that was

dangerous because of fanatical Jerries. Ten minutes later, the euphoria was over, all the aircraft out of sight.[7]

But the food still had to be collected. The Dutch rushed to pick it up. Some tucked in at once, like the prisoners at Belsen, cramming themselves so full that their stomachs promptly rebelled and they vomited. Others pocketed the food for later. The vast majority handed the parcels to the people appointed to make sure that everything was distributed fairly, so that everyone got their share. It had been feared that riots might break out when the food arrived, but there was very little disorder. The black marketeers did not profit. It took so long to weigh everything and distribute it evenly across Holland – up to ten days, for the outlying regions – that a few people died of starvation in the meantime, though not many. The Dutch kept their discipline well and took care of their neighbours as well as themselves.

The most serious casualties on the first day came from falling sacks, not all of which landed in the right place. One killed a German soldier who saw a bag hurtling towards a young girl. There was no time to yell out a warning, so he threw himself on top of her to save her life. The girl survived, but the soldier was hit on the head and died instantly. He had been a decent young man, underneath his Wehrmacht helmet.

———

In London, Queen Wilhelmina of the Netherlands was following the drop with ill-concealed excitement. She had been lobbying for it ever since January, when she had made a personal appeal to Roosevelt, Churchill and King George VI, urging them to act at once to save her people from mass starvation. The Allies had had other priorities at the time, but Wilhelmina had never stopped lobbying. She had kept up the pressure, and now at last something was being done.

Wilhelmina was no great friend of the British. She had supported the Boers in the South African war and had traded with the Germans in the Great War. She had also given asylum to the Kaiser in 1918, repeatedly refusing to hand him over to the victorious Allies. But all that had changed when the Germans invaded her country in 1940. Rescued by the Royal Navy, Wilhelmina had made the difficult decision to seek exile in England rather than remain in Holland under Nazi rule. She had taken her government with her and kept in touch with her people through regular radio broadcasts, raising their morale and reminding them that she would certainly return one day, when Holland was free again.

The day had almost arrived. Wilhelmina had already returned to Holland once, making a flying visit in March to the southern provinces already liberated by the Allies. She had been close enough to the front line to hear shelling and to see the V2 rockets roaring overhead. This time, though, she was going home for good. Now that the Allied food drop had started, Wilhelmina had agreed with that, if the weather held, she would return to her people the next day, 30 April. She had chosen that day because it was her daughter Juliana's 36th birthday. The Dutch were very big on royal anniversaries and it would be a wonderful surprise for them to have their monarch back on Juliana's birthday. It would be a nice surprise for Juliana too.

⁓

Some parts of Holland were already free. The Rhine town of Arnhem, so bitterly contested in September 1944, had finally been liberated in the middle of April. Canadian troops pushing through it had discovered a ghost town, because the Germans had forced its 90,000 inhabitants to leave immediately after the Allied withdrawal in 1944. The Germans had looted their homes as soon as they had gone, keeping the valuables for themselves and sending all the clothing back to Germany for the use of civilians bombed out of their houses.

But the Dutch had come flooding back, once there was no chance of the Germans returning. They had been overjoyed to see the Canadians, who hadn't arrived a moment too soon. Like everyone else in Holland, the population around Arnhem had been half-starved, forced to fry tulip bulbs for food and make soup out of nettle leaves. Very few of the babies born to them in the previous twelve months had survived to see the spring. They had died of malnutrition, while their mothers had watched in despair, powerless to intervene.

Walter Cronkite, a United Press reporter who had parachuted into Arnhem in 1944, had returned to Holland with the Canadians to follow their advance. He shared the Canadians' concern at what they saw as they pressed forward: 'What little food there was, the German Army took. We found the Dutch near starvation. They had been reduced to eating tulip bulbs. Their clothes hung on their gaunt forms. They looked like children in their parents' clothing.'[8]

Food had been so scarce that Baron Aernoud van Heemstra's family, in their country home just outside Arnhem, had had nothing at all to eat on Christmas Day that winter. The Baron's fifteen-year-old granddaughter,

Audrey Hepburn-Ruston, had been so weak from hunger that she had had trouble climbing the stairs to her room. Sick with jaundice, weighing only ninety pounds, her legs and feet swollen from oedema, she had lived for months close to death, waiting like the rest of Holland for the Allies to arrive and bring the ordeal to an end.

Audrey Hepburn had been living with her mother in their own house in Arnhem until the Germans had evicted them. Her mother was a Dutch aristocrat, but her father was British, a descendant of James Hepburn, husband of Mary, Queen of Scots. They had been Fascists before the war, living in Britain and supporting Sir Oswald Mosley's Blackshirt movement, even to the extent of meeting Hitler on a fact-finding trip to Germany. But their divorce had been followed by her father's arrest and internment under British wartime regulations. Rather than stay in England and be bombed, Audrey's mother had taken her home to Holland in order to sit out the war in a neutral country. It was a decision she had come to regret after the Germans invaded in 1940.

Audrey Hepburn had suffered badly during the war. Despite his earlier Fascist leanings, her interned father had never been a traitor to Britain. Her mother's family were no friends of the Germans, either. The Van Heemstras had Jewish blood, several generations back, and had been obliged to accommodate the Kaiser in their castle at Doorn when he sought asylum after the Great War. They had later had to sell the castle to him against their wishes.

Audrey had seen enough of the Germans during the war to last her for ever. The same age as Anne Frank in Amsterdam, she had watched Jews being rounded up, many of them refugees from Germany, and transported to the holding camp at Westerbork for onward transition to Auschwitz. She had been a helpless witness as her own neighbours were herded into trucks and taken away:

> I'd go to the station with my mother to take a train and I'd see cattle trucks filled with Jews ... families with little children, with babies, herded into meat wagons – trains of big wooden vans with just a little slat open at the top and all those faces peering out. On the platform, soldiers herding more Jewish families with their poor little bundles and small children. They would separate them, saying 'The men go there and the women go there.' Then they would take the babies and put them in another van. We did not yet know that they were going to their death. We'd been told they were going to be taken to special camps.[9]

Audrey's own uncle had been executed by the Germans, shot in reprisal for a sabotage attack by the Resistance. She herself had lived in fear of being kidnapped and taken to a military brothel, as so many other girls had been. She had indeed been picked up by the Wehrmacht once, looking for women to work in their kitchens, but had escaped immediately, running away and remaining hidden indoors for the next few weeks.

She had also worked for the Resistance, tripping past German sentries with messages concealed in her shoe. During Operation *Market Garden*, the Allies' attempt to force a passage across the Rhine at Arnhem, she had made contact with a British paratrooper stranded in the woods and put him in touch with Resistance members in the town. With so many friendly troops around, the Dutch had assumed that liberation was at hand, only to be bitterly disappointed when the Allies withdrew and the Germans evicted them from their homes in retaliation. Audrey and her mother had gone to her grandfather's large house at Velp, three miles from Arnhem, but others had had nowhere to go at such short notice. Audrey had watched them with horror: 'I still feel sick when I remember the scenes. It was human misery at its starkest: masses of refugees on the move, some carrying their dead babies, born on the roadside, hundreds collapsing of hunger… 90,000 people looking for a place to live. We took in forty for a while, but there was literally nothing to eat, so they had to move on.'[10]

The situation had worsened as winter arrived. Audrey's mother advised her to drink plenty of water to make herself feel full, and to lie in bed to conserve energy. So many Dutch people had starved to death by the spring of 1945 that there weren't enough coffins to bury them all. And then one day, in the middle of April, the moment they had all been waiting for had arrived at last:

> We were in our cellar, where we'd been for weeks. Our area was being liberated practically house to house, and there was lots of shooting and shelling from over the river and constant bombing: explosions going on all night… Once in a while you'd go up and see how much of your house was left, and then you'd go back under again. Then early in the morning all of a sudden there was total silence. Everybody said 'My God, now what's happening?' We listened for a while, and strangely enough, I thought I could hear voices and some singing – and I smelt English cigarettes.
>
> We crept upstairs to the front door, opened it very carefully and to our amazement our house was completely surrounded by English soldiers, all aiming their guns at us. I screamed with

happiness, seeing all these cocky figures with dirty bright faces and shouted something in English. The corporal or sergeant walked up to me, and in a very gentle English voice – so different from all the German shouting we'd been used to – said: 'We hear you have a German radio station in your house and we've come to take it away. We're sorry to disturb you.' I laughed and said: 'Go right on disturbing us.' Then a cheer went up that they'd liberated an English girl. I was the only one for miles.[11]

CHAPTER 9:
DACHAU

While the British cleaned up at Belsen and the RAF dropped food over Holland, the Americans were advancing into Bavaria. After all the fighting that had gone before, they were beginning to enjoy themselves at last as German resistance crumbled and village after village surrendered to them without a fight.

Desperately short of men and equipment, the German Army was in retreat all along the line. The retreat was led by the Nazis: Gauleiters and high party officials fleeing with their families and as much loot as they could carry, hoping to slip across the border into Switzerland or else hide anonymously in some country place until the danger had passed and they could re-emerge after a few months with a new identity and total amnesia about the past. Nazi officials had never hesitated to throw their weight around during the good years, bullying their own people almost as much as they bullied the rest of Europe. They were a lot more subdued as they joined the columns of refugees fleeing the American advance. No longer did they hoot at everyone else to get out of the way, forcing ordinary people off the road while they roared past in their staff cars. The Nazis rarely had the fuel, for one thing. And the people might turn on them, for another.

Many Nazis had their womenfolk with them, wives and mistresses who had done well out of the war years and were bedecked with fur and jewellery, often looted from occupied countries. Diamonds that had been swallowed by Jews just before they were taken away, to be recovered later and bartered for a few more days of life, had been swallowed again as their new owners became fugitives in their turn. Nazi wives were often fatter than other German women, because they had eaten better during the war. It had proved to be a disadvantage when the Russians came, because the Russians preferred women with flesh on them. Nazi wives had often been the first to be raped, an irony not lost on other women who had had to go without while the Nazis had continued to enjoy the best of whatever was available.

Resistance to the Nazis was growing apace as their regime began to collapse. Germans who had never found the courage before were finding it now as the Nazis shed their uniforms and the Americans appeared on the horizon. Some of the resisters were genuinely anti-Nazi, but others were merely fed up with the war, not impressed by rumours of a proposed last stand in the mountains around Berchtesgaden, where all Germans would be expected to fight to the death in defence of their Führer. Many were simply opportunistic, seeing which way the wind blew and hurrying to establish their anti-Nazi credentials before the war ended. It could surely do them no harm to be in charge of their town or village when the Americans arrived, demonstrating that they had overthrown the Nazis of their own accord, without help from anyone else.

Accordingly, many small towns and villages sported a prominent display of white flags when the Americans appeared, sheets and pillow cases hanging from upstairs windows as the occupants put up their hands and offered no resistance to the invaders. The Americans encouraged them by sending burgomasters ahead from villages already captured to make it clear to the inhabitants that only a mass display of white flags would save their village from destruction. With so much firepower at the Allies' disposal, the Germans had no reason to doubt it. They swiftly got the message and surrendered without a fight.

The Americans bowled straight through if they had no reason to stop, racing from one village to the next through some of the prettiest countryside they had ever seen. After the horrors of the Normandy bocage and winter in the Ardennes, it was good to sit at the wheel of a jeep in the Bavarian spring, with no one shooting at them and the sun glinting off the Alps in the distance. Like the Russians in the East, the Americans kept asking themselves why the Germans had wanted to invade so many other countries, when their own was so rich and beautiful. To farm boys from Idaho and Kentucky, it made no sense at all.

The Americans were on their way to Munich. It was the last great city in southern Germany that hadn't already fallen to them. The city was particularly important because it was the birthplace of Nazism: 'the cradle of the beast', as General Eisenhower liked to call it. At the rate they were going, the Americans were scheduled to reach the outskirts either that evening or very early next morning.

After Munich, they would continue south east towards Berchtesgaden, Hitler's private retreat in the mountains near the old border with Austria. Hitler hadn't been seen in public for weeks, so there was every chance that he might be holed up in Berchtesgaden somewhere, just waiting for the Americans to come and dig him out. More than one GI nursed a fantasy of being the man who did exactly that, dragging the Führer from his hiding place and parading him in front of the world's cameras while millions cheered.

First, though, the Americans had another task. A dozen miles north of Munich lay the little town of Dachau. There was a concentration camp at Dachau, the first the Nazis had ever built. It was in a dreadful mess, according to reports reaching the front line troops. Thousands had already died of typhus and the remainder were due to be killed that day, executed in cold blood before the Americans could arrive to save them. The Americans knew all about Dachau and had been planning to begin relief operations in due course. But the reports of imminent mass murder galvanised them into action. They went that way at once.

———

They were held up by sniper fire as they advanced, then a blown bridge over a railway line. By mid-morning, however, their tanks had found other ways forward and were fast approaching Dachau, aiming to secure the town first before turning their attention to the camp on the outskirts.

The Germans in Dachau were in two minds about how to respond. Civilians in the town were all for raising the white flag, but had been threatened with severe reprisals by their newly appointed burgomaster … just before he fled. The military commander had already withdrawn his headquarters across the river, effectively surrendering half the town to the Americans.

They advanced cautiously and were in the town square some time before midday. From there, tanks set off towards the Amper Bridge, aiming to cross the river that ran through the town and then swing towards the camp on the outskirts.

The Germans put up a token resistance, blowing the bridge just as the first tank was about to cross. They killed several of their own troops in the process, but didn't delay the Americans for long. The railway bridge remained intact, allowing the infantry to flood across. By early afternoon, one company of Americans was securing the town of Dachau, while another headed along the railway line towards the camp, its barbed wire and huts just over half a mile away behind the trees.

The main line led to Munich, with a spur branching off towards the camp. Following it along, the Americans came to a row of rail wagons abandoned at the entrance to the camp. There were thirty-nine freight cars, normally used for transporting coal or cattle. Moving closer, the Americans saw to their horror that each one was packed full of dead prisoners, all in pitiful condition. Their bodies had been lying there for two days, at least 500 in all and perhaps as many as 2,000. Estimates varied, because no one had the stomach for an accurate count. A Red Cross man estimated 500, but *Time* magazine's Sidney Olson counted fifty-three bodies in one car and sixty-four in another, which suggested a lot more in total.

The prisoners had come from Buchenwald. The journey had taken more than two weeks, because of Allied attacks on the line, including at least one on their train. Packed tight into every car, some in open-top gondolas, others in enclosed boxcars with the doors locked throughout, the prisoners had died like flies on the way, some of thirst, some of hunger, some of cold and some simply of disease or exhaustion. The Germans had done nothing for them. As at Belsen, they had just washed their hands of the whole business and left the prisoners to get on with it by themselves. A few had managed to survive the journey, a very few, but the SS had shot them as soon as they arrived, or else clubbed them to death to save ammunition.

The smell was the worst of it for the Americans. That, and the dreadful state of the corpses. Some naked, some in striped prison garb, but all skeletal, all parchment white, all sprawling helplessly in their own blood and filth. Some lay with their eyes still open, staring accusingly at the Americans who had failed to save them, others with their teeth bared and their arms protectively over their faces to ward off the blows that had killed them. 'They were spilled out of the boxcar as if you had taken it and just turned it over and poured the people out onto the side of the tracks,' recalled Private Jimmy Gentry.

> Some of the bodies were still in the train, some were hanging out over the tops of the piles of people outside, and that's when I saw for the first time that they were not soldiers. We were used to seeing soldiers, both American and German soldiers who had been killed, but we'd never seen anything like this. They were striped, dressed in striped clothes, their head was the largest part of their body, their eyes all sunken back. They were ashen white, almost a blue colour also, their ribs would protrude, their arms the size of broomsticks, their legs the same.[1]

'I saw two prisoners lying on the pavement with their brains squashed,' remembered Lieutenant-Colonel Felix Sparks, commanding the battalion of the 45th Thunderbird Division tasked with capturing the camp. 'We didn't do a detailed examination of the bodies in the cars. We looked in to see if anyone was alive and then continued on. I heard later that there might have been a couple of people still alive, but I doubt it very much.'[2]

Like the British at Belsen, the Americans thought they had seen it all in the fight across Europe. But what they had found in the boxcars filled them with a blind, incandescent rage as they pushed past the train and continued into the SS barracks. Almost at once, four soldiers emerged from hiding and surrendered to Lieutenant Bill Walsh, the commander of I Company. But Walsh wasn't having it. Outraged, he ordered the men into one of the boxcars and shot them immediately with his pistol, one after another. Private Albert Pruitt joined him, finishing the men off with his rifle as they lay moaning on the floor. The Americans were in no mood to take prisoners after what they had just seen. It was immediately understood among them that none of the Germans in the camp should get out of there alive. None deserved to live.

Ironically, most of the Germans responsible for the atrocities had already fled the camp. Almost a thousand had left Dachau the previous day, hastily putting a safe distance between themselves and the approaching enemy. Only a few hundred remained behind, some convalescents newly arrived from the front, others too wounded in hospital to move. The distinction between the fighting soldiers of the Waffen-SS, billeted in the adjoining barracks, and the prison guards of the SS-Totenkopf was lost on Walsh. After six months of more or less continuous combat, he had reached his breaking point. He ran amok after shooting the SS, chasing after every German he found, waving his gun and shouting 'You sons of bitches, you sons of bitches!' He had to be knocked to the ground by Colonel Sparks and held down by seven of his men until he had stopped crying and come to his senses.

Later, pulling himself together, Walsh rejoined his company as they advanced through the SS barracks, methodically clearing each building of the enemy. When they reached the infirmary, Walsh ordered all the Germans outside, regardless of their condition. Private John Lee helped to bundle them out:

> Our platoon entered the hospital and searched room to room to
> clear everyone out. Several were in hospital beds with bandages
> on their arms and legs. Some were on crutches, feigning injury.

These were German Wehrmacht and SS guards, dressed as Wehrmacht soldiers. They were moved outside and lined up with the doctors, nurses and medics. There were also four or five inmates working in the hospital who became very helpful in picking out the real SS men, as well as those faking injury.[3]

Lee was helping to separate the SS from the other prisoners when he and his friend Bob McDonnell heard screaming from outside. Rushing out to investigate, they found two prisoners with shovels attacking a medic in a white coat. 'By the time we got there, he was a bloody mess. We ordered them to halt. They said they were Poles, and one of them dropped his pants to show he had been castrated in the hospital and this German was somehow involved in the operation.'

While Lee's platoon cleared the hospital, Walsh lined up sixty of the SS against a wall in the adjoining coal yard. Although they had been disarmed, the SS easily outnumbered the Americans nervously guarding them. Ordering them to keep their hands up, Walsh told Private William Curtin, a machine gunner from M Company, to shoot if the SS refused to stay back. Curtin cocked his weapon obediently. Assuming the worst, the SS allegedly began to run. Curtin and four others immediately opened fire. Colonel Sparks, a few yards away, twisted round to see what was happening:

> I ran back and kicked the gunner in the back and knocked him forward onto the gun, then grabbed him by the collar and yelled: 'What the hell are you doing?' He said they were trying to get away, and then he started crying. I pulled out my .45 and fired several shots into the air and said there would be no more firing unless I gave the order. I told them I was taking over command of the company, and I ordered them to get the wounded into the infirmary.[4]

But it was too late for the SS. Seventeen had been killed, perhaps deliberately murdered. All but three of the remainder lay in a tangled heap at the base of the wall, some wounded, others feigning death. The last three were still on their feet, two with their hands in the air, the third with his arms folded, defiantly awaiting the inevitable.

By some accounts, there was a similar incident later, when a further 346 Waffen-SS were lined up against the same wall and machine-gunned at the order of I Company's executive officer, Lieutenant Jack Bushyhead. A Cherokee from Oklahoma, Bushyhead was said to have directed the fire from the flat roof of a bicycle shed. Afterwards, three or four prisoners were given pistols and went down the line, finishing off the wounded.

Whatever the truth, nobody wanted to discuss the killings in the days that followed. There was talk of courts martial at first, almost certainly scotched by General Patton's refusal to proceed. Stories changed later and accounts grew in the telling, once the threat of legal proceedings had receded. Some soldiers told their stories of Dachau at once, others not for fifty years. A handful left graphic, eyewitness accounts, even though they had been nowhere near Dachau at the time. And the official history told a different story again. All that could be said for sure was that it had been a proud day for the Thunderbird Division when it liberated the camp at Dachau … and for a few chaotic minutes, a shameful day as well.

—

While the men of the Thunderbird Division advanced through the SS barracks, clearing them of the enemy before turning their attention to the prisoners in the adjacent concentration camp, other American troops were approaching from a different direction. An advance party from the 42nd Rainbow Division was probing forward towards Munich, but had been urged by some war correspondents to make a quick detour to Dachau on the way, even though it wasn't part of the plan. With 30,000 inmates in imminent danger of execution, the division's commander had needed little persuading. He had sent Brigadier-General Henning Linden forward to reach Dachau and report back on what he found there.

Linden was a small man brandishing a swagger stick just like General Patton's. Accompanied by a posse of reporters, he followed the railway spur to the abandoned boxcars and then drove east around the perimeter of the camp towards the main gate. They were almost there when they heard shooting. Thinking it was aimed at them, Linden's party abandoned their jeeps and ran for cover in a drainage ditch. The shooting stopped after a while and an SS officer strolled over to make contact. He declined to put up his hands at first, but was persuaded to do so after Henning hit him on the side of the head with his stick.

The Germans were waiting to surrender the camp at the main gate. They were led by Lieutenant Heinrich Wicker, Dachau's new commandant, who had only been at the camp two days. The real commandant had fled the day before, leaving Wicker to surrender to the Americans and take the blame for something that had been nothing to do with him.

Wicker was not a happy man as he stood at the gate, a very junior officer recently arrived from the Russian front and now saddled with the responsibility for appalling crimes committed by other people. He too had wanted to flee that morning, but had been persuaded to stay by Victor Maurer, a Swiss representative of the Red Cross. Maurer had argued that Wicker should continue to keep order in the camp until the Americans took over, for fear that the prisoners would riot into the town otherwise, spreading typhus in all directions and wreaking havoc on the local population. Maurer had assured him that the Americans would give the German garrison safe conduct once the camp had been handed over, allowing them to return unharmed to their own lines. The two of them had negotiated an agreement to that effect, after which Wicker had ordered his men to remain at their posts and offer no resistance when the Americans appeared.

Carrying a white flag on a broomstick, Maurer accompanied Wicker towards General Linden. Wicker saluted and formally surrendered the camp to Linden. The General didn't have enough troops with him to move in at once, so he sent to the rear for reinforcements and stood waiting for a few minutes until they arrived. In an account hotly disputed by others, Marguerite Higgins of the *New York Herald Tribune* then claimed that she and Sergeant Peter Furst of the *Stars and Stripes* were the first Americans to enter the camp, in the company of an SS guide:

> There was not a soul in the yard when the gate was opened. As we learned later, the prisoners themselves had taken over control of their enclosure the night before, refusing to obey any further orders from the German guards, who had retreated to the outside. The prisoners maintained strict discipline among themselves, remaining close to their barracks so as not to give the SS men an excuse for mass murder.
>
> But the minute we entered, a jangled barrage of 'Are you Americans?' in about sixteen languages came from the barracks 200 yards from the gate. An affirmative nod caused pandemonium.
>
> Tattered, emaciated men weeping, yelling and shouting 'Long live America!' swept toward the gate in a mob. Those who could not walk limped or crawled. In the confusion, they were so hysterically happy that they took the SS man for an American. During a wild five minutes, he was patted on the back, paraded on shoulders and embraced enthusiastically by the prisoners. The arrival of the American soldiers soon straightened out the situation.[5]

General Linden too remembered the enthusiasm of the prisoners:

> I moved in with my guards and found that the inmates – having
> seen the American uniform of my guards there, and those of the
> 45th Division approaching the main stockade from the east – had
> stormed to the fence in riotous joy. This seething mass increased
> in intensity until the surge against the steel barbed wire fence was
> such that it broke in several places, and inmates poured out into
> the roadway between the fence and the moat. In this process,
> several were electrocuted on the charged fence.[6]

Colonel Sparks saw what was happening and tried to calm the prisoners
down:

> I told Karl Mann, my interpreter, to yell at them and tell them
> that we couldn't let them out, but that food and medicine would
> be arriving soon. He yelled himself hoarse. Then I saw bodies
> flying through the air, with the prisoners tearing at them with
> their hands. I had Karl ask what was going on. The prisoners told
> him that they were killing the informers among them. They
> actually tore them to pieces with their bare hands. This went on
> for about five minutes until they wore themselves out. I had Karl
> tell them to send their leaders to the fence, where I told them to
> keep calm, that medicine and food would be coming soon. This
> seemed to settle them down.[7]

Jimmy Gentry, who may have arrived later, saw little excitement in the
faces of the prisoners. On a ration of 600 calories a day, most were simply
too apathetic for sustained celebration as the Americans appeared:

> There was not a lot of screaming and yelling and jubilation, not
> at all. They were blank faced, they were stunned. They did come
> up to you and hug you and someone, I don't know who,
> someone in my squad, said 'Don't let them kiss you on the
> mouth.' They had diseases, typhus fever, for example, and they
> would fall down to their knees and hug you around the legs, and
> kiss your legs and kiss your boots. And of course we didn't know
> enough German to know what they were saying and some of
> them weren't German. We just knew they were happy to be
> released, but they were a pitiful sight.[8]

Filth, squalor, bodies heaped in piles. A gas chamber and crematorium. Medical experiments, guard dogs, arbitrary execution. The prisoners of Dachau came from all over Europe, but they had all suffered unimaginably at the hands of the Nazis, the German prisoners as much as anyone else. They were in no mood for forgiveness as they embraced their liberators. Their first thoughts were of revenge, summary justice for the guards who had tormented them. It wasn't enough to have killed the informers in their midst. The prisoners wanted to see their gaolers suffer too, see them writhe in pain and plead miserably for their lives, as the prisoners had done. Some of the inmates had waited years for the day. They were not to be denied, now that it had come.

Lieutenant George Jackson of the 42nd Division couldn't bring himself to intervene as he spotted some prisoners cornering a German soldier who, like Lieutenant Wicker, had probably just come from the front:

> As I entered the camp, I noticed a group of several hundred people on one side of the compound. Going closer, I observed a circle of about two hundred prisoners who were watching an action in their midst. A German soldier with full field pack and rifle who had been trying to escape from Dachau was in the middle of the circle. Two emaciated prisoners were trying to catch him. There was complete silence. It seemed as if there was a ritual taking place, and in a real sense, there was. They were trying to grab hold of him.
>
> Finally, an inmate who couldn't have weighed more than seventy pounds, managed to catch his coat tails. Another inmate grabbed his rifle and began to pound the German soldier on the head. At that point, I realised that if I intervened, which could have been one of my duties, it would have become a very disturbing event. So I turned around and walked away to another part of the camp for about fifteen minutes. When I came back, his head had been battered away. He was dead. They had all disappeared.[9]

The Americans too continued to kill Germans. Many GIs had alcohol with them, a bottle they had been carefully saving for the day the war ended. After half an hour at Dachau, they had decided they needed it at once. One of General Linden's officers snatched a bottle from a soldier of the 45th and threw it into the canal, but others were blind drunk as they lurched through the camp, looking for Germans to kill. And some were mad. Chaplain

Leland Loy was standing by a jeep with his driver when a panic-stricken German came running around the corner with an American GI in pursuit:

> We grabbed him as he came to our jeep, and a 42nd Division soldier came around the corner right behind him. We were standing not more than three feet apart and this 42nd Division man whirled the guy around and said: 'Here you are, you sonofabitch,' and machine-gunned him. I said: 'Look, fella, you're crazy. This guy was a prisoner.'
>
> But the soldier's only response was: 'Gotta kill 'em, gotta kill 'em, gotta kill 'em.' This guy was psycho.[10]

The killing continued well into the evening, when a German counter-attack on the camp was quickly repulsed. The final count of Germans killed at Dachau that day may have reached 500, although no accurate figures exist. The only certainty is that many died, among them the camp's hapless commandant, Lieutenant Wicker. The guarantee of safe conduct that he had negotiated with the Red Cross had turned out to be worthless. Whether the prisoners killed him, or whether the American Army did, Heinrich Wicker's body wasn't found and he was never heard of again.

—

Yet nobody was worrying about the Germans as they advanced through the camp. Dachau had been a model camp once, a Nazi showcase that Hitler's people had been happy to show to the Red Cross. But the disruption caused by the Allied advance had hit Dachau as well as Belsen. Supplies had failed, typhus had broken out and the crematorium had been overwhelmed, leaving hundreds of bodies dumped in piles to await incineration. Dead guards and the corpses of murdered informers added to the picture. It was not a scene the Americans would ever forget as they pushed open the gates and struggled to hold the prisoners back, sometimes firing over their heads to prevent them from storming all over the countryside before food and medication could arrive.

Like other camps yet to be revealed, Dachau had seen medical experiments conducted on prisoners, tests for the Luftwaffe on the limits of human endurance at high altitude or in the freezing cold of the sea. The Americans were taken at once to the medical block, where a Belgian prisoner showed Lieutenant Walsh the place where the experiments had been carried out. The tests had apparently been conducted on criminals condemned to death or Russian prisoners suspected of being political commissars. Nazi doctors had suspended some in compression chambers and a parachute harness and subjected them to the atmospheric conditions of up to 60,000 feet above sea level, sucking the air out of the compression chamber and observing the prisoners' reactions through the glass as they lost consciousness and died. Others they had immersed for hours at a time in a tank of freezing water, leaving some to die of cold, some to be revived by a variety of methods, including the bodily warmth of prostitutes. The experiments had been carefully controlled and perfectly scientific, but the subjects had been human beings, not laboratory rats.

There had been execution squads too, torture chambers, a brothel, all the usual paraphernalia of the Nazi system. It was a scoop for the journalists accompanying the 42nd Division, just what they had anticipated when they had asked to be taken to the camp. The *Herald Tribune*'s Marguerite Higgins had made a nuisance of herself when she arrived, demanding to be allowed in at once to interview some of the prominent figures known to be prisoners there. She had mentioned Kurt von Schuschnigg, the former Austrian Chancellor, Martin Niemöller, the anti-Nazi pastor, Léon Blum, the former French Prime Minister, and various European royals, including Prince Frederick Leopold of Prussia, Prince Louis de Bourbon and Prince Xavier of Luxembourg. It was rumoured that Stalin's son Jacob was in Dachau too, although no one knew for sure.

But Linden and Sparks had refused to allow her in immediately, pointing to the huge crowd of prisoners pressing at the gate. Ignoring them, Higgins had removed the bar holding it shut, only to be overwhelmed as the prisoners poured out. The Americans had had to use force to get them back in while Higgins retreated, chastened, to her jeep. She had filed a story in due course, but not the one she wanted. The important prisoners – the *Prominente* – weren't at Dachau any more. They had been removed a few days earlier and taken south as hostages, to be used as bargaining chips in the hands of the Nazi leaders as they prepared to negotiate a surrender.

———

The *Prominente* were in Villabassa, known also as Niederdorf, a mountain village in the South Tyrol. They had been driven there in a convoy of coaches under the guard of the SS. But they weren't expecting to be used as bargaining chips. While the Americans captured Dachau, the camp's most important former prisoners were expecting to be shot at any moment, executed in a last act of defiance before the Allies arrived to save them.

The *Prominente* were a mixed bunch, high profile prisoners from perhaps 22 different nations across Europe. They ranged in age from four to 73: men, women and children, Greek generals, British agents, a former Hungarian Prime Minister and his cabinet, a grandson of the Italian leader Garibaldi. There was no sign of Stalin's son, but Fritz Thyssen, the German industrialist, was among the prisoners, as was Hjalmar Schacht, the former Economics Minister and President of the Reichsbank. So too were several German generals who had refused to carry out Hitler's orders, and the families of Klaus von Stauffenberg and other conspirators in the many unsuccessful attempts to kill him. They had all been collected from Dachau and similar camps and taken south through the Alps to escape the Russian and American armies converging on them from different directions.

They had passed through Munich first, an eye-opener to those who hadn't set eyes on a city for several years. The place had been heavily bombed by the Allies, pounded so extensively that many houses had been reduced to rubble, with only the odd wall standing here and there. The trams were still running, their smashed windows replaced with cardboard, but the tram stops seemed hard to locate, with few landmarks left to indicate their whereabouts. Allied aircraft ruled the sky, forcing the convoy to stop several times while the guards ran for cover. When they halted for the night, the prisoners had seen fires burning all around. It was obvious that Germany was close to collapse. The war couldn't go on much longer, not more than a few days at most.

After Munich, the *Prominente* had been held at Innsbruck for a while until the last of them had been gathered together. While waiting, they had listened to a group of Polish prisoners singing patriotic songs as one of their number was hanged. Then they had continued south through the Brenner Pass to Italy, guarded by a squad of SS whose arrogance had evaporated markedly as they left German soil behind. Nobody was in any doubt that the SS had orders to shoot the prisoners before the Allies appeared. But it was clear too that the SS were no longer very sure of themselves, with the German Army in disarray and the mountains teeming with Italian partisans.

The Germans' resolve had begun to waver as the convoy approached Villabassa on 28 April. It had stopped by a level crossing a mile short of the village while the guards got out to confer among themselves about what to do. Some had wanted to shoot the prisoners at once and loot their possessions before turning round and heading for home. Others had been reluctant. They had stood arguing among themselves while the prisoners eyed them warily from a distance.

Sigismund Payne Best, a British agent captured in 1939, had decided that bribery was the prisoners' best hope of survival. He was discussing it with Thyssen and Schacht, the two money men among the prisoners, when some passing cyclists recognised Kurt von Schuschnigg, Austria's former chancellor and a native of the Tyrol. Before long, an Italian had appeared, a leader of the local partisans. Introducing himself as Dr Antonio Ducia, he had told the German guards that food and shelter could be found for them all in the village.

Scarcely able to believe it after Dachau, the prisoners had been taken to Villabassa and given food and wine in local hotels. For some, it was the first alcohol they had tasted in years. But their troubles were still far from over. While the others tucked in, Best had joined Fritz, one of the guards, for a drink. After he had had one too many, Fritz had produced Best's death sentence from his pocket.

'Here is the order for your execution,' he had told him. 'You won't be alive after tomorrow.'

'Surely no one is going to be such a fool as to shoot any of us at this stage of the war?' Best had demanded incredulously:

> 'No, it is quite certain. See, here it is in black and white – an order from the Reichssicherheitsdienst in Berlin,' and Fritz pushed a paper under my nose. He waved it about a good deal and I could not read it all, but it was an order that the following prisoners must not be allowed to fall into the hands of the enemy and were to be liquidated should there be any danger of this occurring. Then followed a long list of names which, as it reached to the bottom of the page, was probably continued on the back which I did not see. I saw the names of Schuschnigg, Blum, Niemöller, Schacht, Müller, Falkenhausen, Thomas and Halder, as well as Stevens and myself.[11]

It had been a fraught night thereafter. Warned that his name was on the list, Pastor Niemöller had gone straight to the SS commander and told him that some of the prisoners had weapons and would certainly fight back if attacked. The commander had denied any such intention, but Niemöller – a U-boat captain in the Great War – had been prepared for the worst. So had the other prisoners as they settled down uneasily for the night.

They had been divided by age and sex. Some had been accommodated in hotels, but many of the men had slept on straw in the Town Hall with an SS sentry at the end of every row of sleepers. The prisoners had taken it in turns to remain awake and keep a close eye on the guards. The SS had tried to segregate the British in a room to themselves, only to be told in no uncertain terms that the British were going to sleep in the same rooms as everyone else. They had no intention of being massacred in the night.

Now it was morning again, Sunday morning, and they were all still alive. While the American Army approached Dachau, its most important prisoners were holding a council of war about what to do next. At the suggestion of the partisans, Sante Garibaldi, a general in the Italian Army, was proposing to overpower the SS and remove all the *Prominente* to a resort hotel in the mountains above Villabassa, where they could safely remain until the war was over.

But the partisans were just village boys, no match for the SS. The Wehrmacht were a better bet. One of the German *Prominente*, himself a Wehrmacht officer, had telephoned Wehrmacht headquarters at Bolzano during the night, outlining the situation and asking to be rescued. Alarmed at the thought of important prisoners being murdered on his watch at this juncture of the war, General von Vietinghoff had just sent a company of men to Villabassa to take over from the SS and make sure nobody got hurt.

Unfortunately, there were only fifteen of them when they arrived, not nearly enough for the task. They were led by a very junior officer reluctant to confront the SS. Nevertheless, Best and Bogislaw von Bonin, the man who had telephoned the Wehrmacht, told the young man to set up his machine guns in the square and point them towards the SS truck. The officer complied with great reluctance. Then Best and Bonin walked over to the SS and ordered them to throw down their weapons. To their amazement, the SS agreed at once. The *Prominente* were still far from free, but they were no longer in immediate danger of being shot down in cold blood.

PART THREE:
MONDAY, 30 APRIL

'In my summary, I clearly stressed that in all probability the battle for Berlin would be over by the evening of 30 April...'

Helmuth Weidling

CHAPTER 10:
THE UNITED NATIONS

Winston Churchill spent the weekend at Chequers, the British Prime Minister's official country house just outside London. He had yet to hear the full story about Dachau, but he had already heard the worst about Belsen and Buchenwald. He had ordered that all such atrocities were to be fully investigated and the perpetrators brought to justice without delay. Like the Americans at Dachau, Churchill saw no reason why the guilty shouldn't be put up against a wall and shot in due course, punished to the full extent of the law for what they had done.

Churchill had been watching a film the previous night when news had come through of the German surrender in Italy. He had also learned of Mussolini's death, which he announced to his house guests with the words: 'Ah, the bloody beast is dead.'[1] He had immediately dictated a telegram about the surrender to Stalin, and another to Field-Marshal Alexander, congratulating him and US General Mark Clark on their great achievement. He had stayed up for hours afterwards, chatting happily with his staff and enjoying the news from Italy. He hadn't finally been persuaded to go to bed until three o'clock that morning.

It was getting on for midday when he surfaced again. The weekend papers had been full of good news about the war: 'Himmler offers unconditional surrender', 'Himmler gives Hitler twenty four hours to live', 'Himmler given till Tuesday to surrender'. The Monday papers were equally cheerful, relishing the death of Mussolini and talking of victory in Europe at any moment. Churchill read them all in bed, puffing on the first of many cigars as he pushed his breakfast tray away and summoned Marian Holmes, his secretary, to begin the day's work. It was his habit to dictate to her in bed, wearing only a bedjacket that all too often revealed more of his rear end than she cared to see.

They were returning to London that afternoon, but Churchill had much to do first: a mountain of briefings to read and cables to pore over before he even got up. He had had his first conversation with the new American President a few days earlier, talking to Harry Truman over the crackly transatlantic line. They had got on well, but Churchill remained unsure of Truman's position over the situation in central Europe. He wondered whether the new man at the White House fully understood the danger from the Russians, who were threatening to impose an iron curtain across Austria, Czechoslovakia and other countries recently liberated from the Nazis. The Russians would simply be substituting one totalitarian regime for another if they weren't stopped in their tracks. The American Army was in the right place to stop them, but Churchill had his suspicions that the new people in Washington didn't really understand the problem and weren't alive to the threat. If an iron curtain was to descend across Europe when the music stopped, then the further east the better. The Russians were perfectly capable of annexing Denmark, if the British Army didn't get there first.

Sitting up in bed, puffing on his cigar and spilling ash all over his bedjacket, Churchill began to dictate to Marian. Among the many telegrams he sent out that morning was one to Truman about the Communist threat in Europe:

Prime Minister to President Truman.

There can be little doubt that the liberation of Prague and as much as possible of the territory of Western Czechoslovakia by your forces might make the whole difference to the post-war situation in Czechoslovakia, and might well influence that in nearby countries. On the other hand, if the Western Allies play no significant part in Czechoslovakian liberation that country will go the way of Yugoslavia.

Of course, such a move by Eisenhower must not interfere with his main operations against the Germans, but I think the highly important political consideration mentioned above should be brought to his attention...[2]

And so on, for the rest of the morning. Churchill worked for hours, still spilling ash everywhere. He was so absorbed at one stage that he failed to smell any burning or notice the smoke arising from the collar of his bedjacket. Marian was wondering whether to point it out to him when John Peck, another of his secretaries, came in.

'You're on fire, sir,' Peck said at once. 'May I put you out?'

'Yes, do,' said Churchill.[3]

The smoke was extinguished. The work went on. When they got back to Downing Street that night, it was reported that the red despatch box containing Churchill's official papers had been left by Peck in a 'shocking mess'.

—

Across the Atlantic, the new President of the United States was still feeling his way into the job. After just eighteen days in office, following the unexpected death of Franklin Roosevelt, former Vice-President Harry Truman was working every bit as hard as Churchill, but with far more to learn. He was putting in a full day at the Oval Office every day, then reading a stack of papers several feet high every evening, 30,000 words or more of official text to be studied and absorbed before he could go to bed. Under constant pressure to make immediate decisions, often of crucial importance, Truman felt as if he had already lived through several lifetimes since taking his country's highest office.

He had yet to move in to the White House. His first thoughts had been for Eleanor, Roosevelt's widow, whose home it had been for the past twelve years. Truman had told her to take all the time she needed before moving out. He had been happy to remain in his own apartment at first, only to be forced out when his new security arrangements had caused problems for the other tenants. He was living now in Blair House, the President's official guest house across the road from the White House. He was taking a briefcase of papers there every night until Eleanor Roosevelt had completed her packing and was ready to vacate the premises for him.

As Churchill had surmised, Truman knew little of foreign affairs and had admitted as much to his advisers. Yet he was a shrewd man, far more erudite than his detractors imagined, ready and willing to learn. He understood the threat from the Russians well enough and passed Churchill's telegram about Prague on to his generals as soon as he received it. He also shared Churchill's horror at Belsen and Buchenwald and had just given orders for full co-operation with Britain and the Soviet Union in the hunting down of Nazi war criminals. But he disagreed with the other Allies on how to deal with them. The British were half-inclined to support the Russians in executing Hitler and his gang out of hand, without the bother of a trial first. Truman remained adamant that there had to be due process, a public examination of the Nazis' guilt, albeit 'as short and expeditious as possible'.

He had only been in office a few hours when he had had his first lesson in the awesome responsibilities of a President. Summoned to the White House on the afternoon of 12 April, he had learned of Roosevelt's death from Eleanor Roosevelt in her study. Before he knew it, a Bible had been thrust into his hand and the Chief Justice had sworn him in as the United States' new Chief Executive. That evening, while Truman was still reeling, Secretary of War Harry Stimson had taken him aside and told him something so secret about the United States' military capabilities that it was for the President's ears only. Even as Vice-President, Truman had not been allowed to know. But all that had changed, now that Truman was in the driving seat himself.

The United States had a new weapon, a weapon such as no country had ever had before. It was a bomb of unimaginable power, so immense that a single explosion would be enough to destroy a whole city, if not more. Research was still continuing, but the project was very close to fruition. The scientists working on it were convinced that they would be able to detonate such a bomb within a few months at the latest. After that, if the test was successful, whoever had the bomb would also have the world in the palm of their hands.

Not everyone shared their confidence. Admiral William Leahy, Truman's Chief of Staff, was one of many who hated the idea of such a weapon and was certain it would never work. 'That is the biggest fool thing we have ever done,' he had warned Truman. 'The bomb will never go off, and I speak as an expert in explosives.' But the scientists were equally adamant that it would. And that the effects could be controlled when it did.

As to what to do with this new wonder weapon, Truman had as yet no idea. A bomb of such power had only limited uses. It would have come in handy over Germany, but that war had been won now and most of Germany's cities had already been knocked flat. No doubt the military would find a use for the bomb in due course, after all the money that had been spent developing it. They would surely tell Truman when they had.

Until then, he had people to see that Monday morning – the Governors of Maryland, Oklahoma and Rhode Island – and new officials to swear in that afternoon: the Federal Loan Administrator, the Chief Administrative Assistant, the US Representative on the Allied Reparations Commission, a constant stream of visitors to the Oval Office. They were calling on him at the rate of one every fifteen minutes for much of the day, all wanting to have their photographs taken with the new President before they left. The pressure was so permanent, so unrelenting, that Truman wondered if it was ever going to end. But at least the news from Europe was good, with Mussolini down and Hitler certain to follow within a day or two.

———

In San Francisco, about as far removed from the war in Europe as it was from that in the Pacific, delegates from forty-six countries were meeting to draw up a charter for the United Nations, the new world council that was to replace the old League of Nations once the war was over. The new council was the brainchild of Roosevelt and Churchill, who had dreamed it up soon after Pearl Harbor. One of Harry Truman's first actions as President had been to confirm that the conference would go ahead as planned, even though the chief architect was no longer there to cheer it on.

The conference had begun on 25 April and was scheduled to last for two months. It had been opened by Truman in a radio address from the White House and was being held at a variety of venues across San Francisco: the War Memorial Opera House for large gatherings, and a mixture of hotel suites and conference rooms for smaller meetings as 1,200 delegates from every corner of the free world formed sub-committees and unofficial cabals to discuss their own particular areas of concern. With hundreds of newspaper reporters and lobbyists in attendance, press photographers popping their flashbulbs, party girls prowling the corridors and sightseers crowding the streets, the city of San Francisco had never seen anything quite like it.

Eliahu Elath, a lobbyist for Zionism, was reminded of New York's Times Square as he watched men and women of every race and creed thronging the Opera House. Jan Smuts's son thought it

> the most cosmopolitan medley of mixed humanity the world had ever seen; there were the Whites of Western Europe; there were the Latins and mixed extractions of the twenty South American states; there were the Negroes of Liberia, the Mongolians of the East, the Arab types of Egypt and the Fuzzy-Wuzzies of Abyssinia; there was Bedouin-like Prince Feisal of Saudi Arabia with his quaint head-dress. A member of Feisal's delegation asked the manager of the Fairmont Hotel if he could buy one of the quaint Japanese lift girls to take home with him. He seemed surprised when told that the customs of this country forbade it.[4]

Smuts was accompanying his father, Field-Marshal Jan Smuts, who was representing South Africa at the conference. The old man was one of the most senior figures at the gathering, a veteran of the Versailles peace conference of 1919. Smuts had been a reluctant signatory to the 1919 treaty, arguing that the terms imposed on Germany after the Great War were too harsh and certain to cause trouble in the future. He had been overruled by the Allied leaders, Georges Clemenceau, David Lloyd George and Woodrow Wilson, each with his own gallery to play to back home. But the terms had indeed been too onerous. The rapid collapse of Germany's economy under the weight of the reparation terms had been followed by the rise of Nazism, while Smuts looked on in despair. It had given him no pleasure at all to be proved right.

But the San Francisco conference was not about punishing the Germans again. The delegates were looking to the future this time, planning ahead for a new and better world in a time of peace. Smuts had been given the task of drawing up the preamble to the United Nations charter. With the help of a committee, he was working on a draft that called on the nations of the free world

> to prevent a recurrence of the fratricidal strife which twice in our generation has brought untold sorrow and loss upon mankind, and to re-establish faith in fundamental human rights, in the sanctity and ultimate value of human personality, in the equal rights of men and women of nations large and small, and to promote social progress and better standards of life in larger freedom.[5]

The draft spoke of tolerance, peace and international machinery for the promotion of economic and social advancement. Its tone was lofty, but Smuts was pleased with it so far, although he still had more work to do on the wording before the final version could be presented to the delegates for their approval.

He was less optimistic about the rest of the conference. The meeting was still only in its first week, but already the proceedings were becoming bogged down in a morass of committees, procedural wrangles, walkouts, resolutions and counter-resolutions, all the bureaucracy and jockeying for position of an international jamboree with one eye on its audience at home and another on opinion abroad. Part of the trouble was the lack of dominating personalities in San Francisco. Wilson, Clemenceau and Lloyd George had all been powerful figures at Versailles. They had never allowed the proceedings to slip out of their control, but their successors in San Francisco were pygmies by comparison. There was no one of any great stature to lead the way. Smuts himself was as big a figure as any. He had been appointed President of the General Assembly, but he had just turned seventy-five and was too old to carry the conference on his own. It needed younger men to grab hold of the proceedings and steer them successfully in the right direction.

——

Smuts was not alone in his distaste for the proceedings. Ed Stettinius for the United States and Anthony Eden for Great Britain were equally dismayed, watching through gritted teeth as the delegates wrangled interminably over minor concerns such as seating arrangements instead of turning their attention to more important matters. The issue that Monday morning was whether the pro-Nazi dictatorship of Argentina should have a seat at a conference of free nations: whether it should be formally invited to attend, or merely given permission to participate as an observer. The other nineteen countries of Latin America were agreed that if Argentina couldn't have a seat, then neither should the Soviet Union's two satellite republics, Byelorussia and the Ukraine. But the Soviet Union was adamant that its seats weren't up for discussion. And if Argentina had a seat at the table, then why shouldn't Poland have one too, even though the Russians had installed a puppet regime in Warsaw and had no intention of allowing free and fair elections?

The arguments would run and run. Much of the lobbying went on behind the scenes as the diplomats pursued private agreements behind closed doors. Ed Stettinius was based in the penthouse suite at the Fairmont. The US delegation met there every day to confer with their opposite numbers from Britain, France, China and the Soviet Union. When he wasn't in conference, Stettinius was constantly on the phone to Truman, Eden, Soviet Ambassador Andrei Gromyko and others, consulting some, advising the rest, always trying to move the process forward. Eden too was always either on the phone or deciphering telegrams from Churchill at home or talking to diplomats in quiet corners. It was a tedious, mind-numbing, soul-destroying business, something that nobody enjoyed, not even the career diplomats and professional lobbyists whose lifeblood it was. Yet, for all that it was a talking shop of the worst kind, the United Nations conference had one great, incontrovertible and undeniable factor in its favour. It was better than war.

——

The Russian delegation was led by Foreign Minister Vyacheslav Molotov. He was based at the Saint Francis hotel, where he had been besieged by autograph-hunting bobby-soxers on his arrival from the airport. The Russians had done more than anyone to stop the German Army in its tracks and the free world was grateful. But the good will of the war years was rapidly dissolving as Communists and capitalists came together in San Francisco and failed lamentably to iron out their differences. Wartime co-operation had given way to paranoia and distrust as the Russians squared up to the Western Allies and made it clear that the Anglo-American view of Europe in a post-war world was radically different to what the Soviets had in mind.

The Russians wanted control of all the countries along their European borders: Latvia, Lithuania, Estonia, Poland, Hungary, Czechoslovakia, Romania and any other nations they could lay their hands on, a vast cordon sanitaire between their own borders and any further invasion from the West. After all they had suffered since 1941, they would settle for nothing less. They remained deaf to the objections of the Western Allies, whom they suspected of seeking to bring those countries into their own domain in order to make trouble for the Communists in due course. To the victor, the spoils, in the Russians' view. They wouldn't budge an inch.

Molotov was the embodiment of Russian paranoia. He had spent a few days in Washington before San Francisco, staying at Lee House, next door to the Truman family in Blair House. He had amused them all with his refusal to sit with his back to a door or window. A Russian valet had checked the pockets of his suits when they came back from the cleaners and a Russian had always stood watch when the Blair House staff made Molotov's bed. He had amazed his American hosts still further by prowling the grounds of Blair House at three or four in the morning, long after everyone else had gone to sleep.

In San Francisco he was no better, accompanied everywhere by a phalanx of unsmiling Soviet agents in terrible suits. Molotov seemed determined to put the worst possible interpretation on anything that came his way. He was already doing his best to make trouble at the conference, creating artificial objections to other country's proposals and threatening dramatic walkouts when his own were not accepted. To the dismay of observers, he seemed hell bent on destroying the United Nations before it had even drawn up its charter. The idea of cooperation between nations did not appear to have crossed his mind at all.

He was particularly inflexible on the subject of Poland. The Russians were determined to impose a Communist government on Warsaw, one that would always look to Moscow for direction. But the Anglo-Americans wanted to see Poland free again, as it had been before the war. The issue was especially important to the British, because Poland's freedom had been their reason for going to war.

The British wanted to take Molotov aside and put it to him bluntly that Poland's freedom was non-negotiable. But the Americans wouldn't back them. They feared that a tough line with Molotov might lead to a Russian boycott of the conference. The United Nations needed Russia much more than it needed Poland. Molotov was well aware of it and saw no reason to make any concessions. Why should he, when the Soviet Union had so many millions of troops on the ground?

———

Among the many Americans unimpressed by Molotov's antics was Lieutenant Jack Kennedy, recently of the US Navy. After active service as a torpedo boat commander in the Pacific, Kennedy was preparing for an operation on his back before going to law school in the fall. In the meantime, his father had arranged for him to attend the conference as a reporter for the *Chicago Herald American* and other newspapers owned by his friend William Randolph Hearst.

Joe Kennedy's war had not been nearly as distinguished as his son's. As the US Ambassador to Britain in 1939, he had been very close to Prime Minister Neville Chamberlain, fully supporting his policy of appeasement towards Germany, partly because the Germans had been badly treated at Versailles and partly because the Nazis seemed the lesser of two evils when compared to the Communists. Kennedy had got straight on the telephone to Chamberlain on the day war broke out. He had been with his son Jack at the House of Commons when the air raid warning had sounded, trooping down to the shelter with all the Members of Parliament. But Joe Kennedy's closeness to Chamberlain had not served him well in the months that followed, as the British buckled down to the war. His assertion that they would quickly surrender had proved horribly wide of the mark. Professional US diplomats had lobbied successfully for his recall.

Kennedy's troubles hadn't stopped there. His eldest son, also called Joe, had been killed in an air force accident over Suffolk, taking with him his father's hopes for a Kennedy in the White House. Joe junior had been groomed for the Presidency from an early age, raised to expect it almost as his due. A good war record was deemed essential for anyone seeking the Presidency in future years, but death on active service had played no part in the Kennedys' plan. Joe senior's grief for his son had been the same as any father's, but he had mourned for his family's ambitions as well.

The mantle had fallen now on Jack, the second of his four boys. By arranging for Jack to attend the United Nations conference, Joe was hoping that he might develop an interest in politics or at least learn how history was made. He would also come to the attention of millions by writing for Hearst newspapers 'from the point of view of the ordinary GI'. Bowing to his father's wishes, Jack had installed himself at the Palace Hotel, from where he could report on the conference by day and chase girls by night.

He was not a particularly good reporter. His reputation rested on his book *Why England Slept*, which had been written for him by someone else. But what he lacked in writing skills he made up in shrewdness and common sense. Unimpressed by Molotov, he nevertheless understood the Russian fear of another invasion, the refusal to countenance an anti-Communist government in any of the countries along Russia's western borders: 'The Russians have a far greater fear of the German comeback than we do. They are therefore going to make their western defences secure. No government hostile to Russia will be permitted in the countries along her borders… They feel they have earned this right to security. They need to have it, come what may.'[6] Understanding the other side's point of view was halfway to winning the battle, in Jack Kennedy's estimation.

But he couldn't warm to the United Nations. He disliked 'the timidity and selfishness of the nations gathered at San Francisco', compared to the courage and sacrifice he had seen in the war. Above all, he disliked the way the new organisation was being set up, with a power of veto vested in each of the five permanent members of the Security Council. What that meant in practice was that Britain, France, China, the United States and the Soviet Union would each be able to vote down anything they didn't like, which was surely a recipe for disaster. The United Nations was supposed to be about solving problems in partnership, not stymieing the opposition. Kennedy wondered if it would ever be the right place for the world to settle its disputes, when the set-up was so flawed from the outset.

—

Orson Welles too was covering the conference as a journalist, but not for Hearst newspapers. After his recent performance in *Citizen Kane*, a thinly disguised and none too flattering portrayal of the proprietor, he was never going to find any employment with the Hearst Corporation.

He was writing for a daily newsletter entitled *Free World*, published in English, French and Spanish for the duration of the conference. He was also hosting *The Free World Forum* on radio, interviewing United Nations delegates about the proceedings and occasionally allowing them a word in edgeways. As a long-time political activist, hoping to make a living from politics rather than the cinema, Welles was taking a keen interest in the United Nations conference. He claimed that he was speaking for the whole world in demanding radical change from San Francisco. Whether the whole world shared the radicalism of the changes he demanded was another matter.

But few could disagree with his anger at the concentration camps. Newsreel of generals Eisenhower, Patton and Bradley going round Ohrdruf-Nord, a small camp near Buchenwald, had just been shown to the delegates in San Francisco. Welles had added his own commentary in his column *Orson Welles Today*: 'The heaped-up dead in evidence. The burdened ovens. The ingenious machinery for the gift of pain. The eyeball blinking in the open grave... Patton and Bradley, their eyes choked full of this. Eisenhower, moving slowly, with immense dignity, through the long tableau. A huge black anger knocking with heavy blows on the commander's heart.'[7]

The Americans had also filmed local Germans being shown what had been done in their name. As elsewhere, the civilian population had denied all knowledge of any atrocities, to unconcealed scepticism from Welles:

> The Military Police are gentle with the *Herrenvolk*. You realise that they need to be or they would strike them down, each with a single blow... One place of torture, you will learn, was camouflaged as a madhouse. Here the most grisly of all Grand Guignol conceits was realised: here the wardens were the lunatics... This is a putrefaction of the soul, a perfect spiritual garbage. For some years now we have been calling it Fascism. The stench is unendurable.[8]

On the other side of the globe, in a royal hunting lodge just outside Madrid, Spain's General Franco was following the proceedings in San Francisco with mounting dismay. He was wondering if there was going to be a place for Spain at the United Nations, or whether his country was to be denied admission as punishment for having backed the wrong side in the war.

The omens were not good. So soon after their own civil war, Franco had been careful to keep the Spanish out of the larger conflict — at least until he could be sure that the British were going to lose – but there had never been much doubt as to which side he was on. Hitler had urged him repeatedly to declare war on Britain and allow German paratroopers to seize Gibraltar without delay. Franco had replied that the Royal Navy would seize the Canary Islands if he did. He had resisted all attempts to get Spain in on the Axis side, while making little secret of his admiration for Hitler and Mussolini and offering them plenty of covert help. In the Allies' view, he had given their enemies all the help he could, short of actually entering the war.

But there had been a price to pay in economic isolation and pariah status as the rest of the world proved reluctant to do business with the Spanish. It hadn't been a problem at first, with Germany in the ascendant and everyone else in retreat, but it was rapidly becoming one now that Germany was beaten and Spain had no other friends. Franco had been back-pedalling for months, frantically distancing himself from the Axis and struggling to re-engage with the rest of the world.

The autographed photos of Hitler and Mussolini had been removed from his study, to be replaced by a picture of the Pope. Spanish troops had been withdrawn from the Russian front and German agents evicted from Tangiers. Spain had just broken off diplomatic relations with Japan and was about to do so with Germany as well. To anybody who asked, Franco was letting it be known that his previous flirtation with the Nazis had simply been a ploy, a delicate balancing act to keep his country from being occupied. What else could he have done, with the German Army breathing down his neck and Italy just across the water?

He had written to Churchill and Roosevelt, saying that their countries should be friends. Churchill's response had been chilly. Roosevelt's, mindful of the congratulations Franco had lavished on Japan for bombing Pearl Harbor, even chillier. Between them, Churchill and Roosevelt had made it clear that there was no place for Spain at the forthcoming peace conference nor much chance of Spain belonging to the United Nations under its present regime. The United Nations had no room in its charter for Fascism.

Franco had other enemies in San Francisco, domestic enemies from Spain itself. After his victory in the civil war, many defeated Republicans had fled to Mexico, where they had been welcomed with open arms. The Mexican delegation to the United Nations was heavily influenced by anti-Franco Republicans, openly lobbying to deny Spain a seat at the table. Franco could protest all he liked, but his regime was too closely associated with Hitler and Mussolini for the rest of the world to want him at their conference.

Worst of all was the news just in from Milan. Franco had read the accounts of Mussolini's death that morning with horror. Dangled upside down in front of a baying mob, his face bashed in, his body poked with sticks. Hitler would doubtless be the next Fascist leader to suffer a similar fate. And after that? In a country still bitterly divided by his leadership, Francisco Franco didn't even want to think about it.

He was not alone in his unease. In the royal palace at Oslo, Vidkun Quisling too was afraid that there might be a price to pay for backing the wrong side in the war. As Norway's so-called Minister-President, installed by the Nazis after they had deposed King Haakon and abolished the monarchy, Quisling knew that he could expect short shrift when Haakon returned from exile in England and the Norwegians regained control of their country. The Norwegian government in exile had already announced its intention of calling him to account for the years of collaboration. So had the Norwegian Resistance and many of the ordinary population. Quisling's was a name that had long since passed into the English language as a byword for treason of the worst kind.

Quisling had been the leader of Norway's Fascist party before the war, but he had never won more than two per cent of the popular vote. He had stormed into a radio studio during the German invasion in 1940, proclaiming himself Prime Minister and ordering all resistance to halt at once. The Germans had installed him as a puppet leader, but no Norwegians of any standing had agreed to serve in his cabinet. Quisling had spent the war years in office yet not in power, merely doing the Germans' bidding. He had encouraged Norwegians to join the SS and had assisted the Germans in deporting Norway's Jews. He had also been responsible for the execution of Norwegians in the Resistance, something that was unlikely to be forgotten when peace returned to the country.

His immediate concern was to ensure an orderly transfer of power after the departure of the Germans. He had held a cabinet meeting on 29 April to discuss the radio reports of Himmler's secret approach to the Allies. The reports had been rapturously received in Norway. People had come out onto the streets to celebrate, until advised by the Resistance to keep their heads down and avoid gathering in crowds. With the Nazis obviously disintegrating, Quisling's cabinet had decided to reconstitute itself as a transitional government, one that no longer had any business with the Germans but was merely concerned 'to prevent chaos, civil war and military activity on Norwegian soil' until the war was over. After that, it was anybody's guess what would happen.

Quisling suspected that he was doomed in the long run, but was still hoping for a miracle. Like many Fascist leaders, he had little idea of how much he was loathed by ordinary people. The Germans had offered to put a U-boat at his disposal, and he had friends who could hide him if need be, but he wasn't prepared to cut and run as his time came to an end. Explaining it earlier to his secretary, he insisted that he had done his best for Norway and his conscience was clear:

> I shall remain sitting where I am sitting. A political vacuum would be the worst thing that could happen. In any case, I have the satisfaction of having governed Norway equally as long as Olav Trygvason, and certainly no worse, all things considered. As far as I am concerned, I shall hand over the country in an equally good condition to its future rulers, assuming that they won't be the Russians. Against the Russians, I would mobilise everyone capable of carrying arms, whatever the consequences.[9]

Olav Trygvason had been a Viking king, much admired by his people. Quisling wasn't admired at all. Yet he was no coward. He had decided to turn himself over to the incoming Norwegian government, if the worst came to the worst, and accept whatever fate they decided for him. At best it would be a long spell in prison, at worst execution by firing squad. But Quisling wasn't afraid. He would rather that than run away or kill himself, as so many others in his cabinet were thinking of doing, now that the Nazis were no longer there to protect them.

CHAPTER 11:
ASSAULT ON
THE REICHSTAG

In Berlin, the Russians were preparing to attack the Reichstag. Fighting had continued throughout the night as they struggled to secure the Ministry of the Interior, flushing the Germans out of the vast office complex one room at a time. There was still sporadic shooting on the top floors as dawn broke, but the rest of the building was safely in Russian hands. Cooks in the basement were busily preparing breakfast for the assault troops while their commanders studied the Reichstag through their binoculars and braced themselves for the ordeal ahead.

Germany's Parliament building was only 400 yards away, but it might just as well have been on the moon from where they were standing. The intervening ground was a rabbit warren of shell holes, trenches, railway sleepers, overturned trams, barbed wire and flooded waterways, every kind of obstacle to an advance. The approaches to the Reichstag were heavily defended and the building itself may have had a thousand troops inside. The Germans weren't going to give up their Parliament building without a struggle.

But the Russians were determined to fly their flag over its giant dome before nightfall, in good time for next morning's May Day celebrations in Moscow. The leading units had been equipped with flags specially made for the purpose, Red Banners of Victory with extra large hammer and sickle emblems to be planted over 'the lair of the Fascist beast'. The units were in competition to see who planted their banner first.

The assault began at five am with a preliminary bombardment, every available gun pouring fire into the Reichstag at point blank range. An hour later, the first wave of troops attacked, emerging from cover and charging forward across the rubble. They got fifty yards before being cut down. Others followed and were killed too. Much of the defending fire came from the Kroll Opera House, across the square from the Reichstag. The Russian commanders decided that they would have to capture the Opera House first, before turning their full attention on the Reichstag.

It took them most of the morning, because the nearby buildings had to be secured as well. Reinforcements poured in over the Moltke Bridge, guns and tanks rumbling forward to join the assault. They came under fire from German anti-aircraft guns on the giant concrete flak tower near the Zoological Gardens and from other positions in the Tiergarten. The Russians responded in kind, hitting the Tiergarten with a devastating combination of rockets and heavy artillery that blasted everything in its path. The sun was shining and the birds were singing in the trees, but artillery officer Siegfried Knappe remembered only the destruction as the Russian shells rained down around him:

> Through the springtime foliage of the Tiergarten the shells burst without interruption, destroying everything in their path. Small-arms fire was everywhere. Blinding sunshine lay over a gruesome scene. On the lawns of the Tiergarten, under mutilated age-old trees, I could recognise artillery pieces, all put out of action by direct hits. The gunners who had not made it were lying around, so mutilated that they were hardly recognisable as human beings. Everywhere in the streets, the dead could be seen amid piles of dust-covered debris. Abandoned shoes lay here and there. I remembered the first combat dead I had seen in France so long ago, and how shocked I had been at the sight. Now my sensibilities were so numb that a corpse was little more than an obstacle to step over. When I stopped to catch my breath or wait for a salvo to pass, I could see in gruesome detail the outlines of a human torso, or part of one, between pieces of brick, rock or concrete.'[1]

The firing was so intense that the sun quickly disappeared, blotted out by a rising cloud of smoke and dust. The Russians took the Kroll Opera House by the end of the morning and turned towards the Reichstag in the early afternoon. As with the Ministry of the Interior, every room on every floor was held by a mix of sailors, SS and Hitler Youth determined not to give an inch. The Germans were supported by Frenchmen, traitors to their country, who had volunteered for the SS's Charlemagne Legion and had nothing to lose by fighting on. For some at least, it was Bolshevism they were fighting, not just the Russians. They fought for their beliefs, and because they were desperate, and because they had no future if they surrendered. They also had nowhere left to retreat to, with the Russians already in the Wilhelmstrasse behind them. The defenders of the Reichstag really did have their backs to the wall.

In the noise and confusion, it was difficult to know when exactly the Russians finally reached the Reichstag. Some thought it was about three o'clock, others in a renewed attack just after dark. The doors and windows had been blocked, which meant that they had to blast their way in with artillery and horizontally aimed mortars and then throw in grenades before storming the building. Casualties on both sides were high as the defenders fought back. Some Russian sergeants had apparently pestered their officers for the honour of carrying the Red Banner into the Reichstag and raising it on the roof. Most had known better than to volunteer. Honour and glory was for the generals and political commissars, not the ordinary soldiers. They just wanted to come out of it alive.

There were propaganda considerations too, because whoever raised the banner would be made a Hero of the Soviet Union. That meant no Chechens, Kalmyks, Crimean Tartars or anyone else in exile from their homeland. But it could mean a Georgian, if one was available, because Stalin was from Georgia and the publicity value would be high. The Russians' political officers had already nominated suitable soldiers for the banner parties. All the chosen ones had to do, as darkness fell, was storm up the stairs and plant their flag on the dome.

But the Germans still stood in the way. According to Russian accounts, perhaps exaggerated for propaganda purposes, the Germans responded with grenades and Panzerfausts as the Russians burst in. The grand stone columns of the Reichstag's entrance hall were quickly spattered with blood as the casualties mounted. Fire and smoke filled the building. The Russians advanced over the bodies of their own men, lobbing grenades up the stairs and spraying the Germans with sub-machine gun fire in the dark. Hundreds of Germans retreated to the basement. The rest withdrew slowly up the broad stairs, firing along the corridors and defending themselves room by room, refusing to give ground as they settled in for a long, hard fight. As with the Ministry of the Interior, it would take all night to winkle them out. Perhaps the following day as well.

But the Russians couldn't wait that long. Men of the 756th Regiment, carrying Banner of Victory No. 5, forced their way up the stairs and got as far as the second floor before being pinned down by German fire. They managed to unfurl the banner and wave it from a window, though not from the cupola itself. The fighting continued for hours before the Russians tried again. At some point, they did reach the roof, although exactly when is open to dispute. It was reported to Moscow that the Soviet flag was flying proudly over the Reichstag in time for May Day, exactly as planned. By some accounts, though, the report had been written while the building was still being stormed and then wrongly flashed to headquarters. The only certainty was that the Reichstag was still full of Germans as the night wore on, and they were very far from surrender. On every floor, and in the cellars of the basement, they were fighting to the death.

—

In his bunker at the Chancellery, just over half a mile away, Adolf Hitler had been woken by the guns at five am as the Russian barrage began. Even in his personal quarters, under thirty feet of concrete, the sound was inescapable. The Chancellery was being pounded by artillery so close that the Russians were often firing over open sights. In his dressing gown and slippers, weary and bleary-eyed, Hitler knew that the end could not long be delayed, either for him or for Germany.

He was still in his dressing gown when SS General Wilhelm Mohnke came to his anteroom at six. Mohnke did not mince words when Hitler asked how much longer the bunker could hold out:

> I spoke of one or two days. The Russians were at Potsdamer Platz, less than four hundred metres from the Chancellery, they had reached Wilhelmstrasse and the greater part of the Tiergarten and they had penetrated the subway tunnels under Friedrichstrasse. Hitler listened to me without interrupting, then gave me his hand in parting and said: 'All the best. I thank you. It wasn't only for Germany.' The meeting was over towards 6.30 am and I returned to my command post.[2]

Half an hour later, Eva Hitler went upstairs and took a turn in the Chancellery garden. It was a lovely spring morning. She told the guard that she wanted to see the sun once more. Hitler joined her after a while, but the shelling intensified just as he appeared. Turning round at once, he hurried inside again and disappeared back down his burrow.

His wife followed. The bunker staff were unsure how to address her now that she was married, especially the ones who had always thought her rather silly. Most couldn't bring themselves to call her Frau Hitler and settled for 'gnädiges Fräulein' instead. She told them not to be embarrassed. 'You may safely call me Frau Hitler,' she insisted cheerfully.[3]

Back in her own room, afraid of being alone, she summoned Traudl Junge for a chat. They sat talking about whatever came into their heads, desperately spinning out the conversation rather than sit glumly with their own thoughts. After a while, Eva Hitler opened her wardrobe and took out her favourite silver fox fur, one that she had always loved to wear. 'I'd like to give you this coat as a goodbye present,' she told Traudl. 'I always liked to have well-dressed ladies around me. I want you to have it now and enjoy wearing it.'[4]

Traudl was touched. She had no idea what she was going to do with a fur coat at a time like this, but she appreciated the thought. She thanked Eva profusely, and meant it. She had always liked Hitler's wife.

Time hung heavily as the morning wore on. While the battle raged outside, they were trapped and waiting – but for what they didn't know. At noon, the daily situation report was given in the conference room. It was a bleak experience for those present. General Helmuth Weidling, commanding the Berlin garrison, told Hitler that the Russians were attacking the Reichstag and had penetrated the tunnel in the Vossstrasse, alongside the Chancellery. Weidling was as blunt as Mohnke in his assessment:

> I spoke about the vicious fighting that had taken place during the preceding twenty four hours, about the compression into a narrow space, the lack of ammunition, the lack of anti-tank rockets – an indispensable weapon in street fighting – about the declining supply by air and the sinking morale of the troops. In my summary, I clearly stressed that in all probability the battle for Berlin would be over by the evening of 30 April.[5]

Weidling's assessment was followed by a long silence, after which Hitler asked Mohnke if he agreed. Mohnke did. There was no chance of relief from Wenck's army or anyone else, no chance of a breakout either. They didn't even know where their troops were any more, since they had stopped radioing in to headquarters.

Hitler looked like a man resigned to his fate as he accepted that the situation was hopeless. He had trouble getting out of his armchair as Weidling prepared to leave. Weidling asked him what the defenders of Berlin should do if they ran out of ammunition, which they soon would. Hitler replied that he would never surrender Berlin, but the troops might be allowed to escape in small groups after their ammunition had been exhausted.

The meeting broke up in gloom. It was obvious to everyone that Hitler didn't have much longer to live. He had already told Martin Bormann that he and his wife intended to kill themselves that day. Now he summoned Otto Günsche, his personal adjutant, to discuss the details.

The details were crucial to Hitler. Badly shaken by the death of Mussolini, he did not want the same thing to happen to him. If Hitler hadn't underlined the words 'hanged upside down' on the transcript of the radio broadcast announcing the Duce's death, he had certainly read them. It didn't need much imagination to see a horde of Soviet soldiers lashing out and mutilating his body as they dragged it in triumph through the streets, or doing even worse to Eva. Hitler was determined not to let that happen, as he made clear to Günsche:

> I met Adolf Hitler in the antechamber to his office. He told me that he would now shoot himself and that *Fräulein* Braun would also depart this life. He did not want to fall into the hands of the Russians either alive or dead and then be put on display in a freak show, meaning in Moscow. The bodies were to be burnt. He was charging me with the necessary preparations. The way he expressed it, I was to be personally responsible to him for this! I then assured Adolf Hitler that I would carry out his orders.[6]

Günsche meant what he said. He was a loyal man who could always be relied upon to do what he was told. He gave Hitler his word and promised that Hitler's body would be in safe hands after his death. There was no time to waste. Günsche went off at once to organise petrol for the funeral pyre. Hitler spoke to some other people and then went in to lunch.

———

At Ruhleben, there appeared to be a lull in the fighting. The Russians had already recaptured the Reichssportfeld at the Olympic stadium, but were evidently too exhausted to go any further that day. All seemed quiet as Helmut Altner sheltered in a cellar, glancing idly at a tattered copy of Dr Göbbels' newspaper, the *Panzerbär*, written for the defenders of Berlin. 'We are holding on,' it announced. 'The hours of freedom are coming. Berlin fights for the Reich and Europe.' Göbbels added that Wenck's army was on its way to relieve them, hurrying to save the city. 'Reserves are marching in from all sides,'[7] he claimed. The paper was four days old, but the reserves promised by Göbbels still hadn't arrived.

What had come instead was a gaggle of teenaged girls, recently recruited into the Waffen-SS. Some had been anti-aircraft personnel, but most had been called up a few days earlier to build barricades across the city. As civilians, they had not qualified for military rations, so they had volunteered for the SS in order to eat. But they weren't the kind of people normally associated with the SS. Even in the uniform, they just looked like girls to Altner, few of them older than fifteen or sixteen. They seemed every bit as out of place as he was himself.

There was half a litre of soup for lunch, but only for those fighting men whose name was on a list. Altner ate his in the sunshine outside his cellar. Afterwards, he was summoned to battalion headquarters to witness the commanding officer being awarded the Oak Leaves to the Knight's Cross for the defence of Ruhleben. Others were being given medals too, by order of General Weidling. Scarcely believing his eyes, Altner watched in wonder as his comrades stepped forward one by one to receive their awards. He himself had been upgraded to 'Obergrenadier'. It was possible that he was to receive the Iron Cross as well, although the commanding officer wanted to check first to see if he was allowed to award promotions and decorations simultaneously.

Altner could hardly credit it. With Russians all over Berlin and the capital about to fall, the army was worrying about medals. Who did they think they were trying to kid?

> For me and just about everyone else of my age, a medal used to seem the greatest thing that one could achieve, but I've come so far now that I can only think about how many dead this fuss has cost. I'm not going to be psyched up into holding on just for a piece of tin.
>
> The battalion commander's Oak Leaves have been very dearly bought. Piles of dead – soldiers, Hitler Youth, Volkssturm – have paid for his award, while he sat in his bombproof cellar and chased the runners out into a hail of steel with his orders. And now he's trying to whip up the fighting spirit of the troops with a shower of medals and promotions.[8]

It was all just an 'unending, senseless demand for more sacrifices' to Altner. Like everyone else in his unit, he just hoped that he would still be alive when it stopped.

In the cemetery at Hohenzollerndamm, Hildegard Knef and Ewald von Demandowsky had been digging in since dawn, crouched over their machine gun as they waited for the Russians to attack again. They had been joined by two tearful Hitler Youths, one of whom had promptly been killed by a sniper. His body lay in front of them, the eyes still wide open in death. Hildegard was huddled in her trench when a chicken came over to investigate: 'It flaps, gargles, runs back and forth, head out, head back, ruffles its feathers and stalks haughtily over to the dead boy – oh God, the eyes, if that sod goes for the eyes – I pick up a stone and hit it on the tail, it squeals, sheds a few feathers, and stomps off squawking. Where there's a chicken there's an egg, I say, and am on my way.'[9]

Demandowsky yelled at her to come back, but Hildegard was too hungry to listen. Crawling past the gravestones, she followed the hedge along until she came to three more chickens beside a shed. They had laid two eggs. Scooping them up, Hildegard slithered triumphantly back to her trench. She and Demandowsky pierced the shells and drank the fluid at once.

They were joined later by an old man from the Volkssturm, wounded in the back. Hildegard cut his jacket open and tried to staunch the flow of blood with strips from his shirt. But he collapsed into their trench just as the Russians launched their attack:

> There they are, for the first time I can see them, running towards us, machine guns at their hips, bayonets glinting in the sun; gun and bayonet coming towards me, coming closer, arm's length. Earth spurts up into my eyes, ratatat, it's the gun beside me. I remember the hand grenade – pull, throw, duck – ahhvooom, splinters clatter on my helmet, I fall across the old man. Where's the bayonet? I wait for it, my back tenses, here it comes, must come – the bayonet...
>
> Complete silence. We look at each other over the old man's bleeding back and wait, don't dare to look up... There's a whinnying noise and then a bark, the dry bark of a tank gun. An arm floats past us, an arm without its hand, cemetery arm; we follow its flight, the old man moans, straightens up, splutters, rattles, is dead, can't fall down, leans against us with his head on my shoulder.[10]

The roadway was heaped with dead Russians. The Germans ran over to grab their weapons and then retreated before their attackers could regroup. Clutching at Hildegard's jacket, the young soldier from the Hitler Youth begged to come too. Together they set off through the cemetery and came almost at once to a ruined house that seemed vaguely familiar to Demandowsky. He realised, as if in a dream, that it belonged to a friend of his, Bobby Lüdtke.

They took shelter inside, but were spotted by a Russian tank. It opened up from the corner of the road, blasting everything that moved. The Hitler Youth got lost in the confusion as walls collapsed and beams came tumbling down. Lungs full of dust, Hildegard begged Demandowsky not to leave her behind if she was wounded. He promised to shoot her instead and made her swear to do the same for him.

They wondered if they could hold on until dark. With her throat clogged, Hildegard was desperate for water. There was none in the taps, but the Kurfürstendamm wasn't far away and Demandowsky thought he knew someone there who might have some. He and Hildegard decided to risk it. They set off at once and were overtaken almost immediately by a couple of soldiers with machine guns who called them 'Kamerad' as they passed. Hildegard couldn't help noticing, as the men continued on their way, that both of them were Russian.

While the Soviets advanced on the Reichstag from north of the Tiergarten, others were approaching the Chancellery from the south. They had got to within a few hundred yards of Hitler's bunker and were making good progress as they pushed forward, probing the German defences around Potsdamer Platz. Resistance was stiff, but the Russians' firepower was overwhelming. Marshal Vasili Chuikov had watched earlier as his men pulverised the Germans beside the Tiergarten:

> From my observation post I saw solid clouds of smoke and reddish brick dust rising up above the government buildings. The wind brought one of these clouds right down on me. Then the dimly visible disc of the sun disappeared completely, a twilight set in, and visibility was cut almost to nothing. I had only the shell bursts to tell me that the artillerymen, their guns out and firing direct, were striking at a very limited number of targets. They were firing across the canal and down the length of the streets opposite, blasting a way through the approaches to the squares on the far side of the canal, which had been blocked with barricades.[11]

The Germans were responding with flanking fire, concealing their machine guns in side streets untouched by the bombardment and then opening up from the flank as soon as the Russians appeared. It was a tough, hard, merciless business, but it was not a fight the Germans could hope to win. Every passing moment was bringing the Russians closer to Hitler's lair. The only real question was how much longer the Germans could continue to hold out.

The fighting was fiercest at the Landwehr canal, several hundred yards from the bunker. The canal wasn't wide, but the little hump-backed bridge over it was heavily exposed to German fire. While some Russians rushed the bridge, others were planning to swim across the canal or make rafts out of anything that came to hand. Among them, by some accounts, was Sergeant Nikolai Masalov, a decorated veteran from Siberia.

While his comrades moved up to the canal, Masalov apparently heard a child crying in the ruins the other side. The Russians gave him covering fire as he zigzagged across. Ten minutes later, he returned with a three-year-old girl in his arms. Her mother had just been killed in the fighting.

It was a good story, perhaps even with an element of truth. Marshal Chuikov was certainly pleased when he heard it. Suitably embellished, he knew that it would make excellent propaganda in due course, a useful counterweight to all the tales of rape and mayhem that the Soviet Army was leaving in its wake. But that was for another day, after the fighting was over. First, the Russians had to get to the Chancellery and finish the business in hand.

—

A few hundred yards away, lunch in the bunker was a muted affair as Hitler ate a last meal before his suicide. His wife apparently had no appetite and stayed alone in her room. Hitler ate with his two secretaries and his personal chef instead. Gerda Christian, the senior of the two secretaries, wasn't hungry either as they joined him:

> I suppose it was about 12.30 pm when my relief, Traudl Junge, arrived. This was the usual time – we were still working in shifts – and it was also, again as usual, the familiar signal for lunch. Hitler 'for old times' sake', now invited both of us secretaries, along with Fräulein Manziarly, to join him for lunch at one pm. He came out into the corridor to announce this, and soon Fräulein Manziarly, a mousy but pleasant little *Innsbruckerin* arrived with the food.[12]

They ate at a little table in Hitler's study, the so-called map room. If Gerda Christian's memory was correct, the only other man present was Corporal Schwiedel, an SS orderly. It was an unhappy meal of spaghetti and tossed salad. Nobody felt like saying much as they contemplated a grim future.

> We had often eaten alone with Hitler before, of course, but this was the very last lunch, and everybody knew it. It was a peculiar honour, qualified by the depressing knowledge that, with Hitler soon to be gone, the breakout would be our only hope. This was a harrowing thought for all three of us women. The lurid Berlin rape stories had given us the shudders, so the topic was avoided.[13]

Traudl Junge recalled a bizarre discussion about dog breeding and another about French lipstick being made from grease recovered from the Paris sewers. Other than that, as Gerda Christian said, the conversation was desultory, the same conversation they had been having every day for weeks. Hitler seemed perfectly relaxed throughout, but Traudl still remembered the meal as 'a banquet of death under the mask of cheerful calm and composure'.

Hitler pushed his chair back when he had finished, announcing that it was all over and the time had come. He went to say goodbye to Göbbels, who tried one last time to dissuade him, urging him to flee Berlin instead. There was a tank in the Chancellery garage, aircraft on standby with a range of 7,000 miles. They could fly him to South America at a moment's notice, or Japan or one of the Arab countries. There was still a chance to escape.

But Hitler wasn't going anywhere. He had made up his mind. 'You know my decision, Herr Doktor,' he told Göbbels. 'There's nothing more to be said.' He advised Göbbels to flee instead.

Traudl was having a quiet cigarette in the servants' room when Otto Günsche summoned her to say goodbye. Stubbing her cigarette out, she joined a line of Hitler's closest aides waiting to shake hands, but was so overcome that she could barely register who else was there:

> All I really see is the figure of the Führer. He comes very slowly out of his room, stooping more than ever, stands in the open doorway and shakes hands with everyone. I feel his right hand warm in mine, he looks at me but he isn't seeing me. He seems to be far away. He says something to me, but I don't hear it. I didn't take in his last words. The moment we've been waiting for has come now, and I am frozen and scarcely notice what's

going on around me. Only when Eva Braun comes over to me is the spell broken a little. She smiles and embraces me. 'Please do try to get out. You might still make your way through. And give Bavaria my love.'[14]

Hitler was wearing his uniform jacket with the Iron Cross awarded to him in the Great War. Eva was wearing the dress he liked best: dark blue, with roses at the neckline. She had washed her hair and done it up beautifully for the occasion. Traudl was so upset that she could scarcely bear to look.

Magda Göbbels appeared, begging for a last meeting with the Führer. Visibly annoyed, he agreed to a private word. They had a minute together behind closed doors, while Göbbels waited outside. Magda implored Hitler to think again, telling him that it still wasn't too late, urging him to leave Berlin and live to fight another day. But Hitler wasn't listening any more. He turned her down abruptly and she left in tears.

There was nothing more to be said. It was mid-afternoon now. The Führer's time had come and everyone in the bunker knew it. His wife came to him, following meekly to his room. The others watched silently, not meeting each other's eyes, keeping their thoughts to themselves as the heavy steel door swung shut. They had no idea what would happen next, but they could guess. Once the Führer was gone, they could all start thinking about their own futures, how to get out of the bunker alive and in one piece. But they couldn't do that until the Führer was gone. Until then, all they could do was sit in the corridor and wait.

CHAPTER 12: CURTAIN CALL FOR LORD HAW HAW

While Hitler made his farewells, Admiral Dönitz was on his way to Lübeck for a meeting with Himmler. He was going to find out once and for all if Himmler was secretly negotiating a peace deal with the Western Allies, as reported on foreign radio.

Himmler had been drunk and tearful when Wulff told his fortune the previous day, but he had pulled himself together by the time Dönitz arrived. Having had no response from Hitler, he had evidently decided to bluff it out and continue to deny any knowledge of surrender negotiations with Count Bernadotte. Indeed, he was still expecting to succeed Hitler as Führer, as Dönitz quickly discovered:

> I found that every available senior SS leader had apparently been summoned to the meeting. Himmler kept me waiting. He seemed already to regard himself as head of state. I asked him whether the report was true that he had sought contact with the Allies through the medium of Count Bernadotte. He assured me that it was not true, and that in his opinion it was essential, in these last days of the war, that discord among ourselves should not be allowed to create further chaos in the country.[1]

Dönitz took Himmler at his word. Whatever his private suspicions, he saw no reason not to. They parted on good terms and Dönitz drove back to his own headquarters at Plön, glad of an excuse not to pursue the matter any further. He arrived back at six that evening to find Albert Speer waiting to see him. Dönitz immediately invited him in to supper.

They had hardly sat down when Walter Lüdde-Neurath, Dönitz's aide, burst in with a signal from Berlin. It contained astonishing news:

Grand Admiral Dönitz.

The Führer has appointed you, Herr Grand Admiral, as his successor in place of Reichsmarshal Göring. Confirmation in writing follows. You are hereby authorised to take any action which the situation demands. Bormann.[2]

Dönitz was dumbfounded. So were the others. Dönitz knew the situation was bad, but never in his life had he imagined himself as a successor to the Führer. He was a sailor, not a politician. He had hardly spoken to Hitler in the past year and never alone. Hitler had never given the slightest hint that he was thinking of appointing him as his successor.

He was still gaping at the message when Speer recovered from his own shock and offered his congratulations. But Dönitz's first thought, once he too had recovered, was to wonder what Himmler would make of it. When they had met that afternoon, it had been obvious that Himmler was expecting to succeed Hitler as Führer. He wasn't going to like it that Dönitz had been chosen instead.

Dönitz told Lüdde-Neurath to telephone Himmler and ask him to come to Plön at once. But Himmler refused. It was a long drive in the dark and he had already seen Dönitz that day. He was only persuaded after Dönitz came to the phone in person and insisted that his presence was essential.

The meeting was fraught on both sides. Fearing arrest for talking to the Allies, Himmler arrived at about midnight with a large bodyguard, some of the hardest men in the SS, specially chosen for the task. They drove up in a fleet of open Volkswagens and armoured personnel carriers, maintaining a watchful presence around their boss as he approached Dönitz's headquarters in the blackout.

Dönitz too was wary. He had been warned that Himmler might try to seize control by force. Dönitz had few armed guards of his own, but a detachment of U-boat men concealed themselves nearby as the SS arrived, ready to defend him, if necessary. Heinz Macher, the SS commander, spotted them at once and was not impressed. 'Poor bastards!' he thought. 'We'll blow them away with the greatest of ease.'

But there was no bloodshed. Himmler was received by Lüdde-Neurath and escorted to Dönitz's room. The meeting went off without a hitch, although Dönitz was distinctly nervous at first:

I offered Himmler a chair and myself sat down behind my writing desk, upon which lay, hidden by some papers, a pistol with the safety catch off. I had never done anything like this in my life before, but I did not know what the outcome of this meeting might be.

I handed Himmler the telegram containing my appointment. 'Please read this,' I said. I watched him closely. As he read, an expression of astonishment, indeed of consternation spread over his face. All hope seemed to collapse within him. He went very pale. Finally he stood up and bowed. 'Allow me,' he said, 'to become the second man in your state.' I replied that that was out of the question and that there was no way in which I could make any use of his services.[3]

They talked for a while and then Himmler left, taking his entourage with him. Dönitz turned to other matters. His first task as Hitler's heir apparent was to assess the military situation for himself and find out how grave it really was. There was clearly no stopping the Russians. They had just captured Neubrandenburg, on the main road north of Berlin, and were about to take Ravensbrück as well. The British were coming too, advancing on Hamburg from the other direction. Dönitz's main concern therefore, as he sat contemplating his new responsibilities, was to get as many Germans as possible to safety in the West and then bring the war to an end as soon as he decently could.

—

While Dönitz returned from Lübeck, the staff at Hamburg's radio station were having a party. They had made a bonfire in the courtyard and destroyed all the station's records before abandoning the building to the British. Scripts, files and tapes had all gone up in smoke as the paperwork was hurled onto the flames. Now the staff were having a party, eating and drinking everything they could find so that there would be nothing left for the British when they arrived. Alcohol had been rationed for years in Hamburg, but there was no point rationing it any more if the enemy was at the gates. In common with much of the city, the staff at the radio station were drinking themselves into a stupor instead.

Few were drinking more than William Joyce. An Englishman of sorts, known to his listeners as Lord Haw Haw because of his absurd accent, he had spent the war years broadcasting Nazi propaganda to the British, trying to persuade them that resisting the Germans was futile and they should surrender instead. He had succeeded only in making himself hated by millions, a traitor of the worst kind. With the British Army only a day or two from Hamburg, William Joyce was acutely aware that he could expect no mercy from his countrymen if they found him in the city at the war's end.

The irony for Joyce was that he was deeply patriotic. Born in America, Irish in origin, German by adoption, he nevertheless saw himself as wholly British, a man who loved his country and only wished that his compatriots could see the world as he did, could understand that their future lay with the Germans and National Socialism, working in alliance with the Nazis rather than against them. But the British hadn't understood that and now they never would.

Joyce had spent most of the war in Berlin, working for German radio's foreign service in Charlottenburg. When the bombing disrupted broadcasting in the capital, he and his wife had been among the radio personnel evacuated to the country. They had gone to Oldenburg first, where they had been bounced by a Spitfire, and then to Hamburg, where the city's radio station was one of the few buildings to have survived the air raids unscathed. It was from Hamburg, as he lurched drunkenly into the studio after the party, that Joyce recorded his final message to the British people.

It was an embarrassing occasion. Joyce was so drunk that he kept slurring his words, lapsing into long, maudlin silences as he attempted to marshal his thoughts. The technicians recording the broadcast could only watch helplessly as he slumped in front of the microphone and made his valedictory address to his countrymen:

> This evening I am talking to you about Germany. That is a concept that many of you may have failed to understand. Let me tell you that in Germany there still remains the spirit of unity and the spirit of strength. Let me tell you that here we have a united people who are modest in their wishes. They are not imperialists. They don't want to take what doesn't belong to them...[4]
>
> How modest, how harmless does Germany's request for the return of Danzig seem in contrast to the immense acquisitions of the Soviet Union and the further ambitions of the Kremlin. Stalin is not content with Poland, Finland, the Baltic states, Romania, Bulgaria and Eastern Slovakia. He wants the whole of central Europe, with Norway, Turkey and Persia thrown in. And if these territories fall to him, his lust for aggrandisement will only be stimulated still further.

Such is the attitude of the Red dictator who menaces the security of the whole world, and whose power today constitutes the greatest threat to peace that has existed in modern times. Britain's victories are barren. They leave her poor, and they leave her people hungry. They leave her bereft of the markets and the wealth that she possessed six years ago. But above all, they leave her with an immensely greater problem than she had then. We are nearing the end of one phase in Europe's history, but the next will be no happier.[5]

Joyce rambled on for a total of ten minutes. Drunk or not, much of what he had to say was remarkably prescient. He couldn't understand what the Allies thought they had to gain by backing the Soviet Union against the Germans. It made little sense to him. He wondered if the British and Americans really knew what they were doing in allowing the Communists to rampage unchecked across Europe.

Joyce signed off with a defiant 'Heil Hitler' at the end. The talk was recorded on a disc and put aside to be broadcast later. Joyce left in tears soon afterwards, clutching a bottle of wine and accompanied by two SS officers who had been detailed to accompany him and his wife to Flensburg, on the Danish border. The Germans had originally promised him a U-boat from Hamburg to southern Ireland, where he would have been safe from the wrath of the British, but there was no chance of that any more.

Instead, he and his wife had been issued with false papers in the name of Herr and Frau Hansen and given three months' severance pay from the radio station. Their aim was to go to Denmark, still under German control, and from there to Sweden to seek asylum. But the road to Flensburg was in chaos and Denmark was already full of refugees trying to get to Sweden. The prospects for Joyce and his wife were bleak as they left Hamburg in the middle of the night and set off for the border, desperate to cross into Denmark and make their escape before the British could catch up with them.

—

To the east, the Russians had just liberated the women's concentration camp at Ravensbrück. Their tanks had rolled into nearby Fürstenberg that afternoon, finding it all but deserted as the population vanished. From there, Captain Boris Makarow's men had driven up to the camp gates, where they had been met by Antonina Nikiforowa, a Russian Army doctor who had been captured on the Estonian island of Saaremaa. She told them that without water or electricity, scores of the 3,000 women still in the camp were dying of disease every day. Makarow promised to bring help just as soon as his troops had made the area secure.

As in so many camps, Ravensbrück was strewn with dead bodies dumped in piles because no one had had time to get rid of them. But it was not an extermination camp. It had been designed for slave labour originally – a distinction lost on the many thousands of women who had been shot, strangled, gassed, buried alive or worked to death in the nearby Siemens plant, making parts for V2 rockets. Others had been tricked into sterilisation or used for medical experiments, crippled for life in the interests of science.

Gypsy women had been sterilised. Polish girls, some as young as fourteen, had been used for experiments. Known as rabbits, they had been held down while their legs were cut open and infected with bacteria from shards of wood or glass to test the efficacy of the latest sulphonamide drugs for the Wehrmacht. Others had had nerves cut or bones fractured to test their powers of recuperation. Some had died as a result and others had been killed later when their wounds failed to heal.

The rest had faced execution too as the Germans sought to destroy the evidence of their crimes. Ordered to report to camp headquarters a few weeks before the Russians' arrival, the remaining rabbit girls had vanished instead, tearing off their identification numbers and losing themselves in the crowd. They had been shielded by the other prisoners as the whole camp combined to ensure that some at least should live to bear witness after the war.

Wanda Poltawska had been one of the girls who vanished. Having survived an injection of diseased bacilli into her bone marrow, she and five others had barged through the SS guards coming to get them and then fled for their lives:

> We all six ran through the sudden gap in the SS ranks like bats out of hell. I've never in all my life run faster. Like greased lightning we sped into the middle of a crowd of Auschwitz prisoners who had been watching through a crack in their hangar wall. They rose splendidly to the occasion. Never have I undressed and dressed again with such lightning speed (the Auschwitz women were in civilian clothes). Someone handed me a red coat, gave me a quick change of hairdo and rapidly inked a tattoo mark on my forearm – the number of someone who had died on the long death march out of Auschwitz camp. I was safe.[6]

Others had not been so lucky. The elimination of witnesses had been stepped up as the Russians drew closer. Special prisoners had suffered the worst: saboteurs and Resistance members held in solitary confinement in a punishment block known as the Bunker. They had been taken out and shot in ever increasing numbers as the Germans hurried to eliminate the evidence before the Russians arrived.

Odette Sansom had been one of the prisoners in the Bunker, perhaps the most important of all in German eyes. A Frenchwoman working for the British, she had been betrayed to the Gestapo in 1943, along with her fellow agent Peter Churchill. To save their lives, they had pretended to the Germans that they were a married couple, related to the British Prime Minister. That hadn't prevented the Germans from pulling Odette's toenails out or sentencing her to death, but it had probably prevented the sentence from being carried out. She had been sent to Ravensbrück instead, held in solitary confinement as Frau Churchill, a special prisoner in condemned cell No. 32.

The final days at Ravensbrück had been the worst for Odette. Knowing that the Germans were killing their special prisoners, she had had a nerve-racking time in her cell, listening to the footsteps along the corridor as other people were led away to execution. The Bunker was close to the crematorium, so close that Odette had heard some prisoners putting up a fight as they were clubbed unconscious and then shoved alive into the flames: 'The last few days of the war, I saw people being driven to the crematorium. I could hear them screaming and struggling and I could hear the doors being opened and shut.'[7]

Odette's adopted name had saved her from the flames. There had been a mass exodus of guards from Ravensbrück as the Russians approached, a headlong rush to the West of SS men and women stripping off their uniforms and fleeing the enemy advance. Among them had been Rudolf Höss, the former commandant of Auschwitz, and Fritz Sühren, the much-hated commandant of Ravensbrück. Sühren had taken Odette with him as insurance, a hostage to trade with the Allies in due course. While the Russians liberated Ravensbrück, Odette had just arrived at Neustadt-Glewe, a much smaller camp on the road to Hamburg. After months of solitary confinement on death row, she was back in a hut with other women while Sühren waited for the Americans to appear from the West, so that he could hand over Winston Churchill's 'niece' in return for his own life.

—

The Russians had taken Neubrandenburg as well as Ravensbrück, liberating thousands of Allied prisoners from the cluster of camps north of Berlin.

But liberation by the Russians was a decidedly mixed blessing, as the American prisoners in Neubrandenburg were already beginning to discover.

Russian aircraft had dropped leaflets before their troops arrived, stating simply: 'Rokossovski is at your gates.' The resulting pandemonium was witnessed by Father Francis Sampson, a US Airborne chaplain captured near Bastogne:

> The reputation of Rokossovski's army was enough to panic the Germans. The roads were soon jammed with wagons loaded with cherished family possessions, children, and old people. The Germans headed west, hoping to escape the Russians, preferring anything to falling into their hands.
>
> Many of the guards in the camp deserted and fled in the direction of the American lines. Some asked me for letters stating how kind they had been to the Americans. A few of them had been decent, and a couple actually ran great risks to help us; to those I gave notes telling how they had aided us, and I sincerely hope that this benefited them. About a dozen guards, including the camp commandant, turned themselves over as prisoners and were locked up in the stone blockhouse. The small garrison dug in and prepared to defend the town. We were busy digging trenches to take cover in as soon as the Russians began to shell the town. The events of the next few days were as terrible as I have ever seen.[8]

General Rokossovski's troops arrived in the small hours of 29 April and lived up to their reputation. Less than an hour after its surrender, Neubrandenburg was a sea of flames as everything that couldn't be looted went up in smoke. The town burned throughout the night, lighting up the Americans' camp as bright as day. The Americans kept their discipline after the Russians' arrival, but other prisoners did not. French, Italians and Serbs left the compound as soon as the gates were open and hurried en masse into the town to join in the looting.

The mayhem was still continuing twenty four hours later – worse, if anything, as the Russians drank themselves stupid. The first Russians to arrive at the Americans' camp had been all smiles as they strode through the gates, sorry for the death of President Roosevelt and grateful for all the American equipment used in the Russian Army. But others stripped the American prisoners of their watches and ordered them at gunpoint to dig their latrines. Relations between the so-called Allies had deteriorated so rapidly that Francis Sampson was worried that one of the enlisted men might lose his temper and punch a Russian on the nose, provoking a drunken burst of machine gun fire in response.

Thinking their services might be needed, he and a French colleague decided to go into Neubrandenburg that day to see the destruction for themselves:

> An old French priest-prisoner asked me to go downtown with him. He wanted to see how the German priest and the German people who had not fled were making out. I certainly admired the old man's courage; he apparently feared no one. Expecting the worst, we were still shocked beyond words by what we saw. Just a few yards into the woods from the camp we came across a sight that I shall never forget. Several German girls had been raped and killed; some of them had been strung up by their feet and their throats slit.[9]

It was the same when they reached Neubrandenburg. The streets were piled with debris and most of the buildings were still burning. Bodies lay everywhere, ignored unless they were blocking traffic. The stink of burned flesh was stomach-churning. When Sampson and his colleague got to the Catholic church, they found the German priest slumped on the steps of the rectory in a state of catatonic shock. His mother and his two sisters, both nuns, were indoors. The family had gathered together for protection when the Russians came, but their God hadn't saved them. All three women had been gang-raped while the priest and his father were forced to watch. Standing there amid the flaming ruins, surrounded by dead bodies and violated women, the biblically minded Sampson didn't know what to say. All he could think of was that Neubrandenburg that day looked just like the end of the world and the Day of Judgement rolled in to one.

The American prisoners had been left in their compound as Neubrandenburg fell, but others had been force marched to the West as the Russians approached. Thousands of prisoners from all over Europe were on the road that day, stumbling forward at gunpoint rather than drop out and be shot without compunction. Among them was Micheline Maurel, a member of the French Resistance before her arrest.

After months of slave labour in an aircraft factory, Micheline was so ill with stomach pains and ulcerated sores that she could barely climb the steps to her hut, let alone join the march to the West. But she had been rousted out of her bunk a few hours before the Russians arrived and ordered to join the other Frenchwomen outside as they prepared to evacuate the camp. Micheline had gone with them, supported by three friends determined not to let her die this close to the end of the war.

Jettisoning her clogs and a blanket, she had marched through the night and for all of the following day, wearily putting one foot in front of the other as she struggled to keep up. It had rained throughout and many prisoners had died along the way, but Micheline had somehow managed to keep going. The horizon had been in flames and the roar of guns had drawn ever closer as the Russians approached. The column had been overtaken by increasing numbers of German troops in retreat, so many eventually that the prisoners' guards had panicked. Breaking into a run, they had hitched a ride on a passing truck and fled, abandoning the prisoners to their fate.

Many had scattered at once, heading for the safety of a nearby wood. The four Frenchwomen had lacked the strength to walk that far, so they had spent the night in a field before finding shelter in a barn next day. When the Russians failed to appear, they had continued westwards on the morning of 30 April, against the advice of friendly German farmers. The farmers warned them that they would be shot if they were caught wandering the countryside in prison uniform. They did come across some dead prisoners, but kept going anyway, desperate for something to eat. At length, they reached the outskirts of Waren, a village twenty six miles west of Neubrandenburg. It seemed to be deserted, so Micheline selected the first likely looking house on the left and led the way in:

> The table was still laid, there were cups and saucers, plates with the remains of food on them and, in the middle of the table, a huge pot of strawberry jam. With one bound, and without thinking, I clutched the pot of jam in my arms and began to eat, while the others rummaged in cupboards with little cries of joy. At last we would be able to eat and to get a change of clothing. Then we explored the rest of the house, calling to each other from one room to another, 'Michelle, come and see. Look at the childrens' cribs! Do such things still exist?'[10]

The women were still rummaging when the house's owner appeared. He was a policeman. He disappeared at once and was back in five minutes with four young soldiers. Before they knew it, Micheline and the others had been hustled outside and were lined up against a wall, waiting to be shot. Micheline was so exhausted by then that she really didn't care any more:

> The four soldiers took their places and aimed their rifles. Calmly, I saw they were about to shoot us, and my soul, or what was left of it, accepted the fact, I suppose. It must have been floating above me like a balloon on a string, for I could see everything from without and from above, and yet I was part of it. But I participated with extreme indifference, like an unconcerned spectator. The only question in my mind was whether it would be possible to see the bullet.[11]

Luckily for them, an officer appeared, shouting something about the Russians that Micheline didn't catch. The soldiers lowered their rifles and let the women go. They were taken in by a German woman who found them some shoes to wear and opened her cupboards to show that she had no food to give them. Then she begged them to leave, saying that the police would shoot them all and her too if they were found in her house.

That night, they came to a farmhouse and asked permission to sleep in the barn. The farmer was busy tying a bed sheet to a pole to make a white flag. He told them that the Russians had reached Waren and would be at the farm by dawn. Sure enough, there was a battle during the night as the Germans fought a rearguard action around the farm buildings. But Micheline was too far gone to take any notice. She lay fast asleep in the straw, dead to the world, only vaguely aware of men's voices and the occasional rattle of bullets above her head.

All was quiet again when she awoke next morning. It was already full daylight as the barn door swung open and her friends Michelle and Mitzy told her to come and have breakfast. Stepping outside, Micheline saw to her delight that they were free at last. The Germans had all gone. The yard was full of Russian soldiers: big, friendly men with gifts of honey and chicken for them. As if in a dream, Micheline noticed that the weather was perfect for their liberation. The pear trees were in blossom and there was a heavenly smell of lilac in the air. The Russians could hardly have been kinder as they watched the women bustling about, getting breakfast ready. They had evidently been there some time, because Michelle had already been raped.

CHAPTER 13:
THE AMERICANS
TAKE MUNICH

In Holland, it was Princess Juliana's birthday. The weather had prevented her from returning that day with her mother, as they had planned, but the Dutch were celebrating nevertheless, putting out their flags for the royal family. The little village of Achterveld was a sea of red, white and blue as the Allies arrived at St Josef's School for their second meeting with the Germans to complete the arrangements for the food drop over Holland.

The Allied contingent was led by Walter Bedell Smith, General Eisenhower's chief of staff. He was accompanied by Francis de Guingand and Princess Juliana's husband, who had come with them to represent the Dutch royal family. Prince Bernhard arrived to a cheer from the villagers, even though he was German-born and had flirted with Nazism before his marriage. Bernhard had since taken Dutch nationality and identified himself wholeheartedly with his wife's people. The Dutch were delighted to see him in Achterveld, asking him how the princess was and when she would be coming home. Bernhard in turn produced a camera and stood happily taking pictures of the crowd outside the school as they waited for the German delegation to appear.

It was led by Arthur Seyss-Inquart, the Nazi Reichskommissar of Holland and one of the most important figures in Hitler's Germany. The big fish were beginning to surface as the net closed in. First Hess had flown to England, then Himmler had made a tentative approach to the Allies through Sweden. Now here was Seyss-Inquart in Achterveld, a seedy, limping figure in spectacles who was Austrian by birth and had been a lawyer before the war.

He was hated by the Dutch, hated above all other Germans for the ruthlessness with which he had ruled their country for the past five years. Ordered to strip Holland of anything that might be useful for the German war effort, he had done exactly what he was told, reducing the country to a shell of its former self and leaving the people to starve as he fed the German war machine. There were no cheers for Seyss-Inquart as his car drew up under a white flag and he went in to the school. He was accompanied by his officials and some Dutch civil servants who had come with him from occupied Holland. They were making no secret of their pleasure at meeting the Allies at last after so long under German occupation.

The meeting began as soon as they were all settled. Bedell Smith opened it with a few introductory remarks, after which de Guingand ran through the Allies' proposals for feeding the people of Holland. As well as the air drop, the Allies wanted to bring food in by ship, for onward delivery by road, rail and canal. They needed guarantees that they would not be attacked and that the food would be sure to reach the Dutch. Seyss-Inquart was reluctant to provide the necessary assurances at first. He was only persuaded after the meeting had divided up into several smaller groups to discuss particular aspects of the problem.

De Guingand was reminded of a staff college exercise as the delegates adjourned to different classrooms. British, Dutch and Germans, with some Canadians and a Russian observer, all applying themselves to the logistical difficulties, working out the most efficient ways of getting help to the people. He wondered if he was dreaming as the Germans promised to say where the canals had been mined and agreed to repair the road and rail bridges as soon as possible to allow the food through. The agreements were drawn up in writing and signed by both sides. The Dutch participants were dumbfounded, staggered that the Germans were being so cooperative, overwhelmed too at the extent of the help that was about to come their way.

It was all going so well that Bedell Smith decided to take Seyss-Inquart aside and sound him out about the prospects for a German capitulation. With de Guingand, Prince Bernhard and a couple of others, he sat down opposite Seyss-Inquart and probed him over sandwiches and gin. He put it to him that Germany was beaten and that the German command in Holland would be held personally accountable for any further suffering by the Dutch. To everyone's surprise, Seyss-Inquart freely admitted that Germany was defeated. Bedell Smith followed up at once, calling on him to surrender all German forces in Holland to avoid any further bloodshed. But Seyss-Inquart refused, saying that he had no such orders and disclaiming any responsibility for a surrender. He told them that surrender was the Wehrmacht's business, not his.

'But surely, Reich Kommissar, it is the politician who dictates the policy to the soldier?' Bedell Smith demanded.

Seyss-Inquart shrugged. 'What would future generations of Germans say about me if I complied with your suggestion? What would history say about my conduct?'

But Bedell Smith wasn't interested in the verdict of posterity. He saw that he would have to put it to Seyss-Inquart straight. 'General Eisenhower has instructed me to say that he will hold you directly responsible for any further useless bloodshed. You have lost the war, and you know it. If, through pigheadedness, you cause more loss of life to Allied troops or Dutch civilians, you will have to pay the penalty. And you know what that will mean – the wall and a firing squad.'[1]

Seyss-Inquart, in turn, remained unmoved. Like so many of his countrymen, he was half in love with the idea of a violent death. 'I am not afraid,' he told Bedell Smith, quietly and slowly. 'I am a German.'

There was no more to be said. The meeting broke up.

—

In Bavaria, the Americans had taken Munich. The city had fallen with very little opposition as the inhabitants bowed to the inevitable and hung white flags from their windows. There were isolated pockets of resistance, but little of the fanatical fighting that the Americans had been expecting in the birthplace of Nazism. Instead, some Germans were even welcoming them with flowers.

Munich was the birthplace of Nazism, but it also had a long tradition of resistance to the Nazis. The White Rose group had been formed at Munich University: Sophie and Hans Scholl had been guillotined for distributing anti-Nazi leaflets there. Their mantle had been taken up by Rupprecht Gerngross, a graduate of the university with a doctorate from the London School of Economics. Wounded on the Russian front, where he had been disgusted by the murder of Jews, Gerngross had returned to Munich to form Freedom Action Bavaria in the autumn of 1944. He had recruited hundreds of members to strike when the time was ripe and take control of the city from the Nazis.

Their time had come in the early hours of 28 April. With strips of white cloth tied around their left arms, Gerngross's men had moved into position, soldiers as well as civilians, aiming to arrest Munich's Gauleiter and seize control of the newspapers, radio stations and key Government buildings before the Americans arrived. They had been successful at first, taking over the radio stations and broadcasting a message of defiance to the city, urging everyone to join them in overthrowing the Nazis. Thousands had immediately come out on the streets to celebrate, convinced that Hitler must be dead and the war was over.

But the SS had stood firm. They had prevented the arrest of Munich's Gauleiter and enabled him to make a rival broadcast, declaring that he was still in command and that Gerngross's men would be shot as traitors. The plotters' nerve had quickly failed. By lunchtime, Gerngross's parents had been arrested and he himself had fled the city, escaping to the Alps in a hijacked car with SS number plates. His carefully planned coup had failed.

Yet not for lack of support. It was only the SS who had stood firm. While Gauleiter Paul Giesler had been on the radio, telling the people of Munich that they would never be deflected from their loyalty to Adolf Hitler, crews at the airfield had destroyed their aircraft and soldiers had thrown their weapons into the river. A whole division had considered defecting to Gerngross. It had been obvious from their reaction to the attempted coup that the ordinary people of Munich had no more stomach for the fight.

The Americans arrived in the early hours of 30 April to find the city deeply divided as some Germans tried to fight on while the rest attempted to surrender. For the men of the 45th Division, advancing straight from Dachau:

> It was a question of pouring in heavy artillery fire, attacking behind smoke across city streets, dodging deadly fire from anti-aircraft guns or persistent machine guns – all the usual accompaniments the men had come to expect in clearing rubble-strewn German cities. Even as a big white streamer flew from the highest building in Munich, troops from the 45th Division were fighting from room to room in the SS caserne to dislodge diehard defenders.[2]

Others had it easier. Wolfgang Robinow, a German-Jewish lieutenant in the 42nd Division, encountered very little opposition as his platoon edged forward, but nevertheless found the experience stressful: 'Even if we didn't see anybody at all, we never knew what was hiding around the next corner. We didn't have any dogs or tanks or anything like that. Just jeeps. My soldiers had rifles. I had a pistol. That's all.'[3]

By two o'clock that afternoon, Robinow's men had reached the historic Marienplatz in the heart of Munich, where a crowd of civilians was waiting to welcome them. Raised a Protestant in Berlin, Robinow had learned of his Jewish ancestry for the first time when the Boy Scouts had become the Hitler Youth and he had been kicked out for not being Aryan. He was not impressed by the Germans now trying to be his friend in the Marienplatz:

> Most of them were very old people who were too old for the *Volkssturm*. We were greeted as the great liberators of the city, which, to be honest, really made me angry at the time. This was, after all, the capital of the movement. It was where the Nazi party got its start and where its main propaganda organ the *Völkischer Beobachter* was headquartered. And now they were happy to be 'liberated'?[4]

But at least they weren't fighting. The Marienplatz police surrendered at once, saluting Robinow and handing over their weapons without a struggle. There was still sporadic shooting in other parts of the city as the afternoon wore on, but the historic heart of Munich had fallen to the Americans with barely a shot fired.

—

While the Americans headed into Munich, war photographer Lee Miller was on her way to Dachau with her partner. Driving south from Nuremberg, she and Dave Scherman had been advised to stop off at the camp first, before following the rest of the army to Munich.

They were annoyed at missing the scoop at the camp. Lee and Scherman, also a photographer, were very good at their job, usually the first on the scene when there was anything unusual to be witnessed. They enjoyed a friendly rivalry with Marguerite Higgins, who complained that she always seemed to be arriving at the spot just as they were leaving. But Higgins had beaten them both to Dachau, one of the last big stories of the war. She was already long gone by the time they reached the town towards nightfall and drove up to the camp gates in Scherman's drab green Chevrolet.

Lee Miller was American, a society girl who had spent most of her time in Europe before the war. Choosing to spend the war years in England, she had found her vocation as a photo-journalist, one of very few women photographers on the front line. In the past six weeks, she had been all over Germany with the US Army, from Aachen and Cologne to Bonn, Frankfurt and Heidelberg, from a Gestapo prison to a wrecked bridge over the Rhine and the concentration camp at

Buchenwald. In the process, she had come to hate the Germans more than she had ever imagined possible, loathing them beyond all contempt for their cruelty and arrogance, their refusal to admit to any guilt and their lack of concern for anybody's suffering but their own. She already knew about the shrunken head and lampshades made of tattoos in Buchenwald. She wondered what further horrors awaited as she and Scherman drove through the town of Dachau towards the forbidding barbed wire on the outskirts.

The railway to the camp was lined with large, comfortable houses. White flags hung from the windows, the same windows that had looked out onto the track as the emaciated prisoners from Buchenwald arrived in overcrowded boxcars. The prisoners were still there, their bodies still spilling out of the cars as American medics gaped at the sight, wondering how to begin clearing up. Lee and Scherman captured the GIs' horror on film and then moved into the camp to find themselves mobbed by cheerful inmates as they appeared.

Dutch prisoners were celebrating Princess Juliana's birthday. They had gathered in the square to cheer and sing the national anthem while others climbed on to the roofs and gave the victory salute. They didn't have a Dutch flag, but they had managed to find three strips of red, white and blue material to make one. Lee took their photographs and joined the celebrations for a few minutes. Then she moved on to the brothel to photograph the women who had worked as prostitutes in return for shorter sentences. She took pictures of SS guards who had tried to escape by disguising themselves as prisoners and captured a haunting shot of a dead guard half-submerged in the canal. She photographed the corpses piled up outside the crematorium and the gas chamber with its innocent notice announcing SHOWER BATHS above the door. And she pictured the prisoners in their huts:

> The triple decker bunks, without blankets, or even straw, held two and three men per bunk who lay in bed, too weak to circulate the camp in victory and liberation marches or songs, although they mostly grinned and cheered, peering over the edge. In the few minutes it took me to take my pictures, two men were found dead, and were unceremoniously dragged out and thrown on the heap outside the block. Nobody seemed to mind except me. The doctor said it was too late for more than half the others in the building anyway. The bodies are just chucked out so that the wagon that makes the rounds every day can pick them up at the street corner, like garbage disposal.[5]

The American troops in the camp had been encouraged like Lee to go everywhere and see everything, taking pictures with their own cameras so that they would have plenty of evidence to show to the people when they went back home. It was important that they should be believed when they went home. But the order had had to be rescinded, because the troops couldn't take any more. So many had been overcome by Dachau, one way or another, that they were unable to do their jobs properly. It had just been decreed therefore that the huts and other buildings were to be off limits for the time being to everyone except medics and the press corps.

Lee herself was only too glad to leave once she had her pictures. Loathing the Germans more than ever, she and Scherman put the camp behind them at length and set off down the autobahn for Munich. If Munich was where Nazism had begun, they wanted to be there when the city fell, recording every wonderful moment with their cameras after what they had seen at Dachau: 'The sight of the blue and white striped tatters shrouding the bestial death of the hundreds of starved and maimed men and women had left us gulping for air and for violence, and if Munich, the birthplace of this horror was falling we'd like to help.'

A few miles from Dachau, in the little village of Unterbernbach, Victor Klemperer had been following the Americans' progress for days, listening intently as bombs fell nearby and the sound of guns drew closer by the hour. As a Jew married to a German, he was longing for the Americans to arrive, if it meant that his personal nightmare would be over at last.

Son of a rabbi, Klemperer had converted to Christianity before the Great War, in which he had served with distinction. Being Jewish had never been very important to him. He had always seen himself as German, first and foremost, rather than Jewish. But his patriotism hadn't saved him from the race and citizenship laws introduced by the Nazis. He had lost his job as a university professor in Dresden before the war and had later been forced to move into the ghetto with his wife Eva. They had had to put the cat down, because of a ban on Jewish ownership of pets.

Klemperer had spent the war working in a factory or at manual jobs, shovelling snow. He had watched with dismay as deportation orders were served on the Jewish community in Dresden – curt summonses to report immediately with one suitcase for resettlement in the East. With a good war record and an Aryan wife, Klemperer had been a 'privileged' Jew, one of the last to receive such a summons. But he had always known that it was only a matter of time. And that Jews for resettlement were never heard of again.

But then something wonderful had happened. The Allies had bombed Dresden. More than 700 aircraft in two waves had carpeted the city, dropping a mix of high explosive and incendiaries, killing 25,000 people and reducing one of the most beautiful places in Germany to a smouldering ruin. Klemperer had been separated from his wife in the confusion, running for the Jewish shelter as a bomb exploded nearby. He had found her again next morning, sitting on her suitcase near the Elbe. Dying for a cigarette to calm her nerves, yet without matches during the raid, she had thought seriously of getting a light from a body burning nearby.

Kurt Vonnegut, an American prisoner of war in Dresden, had taken shelter during the raid in an underground abattoir named Slaughterhouse Five by the Germans. He had felt only shame for humanity as he helped them clear up their dead. But Dresden had been a legitimate target ahead of the Russian advance. Among the many buildings destroyed had been Gestapo headquarters, and with it all their files on the Jews. Assured by his friends that the files had gone, Klemperer had seized the opportunity to reinvent himself as a displaced German who had lost his identity card in the raid.

Issued with temporary papers, yet afraid of being unmasked if he remained in Dresden, he had left with his wife to join the flow of refugees to the West, heading for Bavaria. They had ended up at Unterbernbach, just north west of Dachau, where room had been found for them in an attic. They had been there for two weeks, waiting for the Americans to come. Klemperer had found it a fascinating experience as all manner of displaced Germans passed through the village, with widely differing views on the war and how it was likely to end.

There had been two SS men who had demanded accommodation in the same house as Klemperer, threatening to evict anyone who opposed them. They had been followed by two other SS who had been perfectly decent and well-mannered. There had been the deputy burgomaster, loudly proclaiming that he had nothing to fear from the Americans, when everyone else said he had been the keenest Nazi in the village. There had been the Berliner, unaware that Klemperer was Jewish, who had confided his anger at the way the Jews had been treated in Berlin. And there had been the blonde, blue-eyed, stern-looking schoolmistress, who had seemed to Klemperer the epitome of everything the Nazis held dear. She had surprised him with her loathing for them, complaining openly about the atrocities at Dachau, telling him that 13,000 people had died there in three months and the rest were being released because they had nothing to eat.

Everyone was waiting for the Americans to come, longing for the war to be over. The village's electricity had been cut off, so they could no longer follow the war on the radio, but they only had to put their heads out of the window to hear the rattle of machine gun fire and the distant sound of artillery towards Munich. Most of it had died away now, which suggested to Klemperer that the city must have fallen to the Americans. If so, they would be in Unterbernbach soon enough. The burgomaster had already taken the precaution of removing the Nazi swastika previously displayed so prominently on the gable above his office. He had been delighted to see it come down, he told anyone prepared to listen, since he had never actually been a Nazi.

—

Klemperer had chosen not to emigrate before the war, but many other Jews had left Germany as soon as it became clear that the Nazis were there to stay. Private Henry Kissinger's father had lost his teaching job in 1933, but had stuck it out for another five years before finally admitting defeat. He and his family had left Germany in August 1938, going to London first, and then to the United States. They had settled in the Washington Heights area of Manhattan, a place so full of German Jewish immigrants that it was known to everyone else as the Fourth Reich.

Henry was the older of the Kissingers' two sons. He had grown up in Fürth, just outside Nuremberg. While Hitler strutted at his rallies and the SS goosestepped through the streets, Henry Kissinger had been a middle class Jewish boy living in a second floor apartment on Matildenstrasse, in the heart of the Old Town. He had gone to school with German children at first, playing soccer with the other boys like everyone else. But then the Jews had been segregated, sent to their own school and beaten up on the streets by gangs of Aryan youths looking for trouble. Kissinger and his brother had quickly learned to avoid trouble if they saw it coming, always crossing the road to escape groups of youths, stepping off the pavement and walking in the gutter rather than give anyone the chance to take offence. They had watched half-enviously as their erstwhile schoolfellows joined the Hitler Youth and had a high old time marching through the town together and singing patriotic songs.

Kissinger had retained his habits in America at first, a Jew always stepping off the sidewalk if he saw a group of youths coming, steering well clear of trouble. But then he had remembered where he was, a free man in a free country. He had as much right to be on the sidewalk as anyone else. He had adapted readily to his new country, learning the mysteries of baseball and going to night school in order to pursue the American dream and become an accountant.

He had been drafted in 1943, sent to boot camp in North Carolina and sworn in as a US citizen during his training. His new country had expected him to walk for miles in boots and attack dummies with a bayonet, but Kissinger had decided very early on that combat was not for him. His application for medical training had been rejected, but he had soon found a more congenial job in division intelligence. It was as interpreter/driver to the 84th Infantry Division's General Alexander Bolling that Private Kissinger found himself on German soil again at the beginning of 1945.

His progress since then had been stellar. The Rhine town of Krefeld had fallen to the Americans in March. Without gas, water, power or refuse collection, its population of 200,000 had been in dire straits after the hurried departure of its Nazi administrators. Among the Americans brought in to replace them, Kissinger had been the only one who could speak German. Still only a private, he had been put in charge of Krefeld, given the task of restoring order in the town and establishing a civilian administration. He had done it within a week.

Kissinger had developed a taste for the work, solving intractable problems with a few minutes' thought and rebuilding a broken organisation from scratch. He had weeded out the remaining Nazis in Krefeld and arrested all the Gestapo he could find. Expecting them to be monsters, he had been surprised to discover that most were just 'miserable little bureaucrats' looking to ingratiate themselves with their new masters. Wherever Kissinger went, Germans snapped to attention at his approach, the same Germans who had kicked him off the pavement when he had been a boy in Fürth.

Kissinger was enjoying that, yet without bitterness. His parents bore a lifelong grudge against Germany which he did not share, despite the humiliations of his youth. He found it impossible to hate the whole country. He kept his distance from the Germans and refused to fraternise, but he wasn't looking for revenge. Kissinger saw himself as a liberator, not a conqueror, far more interested in solving Germany's problems than in getting his own back. He was just there to get the country up and running again.

He was planning to revisit his old home as soon as the war was over. He owed it to his parents to go back and see how it was. Nuremberg had taken a pasting from the Allied bombing and probably Fürth too. The first chance he got, Kissinger was going to take a jeep and get over there, see if there was anyone left from the old days. Most of his friends had emigrated at the same time as the Kissingers and the rest had disappeared into the concentration camps. There had been 3,000 Jews living in Fürth when the Kissingers were growing up. There were only seventy left in the first full head count after the war.

CHAPTER 14:
ITALY

In Switzerland, the two German officers bringing the Italian surrender terms from Caserta were on their way to Wehrmacht headquarters at Bolzano. In the small hours of 30 April, Eugen Wenner and Viktor von Schweinitz were being driven through the night to the Austrian border at Buchs. A Wehrmacht car was waiting on the Austrian side to take them the rest of the way to Bolzano.

It had been a nightmare journey for the two Germans. After signing the surrender terms at the royal palace in Caserta, they had been flown to Annecy in France, arriving early the previous evening. Annecy was just across the border from Geneva, in Switzerland, but their contact hadn't shown up to help them make the crossing. They had had to bluff their way into Switzerland, claiming that the Swiss general staff was taking a keen interest in their mission. The border guards had allowed them in with reluctance, but the delay meant that they had arrived at Geneva station just as the last train of the night was pulling out for Bern.

There had been no cars for hire, because of the fuel shortage. They had a contact in Geneva, but he had gone out for the evening and wasn't answering his phone. The Germans had ended up sitting in the outdoor restaurant at the station with the surrender documents burning a hole in their pockets. They had rung their man every fifteen minutes until he answered at last. A car had been procured and they had arrived at Bern just before midnight.

Bern was the Swiss base for the United States' Office of Strategic Services. The office was headed by Allen Dulles, who had been closely involved in the secret peace negotiations. He opened the door to find

Wenner, Schweinitz and Gävernitz, their interpreter, looking very sorry for themselves in the cold. They had been up all the previous night, studying the surrender terms, and had had very little sleep since. They were half-dead with exhaustion.

Dulles gave them whisky and sandwiches and thawed them out with hot coffee in front of the fire. They left again after an hour, taking blankets and pillows for the long drive to the Austrian border. Dulles went to bed after they had gone, imagining that it would be plain sailing from then on. He soon learned otherwise:

> Before seven in the morning the telephone rang. Gävernitz was on the other end of the wire calling from Buchs. The envoys had arrived at the frontier, but they were blocked. The Swiss government, by formal action, had hermetically closed the Swiss frontier. No one could enter or leave without special permission. Ordinary visas were of no use, and even the special facilities enjoyed by the Swiss intelligence officers were ineffective. Only direct action by the Swiss government could help us out.[1]

Dulles wasted no time. He rang Switzerland's acting Foreign Minister and asked for an immediate meeting. Sensing his urgency, Walter Stucki agreed to see him at the foreign office as soon as he could get there.

Dulles put his cards on the table when they met. He told Stucki that the Germans at the frontier had signed the surrender of all German forces in north Italy and had the document with them. If they were allowed to proceed to Bolzano, the fighting would stop at once. If the fighting stopped, the Swiss would be spared the prospect of guerrilla warfare in their mountains, followed by an influx of thousands of German soldiers seeking internment or even looting the country on their way home. The situation was too urgent to waste time consulting colleagues. Stucki should let the Germans through at once.

He took the point. Where others would have hummed and hawed and wanted to cover their backs, Stucki gave the order without further delay. Wenner and Schweinitz were allowed through immediately and crossed the border into Austria.

But their troubles still weren't over. A car was waiting to take them to Bolzano, but its driver had a worrying message for them. Ernst Kaltenbrunner, head of the SS security service, and Franz Hofer, Gauleiter of the Tyrol, were opposed to the surrender in Italy. They had ordered the Gestapo to arrest Wenner and Schweinitz as they passed through Innsbruck on their way to Bolzano. For that reason, the driver was going to take them a different way, avoiding Innsbruck altogether but travelling along back roads still covered in snow.

Wenner and Schweinitz were thunderstruck. The prospect of another long drive along dreadful roads was bad enough. Far worse was the knowledge that the Gestapo were after them for signing the surrender agreement. It was the last thing they wanted to hear as they climbed wearily into the car, more dead than alive with fatigue, and settled down for the final leg of their tortuous journey to Bolzano.

—

The Wehrmacht headquarters at Bolzano had been tunnelled into a mountain to protect it from the daily air raids by the US Air Force. The SS headquarters nearby had almost been destroyed by a near miss the previous night. Both headquarters were in turmoil as the German commanders waited uneasily to hear the surrender terms from the Allies. They were in several different minds about what to do if the terms were not to their liking, as they almost certainly wouldn't be.

Some were talking of an Alpine redoubt, a last-ditch stand in the mountains around the Führer's Berchtesgaden retreat. Others were adamant that there could be no surrender if the troops were not allowed to march home afterwards, preferably carrying their weapons. A few, rather more realistic, recognised that the war was lost and they would have to accept whatever terms they could get. All were troubled by their oath to Hitler, divided as to whether they could legitimately repudiate it, or whether it should continue to bind them until the Führer's death.

The situation was complicated by the interference of the politicians. Franz Hofer, Gauleiter of the Tyrol, had initially supported the approach to the Allies, but had now changed his mind, favouring a separate deal instead that would leave him in charge of the Tyrol. Ernst Kaltenbrunner wanted to negotiate a separate peace for Austria, one for which he himself could take the credit. Alarmed at the talk of hanging Nazi leaders after the war, Kaltenbrunner had decided that his best chance of survival was to negotiate a comprehensive surrender package that included his own exoneration among its provisions. That was why the Gestapo in Innsbruck had been ordered to arrest Wenner and Schweinitz before they got to Bolzano.

To add to the confusion, General von Vietinghoff, commanding the German Army in Italy, had just been relieved of his duties. It was Vietinghoff who had reluctantly sent Wenner and Schweinitz to Caserta to negotiate

The guillotine at Dachau. (Getty Images)

'Just look at them now', said an Italian bystander, as the bodies of Mussolini and his mistress are put on display in Milan. (Getty Images)

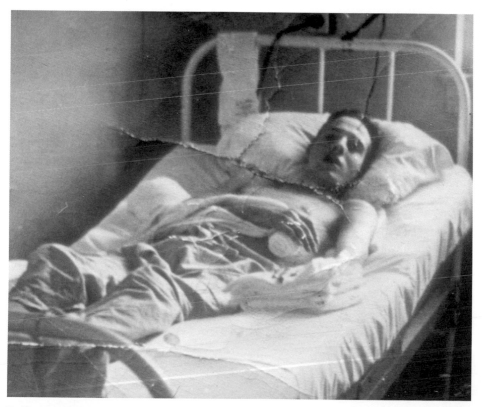

Badly wounded in the Italian mountains, 2nd Lieutenant Bob Dole feared permanent paralysis as news of the German surrender came through. (Sygma/Corbis)

Operation *Manna*. The Dutch cheer as RAF Lancasters drop essential supplies. (RAF Hendon)

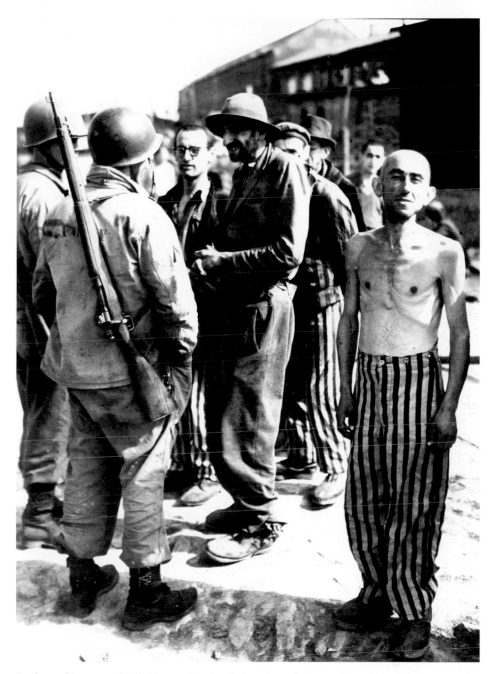

Buchenwald camp is finally liberated in the closing days of the war. (Getty)

Badly traumatised by Dachau, Lee Miller enjoys her first bath for weeks in Hitler's Munich apartment. (Getty Images)

Jack Kennedy was in San Francisco as the war ended, covering the United Nations conference for Hearst newspapers. (Bettmann/Corbis)

Shunned by everyone she knew, Leni Riefenstahl cried all night when she learned of Hitler's death. (Corbis)

Russian troops indicate the probable site of Hitler's cremation in the Chancellery garden. (Getty Images)

The conference room in Hitler's bunker, in the infamous Reichschancellery, after the Nazis had fled. (Time Life Pictures/Getty Images)

Hildegard Knef was in Berlin when the Russians came. She was delighted to end up in the American sector after the war. (Getty Images)

Private Josef Ratzinger deserted at the end of the war and walked home, terrified that the SS would shoot him for cowardice. (Getty Images)

Paula Hitler mourned her brother's death for the rest of her life. (Bettmann/Corbis)

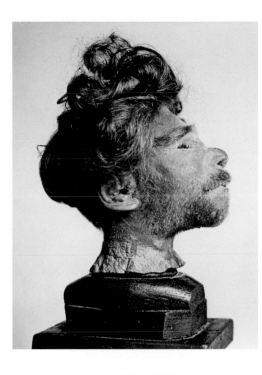

LEFT
The shrunken head of this Polish prisoner, hanged at Buchenwald, was presented as evidence at the Nuremberg trials. (Corbis)

BELOW
The news of the German surrender filled newspapers across Europe. (Getty Images)

DAILY EXPRESS

Coast dim-out 9.59 pm to 5.54 am   SATURDAY MAY 5 1945   Moon rises 4.33 am (Sun.) sets 2.5 pm   One Penny

WAR OVER IN GERMANY, HOLLAND AND DENMARK

GERMANS SURRENDER INSIDE MONTY'S TENT

They argued, they wept, they went and lunched—but said 'Yes' at last

THE MAP CONVINCED THEM

THIS IS IT

Said Monty: If you don't agree I shall go on with the war and shall be delighted to do so

FIELD-MARSHAL SIR BERNARD MONTGOMERY has accepted the surrender of all German forces in Holland, Denmark and North-Western Germany—well over 1,000,000 men, and a quarter of them naval personnel—as from 8 o'clock this morning.

This historic victory of British arms, with the end of the war on the Western Front, was announced from Supreme Headquarters at 8.15 last night. It is the greatest unconditional surrender of this or any other war, even greater than that accepted by Field-Marshal Alexander at Mediterranean H.Q. on Sunday.

A "cease fire" order on the whole of Montgomery's front was expected last night, six weeks after the British crossing of the Rhine.

It will mean that the only areas to be cleansed of the Nazis are Norway, Western Czechoslovakia, a pocket of Germany round Dresden, a strip of Austria and the fortresses on the Atlantic seaboard.

Montgomery signed the agreement with German generals and an admiral in a tent at his headquarters. He did not meet Doenitz. There is no mention of the ersatz Fuehrer in the negotiations which began on Thursday.

THE TERMS —WITH NO ARGUMENT

COLD, RUTHLESS

The surrender was the most dramatic story of the war. Montgomery treated the Germans with cold ruthlessness. He showed them his secret maps to prove that their position was hopeless.

They argued about the terms and only wanted to surrender the forces trapped by the Russians. Monty refused to talk to them. They went away and, what more, had 24 hours later and agreed as ordered.

At once

RUNDSTEDT TELLS—

Why we lost

From WILLIAM TROUGHTON
With Ninth U.S. Army, Friday

GERMANY never had a plan for invading England, knew it was impossible and never made any serious attempt to invade. The great fleet of barges massed along the Channel coast was made up of nothing more than 'apple boats'.

That was Field-Marshal von Rundstedt's considered opinion, expressed to-day at Eisen's.

Rundstedt was captured yesterday and it was in hospital at Bad Tolz, Bavaria, where his German son was with him, that I and a few other war correspondents were allowed to see him.

It is estimated that 50,000 of these are wandering along the west bank of the Elbe and north of the

DRINK ORGY ENDS REICH

Chaos like Dark Ages

From JAMES WELLARD: Ninth U.S. Army, Friday

TODAY marked the high point in the Wehrmacht's collapse. Thousands of German soldiers, in varying stages of drunkenness and accompanied by women, arrived in assorted carts, demanding to be allowed to surrender.

Doenitz off to Norway

Albert Ramson, Swedish Premier, said at midnight: 'I hope that news of Denmark will soon be followed by similar report, equally happy, from Norway.'

From E. D. MASTERMAN
STOCKHOLM, Friday

Doenitz and Himmler are expected to arrive in Norway tonight or tomorrow, after ordering to reopen today from a wireless message.

4.30 a.m. LATEST

KEITEL ORDER NO SCUTTLIN

Field-Marshal Keitel said order of Navy there must be scuttling or destruction of ships at surrender. — Radio.

'BIG 5 AGREEIN ON MANDATES'

SAN FRANCISCO, Friday.— Five hope to reach agreement among major nations on subject trusteeships and mandates. Exchange.

Front Page

Göring, Hess, Ribbentrop, Keitel, Speer and Dönitz were among the top Nazis tried at Nuremberg from November 1945 to October 1946. (Getty Images)

Dr Klaus Schilling about to leave the stage. He was hanged at Landsberg Prison in May 1946 for conducting experiments on prisoners at Dachau. (Getty Images)

the surrender. But Vietinghoff had been sacked that morning by Field-Marshal Kesselring, a Hitler fanatic determined to keep the war going until all the German soldiers on the Russian front had successfully escaped to the West. While Wenner and Schweinitz drove to Bolzano with the surrender terms, Vietinghoff was on his way to Lake Carezza in the Dolomites to face a court-martial for dereliction of duty. Thus were the deck chairs being rearranged on the *Titanic*.

———

In the mountains above Villabassa, the *Prominente* from Dachau were enjoying their first taste of freedom after their release from the SS. Now under the protection of the Wehrmacht, they were being ferried in relays to the Hotel Pragser-Wildsee, a lakeside watering hole in the snow, 5,000 feet above sea level. Known also as the Lago di Braies, the hotel had been closed since the beginning of the war, but had been reopened by the partisans as a place for the *Prominente* to remain in safety and a modicum of comfort until the Americans arrived or the war ended, whichever happened first.

The *Prominente* could hardly believe their change of fortune. After years in Dachau and other prisons, knowing that they could be taken out and shot at any moment, it seemed unreal to be walking in the grounds of a tourist hotel, with a beautiful lake in front of them and a wonderful view of the mountains behind. Snow lay thick on the ground and the hotel was freezing cold after being shut up for so long, but the *Prominente* hardly noticed. It was enough just to be free again, able to come and go as they pleased. They were still under guard, but the guards were for their own protection, sentries discreetly patrolling the forest to shield them from marauding deserters or a counter-attack by the SS.

It was still possible that the SS might try to kill the *Prominente* before they fell into Allied hands. Some Gestapo men who had accompanied the *Prominente* to the hotel had a list of people to be executed on Himmler's orders. They had shown it to Kurt von Schuschnigg, the former Chancellor of Austria. He had not been surprised to see his own name on it, and his wife's too. He presumed the Gestapo had shown him the list to frighten him, but they may have been trying to curry favour, letting him see their orders and then conspicuously failing to carry them out in the hope of getting a good report from him when the Americans appeared and took them prisoner.

But the Gestapo were unlikely to get a good report from Schuschnigg. He knew the Gestapo from old, since the Anschluss of 1938, when the

German Army had marched into Austria to overthrow the government and annex the country to Germany. Chancellor von Schuschnigg had been arrested by the Gestapo and kept in solitary confinement at Gestapo headquarters in Vienna for seventeen months. A cultivated man, intellectual and upper class, he had been bullied by the SS guards, forced to empty their slop buckets and clean the latrine after they had deliberately fouled it. The guards had read his letters, aimed their guns at him, threatened to shoot him if he went near the window, banged the table for an hour at a time to annoy him and denied him permission to attend his father's funeral. Schuschnigg's only crime had been to stand in the way of Adolf Hitler, but he had paid a heavy price for it at the hands of the Gestapo and their goons.

Yet times had changed since then. Hitler's star was no longer in the ascendant. As soon as the *Prominente* had all arrived at the hotel, they were called to a meeting in the lobby. Captain von Alvensleben of the Wehrmacht stood up and told them that they were no longer prisoners, that he and his men were only there for their protection. Schuschnigg and the others listened incredulously as Alvensleben was followed by an Italian partisan who invited them all to consider themselves guests of the Tyrolean district government: 'We are dumbfounded. We look at each other somewhat diffidently, somewhat afraid that this is merely a dream. Soon we shall wake again to reality. But the impossible has happened. The dream is a reality – we are almost free! And we are home! They have spoken to us like human beings! Oh, God, dear God, it is true.'[2]

There was a little chapel in the forest close to the hotel. A devout man, Schuschnigg went there to give thanks after the meeting was over. So did quite a few of the other prisoners.

—

A hundred miles to the south, the fighting was still continuing as the Allies raced eastwards around the Gulf of Venice. They had just taken Venice itself and were on their way to Trieste, aiming to secure the port for the Allies before Josip Tito and his Yugoslav partisans could reach it from the other side.

Venice had fallen on 29 April. It had fallen not to the Allies but to the Italian partisans in the city, who had risen against the Germans and liberated themselves. There had been pockets of resistance, as always, but these had been swiftly mopped up before the arrival of British and New Zealand troops from the Eighth Army. The Italians had rounded up almost 3,000 German soldiers still in the city and imprisoned them in a large garage. Then they had come out on the streets to greet the first troops of the

Queen's Brigade driving in over the causeway from the mainland. The whole operation had gone so smoothly that Geoffrey Cox, a New Zealand intelligence officer who arrived early on 30 April, found the city virtually untouched by the fighting:

> In St Mark's square the scene was almost fantastically normal. Women sold food for the pigeons to the few Allied troops who had got into the city. In the entrance to the Campanile they were taking down the German price lists for the lift and putting them up in English. All the shops were still shut, but the crowds walked to and fro quietly. Enormous flags – the winged lion of Venice and the Italian tricolour – hung from the standards in front of St Mark's. There was a moment of excitement as a group of partisans came from a side street escorting a Fascist, surrounded by a curious, shouting crowd. The Fascist was a miserable specimen in all sooth, a meagre man in his late thirties with a blue cap on his head, looking like a railway porter. He carried a paper parcel under his arm and his face was white. He grimaced constantly, from either fear or indifference. They took him across the bridge which runs parallel to the Bridge of Sighs, and into the prison.[3]

Cox went to the Hotel Danieli for lunch. He found the restaurant full of rich Italians, elegant men squiring women covered in jewels, who looked as if the war hadn't touched them in the slightest. Venice was where the rich of Italy had come to escape the bombing, where the Fascist leaders had sent their wives and mistresses for safety. The only casualties Venice had sustained from the war had been from people falling into the canals during the blackout.

A British soldier from the Queen's Brigade, arriving a few hours after Cox, shared his contempt for the Italians they saw sitting out the war:

> So this was Venice. We all thought it a dump. The gondoliers put up their prices immediately. They must have thought we earned as much as the Yanks. I had heard a lot about this so-called beautiful city. To me it was a waterlogged dump smelling of damp and drains. Nor did the Eyeties there like us. The main square was filled with little tables and chairs and on every chair, all day long, there was either some old woman dripping with pearls or some well-dressed nancy boy in a silk shirt and ponced-up hair. We had been out since well before Alamein and on those bloody chairs in the main square of Venice were the people whom we had sweated to liberate. They

163

didn't want to be liberated. They told us so. And the waiters hated our guts too, because we weren't like the pre-war British.[4]

Cox thought the Italians should start in the restaurant at the Danieli, if they wanted to go looking for Fascists. He was glad to get away after lunch, driving back to the mainland and taking the road to Trieste. The port was still in German hands, but was threatened by the Yugoslavs from one direction and the Allies from the other. The question for the Allies, as Cox's truck turned towards the front line, was whether they could get there first, or whether Tito's Communist troops would beat them to it, seize the port facilities and then claim Trieste for Yugoslavia.

———

In Milan, General Willis Crittenberger of the US Army's IV Corps had arrived that afternoon to find the city still in chaos as the last of the Germans surrendered and the Italian Fascists continued to be hunted down. Partisans were roaming the streets, flourishing red scarves and waving their rifles about to impress the girls. Upwards of 500 people had been 'executed' before the violence subsided. Their bodies were left in the gutter or else dumped at the city morgue or the cemetery, often without any identification marks of any kind. In the words of the British Ambassador: 'It is therefore difficult to say whether the victims are Fascists executed by partisans, or partisans executed by Fascists, or just victims of personal vendettas.'

But at least in the Piazzale Loreto, the bodies of Mussolini and his accomplices were no longer dangling from a girder. They had been taken down the previous night. The other bodies were being prepared for burial, but Mussolini's had been removed to the Policlinico hospital for an autopsy. While rifle shots continued to reverberate around the city, Benito Mussolini was lying naked on a porcelain slab, surrounded by Italian doctors sharpening their scalpels and a group of American cameramen catching every stage of the procedure on film.

Mussolini's head was still a mess as a result of the beating he had taken. 'Skull misshapen, because of destruction of the cranium. Bone slivers forced into the sinus cavities. Eyeball crushed and lacerated, with escape of vitreous fluid. Upper jaw fractured, with multiple lacerations of the palate. Cerebellum, pons, midbrain, and part of the occipital lobes crushed. Massive fracture at the base of the cranium.'[5] The Italian dictator was not a pretty sight.

An assistant sponged away the haloes around the bullet holes in Mussolini's chest. Then the doctors sawed off the top of his skull and slit him open from throat to abdomen. The procedure was routine, but it left the cameramen shaken. The doctors examined Mussolini's stomach and found an ulcer. They searched his aorta for any sign of the stellar white maculas indicative of syphilis, but apparently found none, which suggested that his enemies had been wrong when they claimed that an advanced case of venereal insanity had contributed to some of the Duce's wilder political posturings.

The whole operation took four hours. The doctors stitched Mussolini up again when they had finished. His brain was in pieces, but the Americans took a portion of it away for further analysis in the United States. If there was anything to be learned about dictators from a study of Mussolini's cerebrum, the scientists at St Elizabeth's psychiatric hospital in Washington had their microscopes poised to find it.

—

While her husband was being sewn up, Rachele Mussolini was still in gaol in Como, expecting to be shot at any moment. Her worst fears appeared to be confirmed that evening when a priest arrived, bringing her children Romano and Anna Maria with him. They hadn't been reunited for long when a policeman arrived in turn, politely asking Rachele to come with him. The excitable Rachele assumed at once that she had been allowed to see her children one last time and was now being led away to her death.

Instead, she was put in a car and taken to American headquarters in Como. An Italian-speaking officer received her civilly and took her to a room for a long talk. He confided that he was already finding the administration of Como a strain. 'How on earth did Mussolini manage to govern these people for twenty years?' he wanted to know.

Later, he took her to the officers' mess. Rachele was in tears, worried about her children, but the American was very kind, assuring her that they were being properly looked after:

> He gave me the place of honour and there was respectful sympathy on all sides as the tears rolled silently down my cheeks. I was thinking of Romano and Anna Maria. I was safe, but what about them? Somebody said in Italian, 'You're not to worry; you eat.' I managed to make them understand that I was wild with anxiety about my children, and they succeeded in convincing me that they were being taken care of too. I had plenty of smiles to cheer me up.[6]

CHAPTER 15: HITLER GOES TO VALHALLA

At the Chancellery, they were having a party. While Hitler retired to his room to kill himself, the soldiers in the upstairs canteen were drinking and dancing, enjoying a frenzied release of tension as they waited for him to die. There had been a series of increasingly frantic drinking sessions in the past few days as the Russians tightened their grip and the Chancellery staff abandoned all hope of escape. Shedding their inhibitions, some men had got married in a hurry, while others had taken to the bottle or sought distraction in sex. With the Chancellery full of secretaries and female refugees from the surrounding streets, there had been no shortage of sex for those who wanted it. Ernst-Günther Schenck, an SS doctor at the Chancellery, was an eyewitness:

> There was a kind of contagious mass-hysteria seeking a group outlet. Many of the same wild, red-eyed women who had fled their Berlin apartments, in terror of rape by Red Army soldiers, now threw themselves into the arms, and bed rolls, of the nearest German soldiers they could find. And the soldiers were not averse. Still, it came as a bit of a shock to me to see a German general chasing some half-naked signalwoman between and over the cots. The more discreet retired to Dr Kunz's dentist chair upstairs in the Chancellery. That chair seemed to have had a special erotic attraction. The wilder women enjoyed being strapped in and made love to in a variety of novel positions.
>
> I was sceptical as that story made the rounds. But then one of the women involved, drunk and hysterical, gave me the clinical

details. I dosed her with sedatives. She told me she had been twice raped before fleeing to the Chancellery, took to drinking, could not hold her liquor. Towards the end, she lost all inhibitions. Another diversion was group sex, usually off in the dark corners.[1]

Traudl Junge shared Schenck's bemusement: 'An erotic fever seemed to have taken possession of everybody. Everywhere, even on the dentist's chair, I saw bodies entwined in crude sexual embraces. The women had abandoned all modesty and were freely exposing their private parts.'[2]

But they had lost the appetite for exposing themselves as they waited for Hitler to die. Instead, music blared out from the canteen: *Tipperary*, *The Lambeth Walk*, American swing, all the 'Jewish, jungle music' that Hitler despised. It was so loud that Otto Günsche, standing guard outside Hitler's room, ordered Rochus Misch to ring the canteen and tell them to be quiet while the Führer was trying to kill himself. Misch rang several times, but got no answer. 'They probably couldn't even hear the phone. So I told the orderly to run up and tell them, but I'm sure he was too late.'[3]

The music was still playing when Traudl Junge decided she couldn't bear the tension any longer. 'When that door closed behind Hitler and Eva, all I wanted was to get out. I felt I was suffocating. I craved quiet and sleep. I wanted terribly not to be so frightened.'[4] Desperate to get away, Traudl ran for the stairs to the upper bunker, only to find the Göbbels children sitting on them, looking lost. No one had given them any lunch, so Traudl went to get them something to eat. Returning with a jar of cherries, she kept talking as she buttered bread and made ham sandwiches for them all:

I talk to them to distract them. They say something about being safe in the bunker, and how it's almost fun to hear the explosions when they know the bangs can't hurt them. Suddenly there is the sound of a shot, so loud, so close that we all fall silent. It echoes on through all the rooms. 'That was a direct hit,' cried Helmut, with no idea how right he is. The Führer is dead now.[5]

Traudl was certain that the sound she had heard was Hitler shooting himself, but others were unconvinced. The artillery fire, the humming of the ventilation system and the constant pounding of the generators in the machine room made it almost impossible to distinguish individual sounds in the bunker – especially through a bomb-proof steel door. Whatever the truth, it was just after three in the afternoon, by Traudl's watch. Desperate to be alone, she sent the children back to their room and reached for the bottle of Steinhäger on the table. There was an empty glass beside it. Traudl grabbed the glass without thinking and poured herself a stiff drink to calm her nerves.

Others were drinking too. Heinz Linge, Hitler's orderly, had had several glasses of schnapps at the party in the canteen as he waited for his master to die:

> I then returned to the lower bunker. My instinct told me that now was the time. In the central corridor of the lower bunker I met Günsche, to whom I said it must now have happened. I then went into the antechamber to Hitler's room, where I found the door to his room closed and smelt powder smoke. In order to have a witness with me before going into the living room, I returned to the corridor, where I found Bormann standing at a table. I addressed Bormann with the words 'Herr Reichsleiter, it has happened!', whereupon we both immediately went into the living room.[6]

As Linge remembered it, the bodies of Hitler and his wife were slumped on the sofa against the wall facing the door. He had evidently shot himself in the head:

> The bodies of Adolf Hitler and Eva Braun were in a seated position on the sofa standing against the wall opposite the door from the antechamber. Seen from this door, Adolf Hitler sat on the left side of the sofa. His head was bent to the left and slightly forwards. His lower right arm was between the armrest of the sofa and his right thigh, and his open hand lay on his right knee, palm upwards. His feet were on the floor. They were pointing forwards and were about thirty to forty centimetres apart. Hitler was dressed as usual in a uniform jacket, black trousers, black socks and black gloves.
>
> On his right temple I noticed a dark circular spot about the size of a ten pfennig piece. From this spot, a streaked trail of blood ran down to about the middle of his cheek. Directly next to the sofa I saw a puddle of blood about the size of a medium-sized plate, from which drops had splattered on to the frame of the sofa and the wall. Hitler's eyes were open.
>
> About thirty centimetres away from Hitler was the body of Eva Braun-Hitler. She had drawn her legs up on to the sofa. The legs pointed to the left. Her upper body rested against the back

of the sofa. The head was upright. Her eyes were open and her lips were compressed. The body was dressed in a blue dress with a white collar and stockings. The shoes stood side by side on the floor in front of the sofa. Her face appeared completely unchanged. There were no injuries. There were also no traces of blood.[7]

Eva had presumably taken poison. But Günsche, who entered the room right behind Linge, remembered the details differently:

> Eva Braun was lying on the sofa standing against the wall opposite the door from the antechamber. The head was on the left side of the sofa as seen from the door to the antechamber. She was lying on her back. Both lower legs were drawn up slightly. The body was completely still. The eyes were open. My immediate impression was that Eva Braun, as well as Hitler, was dead. The body was dressed as before in a blue dress with white facings and stockings. The shoes were lying on the sofa a short distance away from her feet.
>
> Hitler himself sat in an armchair standing to the left and slightly forward – as seen from the antechamber – but very close to the sofa. His body was slightly sunk together and slanted slightly to the right over the armrest. The right arm hung down over the armrest. The head was bent slightly forward to the right. I noticed an injury to the head slightly above the outer end of the angle of the right eyelid. I saw blood and a dark discolouration. The whole thing was about the size of an old three mark piece. The mouth was slightly open. There was a small pool of blood on the floor to the right of the armchair.[8]

Photographs of the bloodstains suggest that Linge's memory was more accurate. Hitler had almost certainly shot himself in the temple, rather than the mouth, while his wife had taken cyanide – actually prussic acid – leaving a strong smell of burnt almonds in the room. Death for both must have been instantaneous.

Linge and Günsche needed a couple of minutes to recover themselves. Then Linge fetched a blanket to wrap up Hitler's body, while Günsche went to the conference room to announce the death. He found Göbbels waiting for him, with Generals Krebs, Burgdorf and a few others. Clicking his heels, he brought himself up to attention. 'I must report. The Führer is dead,' he told them.

Wordlessly, they followed him back to Hitler's room. The body was carried past them, its legs dangling from the blanket as it was taken to the conference room. Eva's body followed, carried by Martin Bormann. Göbbels was so upset that he announced his intention of leaving the bunker at once to seek his own death outside at the hands of the Russians.

The rest stood around, wondering what to do next. They were still discussing it when Erich Kempka, Hitler's chauffeur and manager of the motor pool, arrived. Günsche had contacted him earlier, asking for jerry cans of petrol to be delivered urgently to the bunker. Kempka had managed to get some cans together, but wanted to know what they were for, when fuel was so very hard to come by. He also wanted to know why they had to be delivered so urgently, in the middle of the shelling.

'The chief is dead,' Günsche told him.

'How could that be?' Kempka demanded. 'I spoke to him only yesterday. He was perfectly healthy and alert.'

They explained. Once he had got over the shock, Kempka helped carry the bodies upstairs. By his own, much-embellished account, Kempka was disgusted to see that Eva Braun's was being carried by Martin Bormann. The two had heartily disliked each other in life. Bormann's solicitude for Eva in death sickened Kempka:

> That lout Bormann was carrying the body of Eva Braun, clutching her breast with his apelike paw. He was carrying her as if she were a sack of potatoes. Just as they all started to go up the stairs, I reached the bottom. So I grabbed the body of Eva Braun-Hitler from Bormann and began to carry her upstairs myself. I think if Bormann had tried to stop me, I would have hit him. But he made no protest.[9]

The plan was to burn the bodies at once in the garden, secretly, without the rest of the Chancellery knowing. It was easier said than done, with artillery fire raining down. The barrage was so heavy that they were several times forced back inside the bunker. Eventually, however, Hitler's corpse was dumped in its blanket three or four yards from the entrance. Then Günsche followed with Eva's body, which he had taken from Kempka:

> I placed Eva Braun's body directly next to Hitler's, to Hitler's right. The rest of the garden looked like a field full of shell craters, but the spot where the bodies had been deposited was still level. Just as I was laying Eva down, Bormann stepped up to Hitler's

body and uncovered his face. While I was still bending over after putting Eva down, I got another glimpse of Hitler's head. The bloodstains from the temple had spread over his face. But the face itself was still clearly recognisable.[10]

Petrol was sprinkled over the corpses. Göbbels proffered a box of matches, but the bodies stubbornly refused to ignite. Günsche thought of throwing a stick grenade at them, but opted instead for a rag dipped in petrol. While he was getting it ready, he saw that Linge had produced one of the paper spills that he used for lighting the emergency butane lamps in the bunker. Bormann lit the spill and Linge threw it out into the open, hurriedly shutting the bunker door behind him as the bodies burst into a sheet of flame.

Opening the door again, they saw that Hitler and Eva were well and truly alight. Stepping sombrely forward, they snapped to attention and gave the Nazi salute, some from outside the bunker, others from just inside the doorway. The heat was so intense that Hitler's body was already beginning to shrivel as it burned, his arms and legs jerking like a marionette's as the flames took hold. Heinz Linge watched fascinated through a slit in the door: 'One thing that has stuck in my mind is that within a very short while one of Eva Hitler's knees was lifted up. One could see that the flesh of the knee was already being roasted.'[11]

Later, Eva Hitler sat up as well, according to some accounts, her body jack-knifing under *rigor mortis* into the classic equestrian position, arms outstretched as if she was holding a pair of reins. But Linge didn't stay to see that. He remained only a few minutes at the bunker entrance and then hurried back downstairs, unable to take any more.

—

While the bodies were being burned, Traudl Junge sat alone for a long time, trying to come to terms with her thoughts. Then, she plucked up the courage to go and see where her master had died:

The door to Hitler's room is still open at the end of the corridor. The men carrying the bodies had no hands free to close it. Eva's little revolver is lying on the table with a pink chiffon scarf beside it, and I see the brass case of the poison capsule glinting on the floor next to Frau Hitler's chair. It looks like an empty lipstick. There is blood on the blue and white upholstery of the bench where Hitler was sitting: Hitler's blood. I suddenly feel sick. The heavy smell of bitter almonds is nauseating. I instinctively reach for my own capsule. I'd like to throw it as far away as I can and leave this terrible bunker.[12]

Still desperate to be alone, Traudl ran away again. Hurrying along the corridor, she left the Führerbunker and went across to the New Chancellery. She found to her dismay that the Chancellery too was full of people, cheerful secretaries bravely carrying on with their work as if the Russians weren't just outside. They didn't know that Hitler was dead and Traudl certainly wasn't going to tell them.

Instead, burdened with her terrible secret, she made her way to the room that she shared with several others. Her suitcases were there, packed and ready to go. Traudl flung herself down on her camp bed, angry at Hitler for deserting them all, furious with him for killing himself and leaving everyone else behind. She lay on her bed wishing that she could feel the wind again and breathe some fresh air, hear the trees rustling in the breeze. Freedom, peace and calm were all she wanted, an end to all the strife and discord. But freedom, peace and calm were far out of reach as Traudl lay on her bed, tossing and turning distractedly. It was still only early evening as she fell into an exhausted sleep.

—

The bodies took until nightfall to burn. SS men emerged at intervals to keep the fire going. The doors to the garden had been locked to prevent anyone seeing, but various bunker guards spotted what was happening and watched discreetly as the men stoked the flames and poured on more petrol. They all had different memories when they recounted it later.

Harry Mengershausen claimed to have seen Hitler's feet burned off as far as the mid-calves, while the rest of him was still recognisable. Herman Karnau claimed to have witnessed the bodies at five pm:

I saw that both corpses had burned down to skeletons. There were no more flames to be seen, but there were still flakes of white ash blowing upwards. Intending to consign the remains to the earth in a crater a meter away and half a meter deep, I tried to shove them in with my foot. At the first touch both skeletons crumbled. I then had to abandon the attempt because very heavy artillery fire set in again.'[13]

Karnau changed his story later, saying he had seen no bones, only ash. But Erich Mansfeld, who joined him at six pm, remembered more than ash: 'We went to the site of the fire. There we saw two charred and shrunken corpses that were no longer identifiable.'[14]

The one thing they all agreed on was that Hitler had been reduced to a pile of ash by the end, leaving no identifiable remains that his enemies could disinter. Others suspected that enough of him had survived to be wrapped in a tarpaulin, or perhaps the blood-stained rug from the bunker, and buried in the garden after dark, by the light of burning buildings. There was talk of Hitler's skull surviving, or at least the bones of his jaw, identified later by their gold and porcelain bridges. Otto Günsche admitted that Hitler had not completely disappeared by nightfall, but was adamant that what little remained had been scattered across the garden and then dispersed by shellfire. The truth is that nobody really knew or cared any more. With Hitler gone and the Russians closing in, they were all far more concerned with their own futures, wondering how they were going to get safely out of the bunker and make their escape, now that they were free to leave at last.

A meeting was held to discuss it. Gathering in the conference room, Göbbels, Bormann and Generals Krebs, Mohnke and Burgdorf debated what to do now that Hitler was gone. They lit cigarettes as they did so. Hitler had always forbidden smoking in his presence, but the rule had been relaxed in the past few days and now it didn't apply at all. His henchmen were free at last to do as they pleased and address the situation as they thought fit, dealing with it calmly and rationally without any ranting from the Führer.

The first question was the succession. Dönitz was in command of the nation, now that Hitler was gone. But they didn't need reminding that the new Führer was in Plön, far removed from Berlin. There was no one to take the lead in the bunker as Hitler's followers, rudderless and distraught, dragged on their cigarettes and wondered where they went from here.

Bormann was for breaking out immediately, getting several hundred troops together and fighting through the Russian lines that night under cover of darkness. But the generals poured scorn on the idea, knowing it would never work. They understood all too well that they were trapped where they were, with no possibility of escape.

After a long discussion, they decided that their only hope of survival was to approach the Russians, who didn't know that Hitler was dead, and try to make a deal of some kind, one sovereign government talking to another.

Under the terms of Hitler's will, Göbbels and Bormann were still both members of the government. If they offered to surrender Germany to the Russians, perhaps the Russians would allow them safe conduct to Plön, to have the offer ratified by Dönitz.

It was a slim prospect, but it was all they had. After further discussion, it was decided that General Krebs would be the best person to make contact with the Russians. As a former military attaché in Moscow, Hans Krebs spoke the language and had once been publicly hugged by Stalin, an event recorded on newsreel for German viewers. The Soviet leader had told him that Germany and Russia should stand together and always be friends.

A call was put through to Colonel Refior at the Wehrmacht's Bendlerblock headquarters in the Tiergarten. He was ordered to send a radio message to Red Army command, asking if they would be prepared to receive a representative of the German government. The Russians took a while to respond, but proved agreeable. A messenger went through their lines to discuss the details, after which a temporary ceasefire was arranged in the sector south of the Chancellery, near what remained of the Anhalter station.

Krebs took an interpreter with him and a staff officer, Colonel von Dufving. Carrying a white flag, the three of them set off after midnight, walking cautiously forward until they came at about two am to the Excelsior Hotel, across the road from the station. Russian soldiers met them there and led them to the command post of the 102nd Guards Rifle Regiment. A few minutes later, after refusing to surrender their personal weapons, Krebs and his companions crossed the suspension bridge over the Landwehr canal and were taken in a jeep to meet General Chuikov at his forward headquarters near Templehof airport.

PART FOUR:
TUESDAY, 1 MAY

'It is announced from Führer Headquarters that our Führer Adolf Hitler fell for Germany at his command post at the Reichs Chancellery this afternoon while fighting against Bolshevism to his last breath...'
German proclamation

CHAPTER 16:
THE GERMANS
WANT TO TALK

Chuikov's command post was a five-storey apartment building off Belle Alliancestrasse, named for the Anglo-German victory over Napoleon at Waterloo. It was an ugly place with smashed windows and a cement eagle over the entrance, carrying a swastika in its claws. Chuikov's men had installed field telephones in one of the dining rooms and laid out a large map of Berlin on the table. The hall was adorned with a pair of large black pillars. It was here that Chuikov waited in the early hours of May Day for the German surrender party to arrive.

He was not alone as he paced the room. War correspondent Vsevolod Vishnevski had persuaded him that there ought to be some journalists present to record the scene. Vishnevski had joined him with Yevgeni Dolmatovski, a poet in civilian life, and Matvei Blanter, a composer who was in Berlin to write an anthem for the forthcoming victory.

Blanter wasn't in uniform, so he was told to hide in the cupboard when the Germans appeared. The other two correspondents stood with Chuikov's aide-de-camp and posed as a trio of important-looking staff officers advising their boss. It was thus that Krebs and his party found them when they arrived at ten minutes to four that morning, just as the sky was beginning to lighten in the east.

Chuikov was the hero of Stalingrad, the man who had masterminded the single biggest defeat in German history, but he did not introduce himself when Krebs was shown in. He had decided beforehand to play his cards very close to his chest, giving nothing away and showing no surprise at anything Krebs might say. The bemedalled German gave the Nazi salute with one hand and proffered his service book with the other, to show who he was. Chuikov said little in return, an anonymous Russian peasant keeping his own counsel and deliberately failing to respond in kind.

Krebs saw that he would have to make the running. He didn't mind, because he had a scoop that he knew would shake Chuikov out of his reticence. He delivered it with a flourish: 'I shall speak of exceptionally secret matters,' he announced grandly. 'You are the first foreigner to whom I give the information that on 30 April Hitler passed from us of his own free will, ending his life by suicide.'[1]

Krebs paused dramatically, expecting astonishment on all sides. But Chuikov wasn't impressed. 'We know this,' he lied.

Krebs was visibly taken aback. Chuikov let him stew for a bit before asking how it happened. Krebs told him and then produced Hitler's will and a letter from Göbbels requesting peace negotiations.

'Do these documents relate to Berlin or to the whole of Germany?' Chuikov demanded.

Krebs said he could only speak for the army. Dönitz was the new head of state, the man the Russians must deal with to end the war.

Chuikov decided to consult Marshal Zhukov. Going to another room, he rang his superior at Strausberg, just outside Berlin, and told him that Hitler was dead and the Germans wanted to parley. Telling Chuikov to remain on the line, Zhukov in turn got in touch with Moscow. It was beginning to get light in the Russian capital, but Stalin had only just gone to bed at his dacha at Kuntsevo, snatching a few hours' sleep before the May Day parade. Zhukov told the duty officer to get him up again.

Coming to the phone, Stalin was happy to hear of Hitler's death.

'So that's the end of the bastard. Pity he couldn't be taken alive. Where's his body?'

'Krebs says it was burned.'[2]

Stalin wanted to know when Hitler had died. Zhukov put the question to Chuikov, who put it to Krebs. Krebs said half past three on the afternoon of 30 April. The information was relayed back to Stalin. Then came another question.

'Ask Krebs whether they want to lay down their arms and surrender, or just want to start talking.'

After much obfuscation, Krebs decided that the Germans were seeking a temporary ceasefire in order to conduct peace talks. But that wasn't good enough for Stalin.

'There can be no negotiations,' he told Zhukov. 'Only unconditional surrender. No talks either with Krebs or any other Hitler types. Unless anything else happens, don't call me again until morning. I need to get some sleep before the parade.'

Stalin went back to bed while the discussions continued. To concentrate the Germans' minds, Zhukov announced that he would unleash all the firepower at his disposal if they hadn't agreed to unconditional surrender by ten am. But Krebs was adamant that he had no power to surrender. Instead, he urged the Russians to recognise the new German government and then negotiate a peace agreement, perhaps excluding the British and Americans. Chuikov replied that there would be no negotiations and no separate peace. Unconditional surrender was Germany's only option.

The talking continued well into the morning, while Vishnevsky scribbled in his notebook. A breakfast of tea and sandwiches was served, with a glass of cognac for Krebs which he drank with shaking hands. He had learned by now that his host was Chuikov, the victor of Stalingrad. Towards the end of the meeting, the composer Blanter collapsed and fell out of the cupboard, having apparently fainted from lack of air. What Krebs made of an unknown civilian being carried out of the room in the middle of the discussion is a secret that died with him.

Chuikov was relaying every word back to Moscow, where the final decisions would be taken. But there was unlikely to be a swift response, with Stalin asleep and the May Day parade occupying everyone's thoughts. Chuikov decided to take advantage of the lull by setting up a telephone line between his headquarters and the Chancellery, so that he would be able to speak directly to Göbbels and Bormann when the time came. It was arranged that Dufving and Lieutenant Neilandis, the two officers who had accompanied Krebs, should return to the German side of the line with two Russian signallers and a length of telephone cable to make the connection. They set off soon after first light with a white flag, leaving Chuikov and Krebs to continue talking at Chuikov's headquarters. Neither man was prepared to give an inch as Krebs kept refusing to surrender and Chuikov waited for confirmation from Moscow that Krebs's stance was unacceptable and only unconditional surrender would do.

———

While Krebs talked to Chuikov, other Germans were also seeking peace, quite independently of anything going on at the bunker. At half past four that morning, a German radio station calling itself the headquarters for the defence of Berlin sent a message to the Russians asking for a Soviet officer to come to the north east corner of the Zoological Gardens.

Representatives of the Wehrmacht would meet him there to discuss the terms for a ceasefire.

Major Bersenev duly presented himself. Carrying a flag of truce and a demand for unconditional surrender, he reached the Zoo at five am and stood waiting for twenty minutes, uncomfortably aware that the Germans had him in their sights but had promised not to shoot. Bersenev was bitter about what happened next:

> At last I saw two Germans with a white flag come round the corner of the street about two hundred metres away, and walk towards me.
>
> I took a few steps forward, towards them. Suddenly one of them dropped, and straight away I heard shots, bullets were whistling round me. The firing was coming from the Germans' direction. I felt a blow in my left hip and in my knee, and I fell. As I fell I hit my head hard against the pavement, and lost consciousness.
>
> I came to near my car. My orderly had risked his life to drag me out of range, and then he and my driver lifted me into the car. My leg was hanging limp and my head was ringing. I just said 'Take me to the Divisional Commander', and then lost consciousness again.[3]

It was a familiar story. Some Germans wanted to surrender, but others wouldn't let them. Much the same happened to Neilandis and Dufving as they tried to run their cable to the Chancellery. They had reached Prinz Albrechtstrasse, waving a white flag and yelling at their own people not to fire, when the Russian officer unrolling the telephone line was shot in the head. Neilandis picked up the extension reel and carried on, while Dufving went ahead with the flag. But the firing continued from the German side, making it impossible for them to cross. Dufving therefore remained with the Russians at the front while Neilandis hurried back to Chuikov's headquarters to complain. They got across eventually, but it was lunchtime before they managed to establish a telephone link with the Chancellery.

———

Just up the road, the fight was still going on at the Reichstag, even though the Red flag now flew from the roof. Choked with dust and smoke, desperate for water, the German defenders were doggedly refusing to give in. The upper storeys of the building had been cleared, but the cellars and the dressing station in the basement remained in their hands. It wasn't until late afternoon that they decided they had had enough and called for a senior Russian officer to come and negotiate. With a coat covering his badges of rank, Lieutenant Berest went forward and introduced himself as a colonel. The Germans laid down their arms soon afterwards, emerging nervously from the basement with their hands in the air as they stepped uncertainly into the daylight.

Almost 300 came out, 'smiling like obedient dogs' as they wondered if they were going to be shot. A total of 200 had been killed in the fighting and another 500 lay wounded in the basement. The German defence of the Reichstag had been stubborn and fanatical, according to the Russians, but a German survivor later claimed that they had greatly exaggerated the fighting for propaganda purposes and he himself had seen very little. Yet some Germans had certainly fought stubbornly, because a handful still refused to surrender and were not finally persuaded to lay down their arms until their own side ordered them to the following day.

But the Reichstag had fallen, to all intents and purposes. So had the Spandau Citadel, a 17th-century fortress at the junction of the Havel and Spree rivers. The flak tower in the Zoological Gardens was in the process of surrendering. The only significant building that remained in German hands on the afternoon of 1 May was the Reichs Chancellery. It was an object of even greater interest to the Russians now that they had learned from Krebs that there was an underground bunker in the garden, where Adolf Hitler had spent his last days. All eyes were turned in that direction and all guns were trained on the target as Zhukov's deadline for a surrender passed and the Russians opened up on the Chancellery with every weapon they had.

———

At Ruhleben, there was very little fighting that day as the Russians bypassed the area around the Reichssportfeld and concentrated their fire on the Chancellery. With life hanging by a thread and a gaggle of SS girls in their midst, the men in Helmut Altner's unit had followed the Chancellery's lead as they waited for the next attack. Sent to wake up a man for sentry duty, Altner found him under a blanket with a naked girl. Her firm breasts hit Altner full in the eyes as the man got up and the blanket slipped from her shoulders.

Later, if Altner's memory was correct, his friend Windhorst showed him a proclamation for the armed forces that had been printed during the night. Due to be broadcast on the radio next morning, it was still supposed to be secret and should never have fallen into Windhorst's hands:

> It is announced from Führer Headquarters that our Führer Adolf Hitler fell for Germany at his command post at the Reichs Chancellery this afternoon while fighting against Bolshevism to his last breath. On 30 April the Führer appointed Grand Admiral Dönitz as his successor.[4]

Altner was shocked, but only for a moment:

> I feel as if I had been hit on the head. But then it is all the same to me, it hardly bothers me, for the time is over when I once thought that the heavens would collapse if that man no longer lived. Then we discuss it, and the news that is so meaningful begins to pale. Only the thought that I must really be free now, as the man to whom I swore an oath is no longer alive, makes me happy. But Windhorst says that Hitler has declared that the oath applies to his successor.

Other soldiers took the news harder than Altner. A heated discussion broke out in the cellar as Sergeant Major Kaiser spread the word that Hitler was dead. It was followed by a gasp and then a sudden silence when Kaiser suggested that, far from fighting Bolshevism to his last breath, Hitler might have taken poison to avoid being beaten to death by the troops. Kaiser's words would have been treasonable once, grounds for immediate execution. But not any more.

Everyone wondered if Hitler's death meant the end of the war. Not for the moment, certainly, because it was still going on outside. Some new SS girls arrived after lunch, unfamiliar faces flirting with the soldiers around the table in the knowledge that they would probably all be dead by tomorrow. Altner was surprised that the company commander was tolerating the situation, until he saw that the company commander had a girl too. He told himself that if they all carried on like that, the girls who had arrived yesterday would be disappointed that night. They would have to hang back and wait their turn until the new ones had been 'tried out'.

Hildegard Knef was in a deep sleep. After a dreadful night dodging the enemy, she and Ewald von Demandowsky had reached the Kurfürstendamm at dawn. It had been Berlin's most fashionable street once, but it was a war zone now as the Russians approached. They had found shelter with a friend of Demandowsky's mother, an old lady of 82. While a tank trundled past with a dead man dangling from the turret, the old lady had taken them to her apartment and given them water, smiling cheerfully and chatting as she made them a cup of coffee. The old lady was so serene and unruffled that Hildegard wondered if she had any idea of what was happening in the street outside.

The house was rolling like a trawler in the barrage. Looking in the mirror, Hildegard failed to recognise the blood-stained, sweaty figure, with a dirty face and torn hands, that she saw in the glass. Certain that she was about to die, she had tried to write a last letter to her mother, telling her that it was all over and there was no way out, thanking her for a nice life. But the words hadn't come and her tears had stained the page. Hildegard had torn the letter up and fallen asleep instead.

Now she was being woken again, sitting bolt upright as the old lady told her that the Russians had arrived and were in the cellar next door. They had to leave at once. The Russians would destroy the house if they found any soldiers there.

'I'm terribly sorry,' the old lady apologised. 'You'll have to leave. The other tenants insist on it.'[5]

She thrust some cigarettes into Demandowsky's hands as compensation. He and Hildegard stood on the doorstep with no idea of where to go. The other tenants swore at them through the cellar grating, telling them to disappear before the Russians spotted them. They ran off up the road, past a blue-faced boy with a swollen tongue, hanging from a tree. 'I am a coward,' said the placard on his chest. 'I was too afraid to fight for my fatherland.'

They hadn't got much further when they ran into an officer with clusters on his collar.

'Where have you come from?' he demanded.

'Schmargendorf. We lost the others.'

'When?'

'Yesterday, yesterday morning.'

The officer was sceptical. Hildegard and Demandowsky looked like deserters to him. 'Follow me,' he said.[6]

They were taken to a command post on Albrecht Achillesstrasse. Another officer ordered them to stand in line and await sentence. They had deserted their company in the face of the enemy. They didn't need to be told that the sentence for that was summary execution.

—

Back in the bunker, Colonel von Dufving had managed to get through with the telephone line. He had been arrested by the SS as a traitor when he returned to his own lines, but had talked his way out of it. The telephone cable had proved to be too short, so an extension had been added, only to be cut in half by shellfire. But Dufving had persevered and now there was a line connecting the Chancellery with Chuikov's headquarters near the airport.

Krebs was on the phone at once, asking to speak to Göbbels. Göbbels told him to come back to the Chancellery, bringing the Russians' demands with him, so that they could discuss it in person. To prevent any misunderstandings, Krebs repeated the list of demands to Chuikov before he left:

1. Surrender of Berlin
2. All those surrendering to give up their arms
3. The lives of all ranks to be spared
4. Help for the wounded
5. Talks with the Allies by radio

Chuikov nodded his agreement. It was eight minutes past one, by his watch, when Krebs set out. He appeared very reluctant to go, searching for his gloves and then a non-existent haversack, looking for any excuse not to leave the safety of Russian headquarters. It seemed to Chuikov that Krebs was longing to be taken prisoner, preferring to take his chances with the Russians rather than go back to the madhouse and die like a rat in a trap with the rest of them. But Chuikov wasn't going to help him out. Krebs was more use to him in the bunker.

Göbbels wasn't pleased to see him when he got back. Krebs was supposed to be returning with a guarantee of safe conduct for them all, a ticket out of there for anyone of any importance in the bunker. Instead, all he had come back with was an invitation to surrender. 'Surrender?' Göbbels barked. 'I'm not going to use the few hours I have left as Chancellor to sign an instrument of surrender.'[7]

The others agreed. There was nothing for them in surrender. What they wanted was safe passage out of there, not surrender.

They decided to reject the Russians' terms and fight on. It would be dark in another few hours. They could escape then, leaving their dimmer retainers to hold the Russians off while they slipped down the U-Bahn line and disappeared into the network of tunnels. It wasn't much of a prospect, but it was better than putting up their hands and waiting to be hanged by the Allies.

Watching Göbbels and the others as they decided against surrender, news reader Hans Fritsche saw that they were all mad, completely cut off from reality. Fritsche was a popular broadcaster and a senior official in the Propaganda Ministry, but he retained a sense of proportion. He knew that surrender was the only sensible option left for Berlin. With the rest still refusing to countenance it, he decided to take matters into his own hands. Heading back to the ruins of his office on Wilhelmplatz, he sat down to compose a surrender offer of his own to Marshal Zhukov.

He hadn't got very far when General Burgdorf burst in, drunk and trembling with rage. 'Is it true that you're going to hand the city over to the Russians?' Burgdorf demanded.

Fritsche nodded, whereupon Burgdorf announced that he would have to shoot him, because Hitler's order forbidding surrender was still in force. He produced a pistol, only to have it knocked out of his hand by the radio technician who had shown him to Fritsche's room. Burgdorf was overpowered and escorted back to the Chancellery, leaving Fritsche free to continue with his approach to the Russians.

While he went ahead, the people in the bunker prepared to make their escape. The vast majority had chosen to join the breakout, but one or two preferred to remain behind and take their chances where they stood. The plan was for the escapees to slip away in groups of twenty or more, crawling out of the cellar window underneath Hitler's reviewing balcony at the Chancellery, then sprinting across Wilhelmplatz into the Kaiserhof U-Bahn station. From there, it was a matter of fanning out along the railway tunnels, putting a safe distance between themselves and the bunker before daybreak and hoping that they didn't bump into any Russians coming the other way.

Traudl Junge was one of those who had elected to go. Konstanze Manziarly, Hitler's personal chef, was another. She had had to make Hitler's supper the previous night, trying hard not to cry as she ostentatiously cooked fried eggs and creamed potatoes for him so that no one would know he was dead. The two women were issued with a pistol each and boots, trousers, steel helmets, everything they needed for a breakout. The bunker's storerooms were opened and supplies freely distributed: canned food, wine, champagne, chocolate, all sorts of luxury items that hadn't been seen for ages. At any other time, the women might have gorged themselves silly, but luxury items were no use to them now, in the middle of an inferno. They were far better off with ration packs and a water bottle.

A few people had decided to stay behind in the bunker. General Burgdorf was too drunk to go anywhere and General Krebs too exhausted after his trip to Chuikov's headquarters. Göbbels too had chosen to remain. With a club foot and six small children, he knew he had no chance of slipping through the Russian lines. He and his wife had elected to commit suicide instead, killing their children before the Russians came and then themselves. Several people had offered to take the children out with them, keeping their identity secret from the Russians, but the Göbbels had refused. 'I would rather have my children die than live in disgrace,' Magda Göbbels had told Traudl Junge. 'Our children have no place in Germany as it will be after the war.'[8] The Göbbels family had lived together as a single unit and they were going to die together as well.

But it wasn't time for that yet. Göbbels still had his diary to complete. He had kept a diary for many years, a daily account of his life at the heart of the Third Reich. Shutting himself in his room while his wife sat with the children and the rest of the bunker waited for dusk, Göbbels took pen and paper and settled down to make the final entry in the story of his life. It was a seven-page summary for posterity of everything that he and Hitler had been trying to achieve when they embarked on the course that had now ended so disastrously for both of them.

CHAPTER 17:
THE NAZIS REGROUP

Far away in Plön, Admiral Dönitz was still bug-eyed from lack of sleep after talking to Himmler through the night. But there was no time to rest. He was hard at work with his staff when he received another signal from Martin Bormann in the bunker. Despatched at twenty minutes to seven that morning, it reached Dönitz just before eleven: 'Will now in force. Coming to you soonest. Until then, in my opinion, withhold publication.'

Dönitz was stunned. *Will now in force.* That could mean only one thing. Hitler was dead. Something had happened to him in Berlin and now Dönitz was the new Führer.

Reaching for the phone, he rang Albert Speer at his trailer near Lake Eutin. One of Speer's secretaries answered, to be told curtly that the Führer was dead. A few minutes later, Speer set out to join Dönitz at Plön. He was with him later when a follow-up cable arrived from the Chancellery:

Grand Admiral Dönitz (personal and secret). Officer's eyes only.

Führer died yesterday, 1530 hours. Testament of 29 April appoints you as President of the Reich, Göbbels as Reich Chancellor, Bormann as Party Minister, Seyss-Inquart as Foreign Minister. By order of the Führer, the will is being sent from Berlin to you and Field Marshal Schörner for safe custody. Bormann will try to reach you today to explain the situation. Form and timing of the announcement to the public and the armed forces is left to your discretion. Acknowledge. Göbbels, Bormann.

So there it was. Hitler was dead: presumably by suicide, since the signal said he had died rather than fallen in battle. Now it was up to Dönitz to hold the German people together and bring the war to an end. Not only that, he would have to do it with Göbbels and Bormann, if the terms of Hitler's will were to be honoured. But Göbbels and Bormann were the last people he wanted around him as he grappled with Germany's collapse and struggled to secure an acceptable peace. With them around, he would be dead in the water before he had even begun.

Watching him, Speer sensed the admiral's irritation at being saddled with Göbbels as Germany's Chancellor and Bormann as Nazi Party Minister at a time like this:

> 'This is utterly impossible!' Dönitz exclaimed, for it made a farce of the powers of his office. 'Has anyone else seen the radio message yet?'
>
> Except for the radio man and the admiral's adjutant, Lüdde-Neurath, who had taken the message directly to his chief, no one had. Dönitz then ordered that the radio man be sworn to silence and the message locked up and kept confidential. 'What will we do if Bormann and Göbbels actually arrive here?' Dönitz asked. Then he continued resolutely: 'I absolutely will not cooperate with them in any case.'[1]

Thinking it over, he decided that Bormann and Göbbels would have to be arrested if they showed their faces in Plön. But they would have to get to Plön first. More immediately, Dönitz decided to keep Hitler's death secret for the next few hours, until he had had time to adjust to the situation. He had already summoned General Jodl and Field-Marshal Keitel to Plön to give him an assessment of the military situation. Now, as the new Führer, he summoned other generals and various Nazi officials as well. While Albert Speer drafted an announcement for Dönitz to broadcast to the nation that night, Dönitz spent the rest of the day consulting as many senior people as possible before going public with the news and revealing the death of Germany's Führer to the world.

—

Field-Marshal Keitel was already well on his way to Plön. He had been on the road since four that morning, moving his headquarters again to keep one step ahead of the Russians. Driving first to Wismar, on the Baltic coast, he had twice had to abandon his car and run for his life as the RAF strafed the long columns of retreating Wehrmacht. Keitel had been shocked to see RAF fighters wheeling freely overhead. It meant that the British were coming too, closing in on the Germans from one side while the Russians closed in from the other.

Keitel was not a front line soldier. He was Hitler's creature, a staff officer held in deep contempt by real soldiers. He had been promoted far above his natural ceiling, a dim-witted man who should never have risen above colonel. But field-marshals held a special position in German society and Hitler needed to keep his generals close. He had promoted Keitel because he could always be trusted to say 'Ja, mein Führer' and do exactly what he was told, instead of seeking to query his orders, as more independent officers sometimes did.

But Hitler was trapped in Berlin, so far as Keitel knew, and Dönitz was the man of the moment. When he got to Wismar, Keitel conferred with General Jodl and General Kurt Student about the need to keep the Baltic ports open for the shiploads of troops and refugees pouring in from East Prussia. Then Keitel and Jodl drove separately to the naval barracks at Neustadt, north of Lübeck, where they expected to find Dönitz. Learning that he was at Plön, Keitel continued there that afternoon to find the admiral already in conference with another officer about the coastal defences along the North Sea.

Hannah Reitsch was there too, Hitler's favourite pilot. After escaping from Berlin with Greim, she had flown the new head of the Luftwaffe to Plön for a meeting with Dönitz. Talking to her as he waited his turn to see the admiral, Keitel was shocked to hear of Fegelein's death at the bunker, shot on Hitler's orders without even the pretence of a trial. The situation had obviously reached crisis point if officers that close to Hitler were being taken outside and executed on a whim.

Keitel was shown in to Dönitz. The admiral was polite enough, but he wasn't particularly pleased to see the field-marshal. He shared the Wehrmacht's view of him as a 'golden pheasant', one of those useless officers in glittering uniforms who strutted about behind the lines while the real men got on with the war. He had given orders for Keitel to be replaced as Chief of Staff by Field-Marshal von Manstein. But Manstein couldn't be found for the moment, so Dönitz was stuck with Keitel until he could be relieved. He would have preferred an officer with a better grasp of the conditions at the front.

They had a long discussion, mostly about the hopelessness of the situation. Without revealing its significance, Dönitz showed Keitel the first signal from Bormann and told him that Hitler's last will and testament was apparently on its way to Plön as they spoke. It was obvious to both of them that Berlin couldn't hold out much longer. Dönitz wanted the German Army in Czechoslovakia to begin an immediate withdrawal towards the West, so that it could surrender to the Americans in due course. Keitel disagreed, arguing that any withdrawal would rapidly turn into a rout as the Germans fled and the Russians chased after them. Against his better judgment, Dönitz agreed to postpone the decision until he had discussed it with Field-Marshal Schörner, commanding the troops in Czechoslovakia.

Keitel drove back to Neustadt after the meeting. He was delayed again by the RAF, attacking the villages around the naval headquarters just before dark. He called for General Jodl when he got back and compared notes over their meetings with Dönitz. Jodl shared his view that Germany should keep fighting until everyone had been evacuated from the Russian front and could safely surrender to the Allies in the West. It seemed to Jodl that the British and Americans were bound to fall out with the Russians in due course. If the Germans could hold on for another few days, they just might be able to force the issue and drive a wedge between the democratic countries and the Bolsheviks. It could only be to Germany's advantage if they succeeded, because the Western Allies would surely want the Germans in their camp, if it ever came to a stand-off between them and the Russians.

At his new headquarters near Travemünde, Heinrich Himmler was in despair as he sat down to breakfast after returning from his midnight meeting with Dönitz. He had been bitterly disappointed to learn not only that he was not to be the new Führer, but that there was to be no place at all for him in the new government. He had been suicidal when he reached his headquarters and was little better after a few hours' sleep. Joining him after a brief trip to Copenhagen, Walter Schellenberg found Himmler very nervous and distracted as they discussed the situation in Scandinavia and Count Bernadotte's proposals for a peaceful German withdrawal from Norway and Denmark.

Himmler decided to visit Dönitz again after breakfast. He had been so long at the centre of the Nazi web that he didn't know what else to do, now that he no longer had a job. He had convinced himself that he would still be needed in some capacity or other, if only because the Allies would depend on the SS to keep order after the war. Eisenhower and Montgomery would surely need police chief Himmler's services as 'an indispensable factor for law and order' as they grappled with the chaos of post-war Germany. In his wilder moments, he even saw himself as the Minister of the Interior in a post-war world, not just of Germany, but of the whole of Europe.

Taking Schellenberg with him, Himmler set off at eleven. They travelled via Lübeck, but the roads were so congested that even with an SS escort clearing the way they didn't reach Plön until two. Unexpected and uninvited, Himmler had no appointment with Dönitz. With so many other people waiting to see the admiral, he was forced to cool his heels while he waited his turn, wandering disconsolately around the headquarters with nothing to do. Keitel saw him and wondered what his game was. 'I have no idea what his real intentions were, but it seemed to me that he wanted to put himself at our disposal for further duties and keep himself briefed on the situation.'[2] Others saw him too and wondered if the radio reports were true, that Himmler had been negotiating with the Allies behind their backs.

Dönitz had little to say to Himmler when at last he found time to see him. He disliked the man and feared him, because Himmler still had the SS at his disposal, but he repeated, beyond any shadow of doubt, that there was no room for him in the new administration. Himmler still didn't believe it. Convinced that he would be needed sooner or later, he decided to stick close to Dönitz's headquarters for the next few days, so that he could be there at a moment's notice, if necessary. Hans Prützmann was his liaison officer at Dönitz's headquarters. Leaving strict instructions for Prützmann to keep him posted, Himmler returned to his motorcade at the end of a most unsatisfactory day and set off back to his own headquarters to bide his time and await developments.

—

Ribbentrop was in Plön too. After several days on the road, he had finally arrived from Berlin and established a headquarters of his own just outside the town. In common with Himmler, he was convinced that Dönitz would need a man of his experience in the new administration. He had sat by the telephone ever since his arrival, waiting for the call that was certain to come. He was sure the admiral would want to give him an important job, in all probability the same job of Foreign Minister that he had held under Hitler.

The telephone did ring, in due course, but not with the offer that Ribbentrop wanted. Dönitz had decided to reappoint Ribbentrop's predecessor, Konstantin von Neurath, as both Foreign and Prime Minister in his new government. But Neurath couldn't be found, so Dönitz's aide rang Ribbentrop to ask if he knew where he was.

Ribbentrop didn't. Furthermore, he was outraged to hear that Neurath was going to be offered his job. He went round to see Dönitz at once, probably on the evening of 1 May, arguing that he was still legally Foreign Minister and should be allowed to remain in the position, particularly as he had been ordered by Hitler to make an approach to the British. He pointed out that he had been the Ambassador in London before the war and knew the British well. They liked and respected him. He was the right man for the task, if there were to be negotiations with the British in the days and weeks ahead.

But Dönitz shared London's assessment of Ribbentrop as a posturing ninny. He wasn't about to give the job of Foreign Minister to the man who had assured Hitler that the British would never fight. He brought the interview to a close by pretending to seek Ribbentrop's help in choosing a new Foreign Minister. If Neurath couldn't be found, someone else would have to take his place. Dönitz was thinking of Count Schwerin von Krosigk, a former Rhodes scholar at Oxford, but he was open to other suggestions. He asked Ribbentrop to go away and think of some other candidates overnight. Ribbentrop did so, promising to report back with a list of names the following day.

———

At Mauterndorf, the SS detachment guarding Hermann Göring in his castle had just received orders to kill him. The orders had come from Martin Bormann in the bunker. After sending a signal to Dönitz to say that Hitler's will was in force, he had sent another to Mauterndorf, couched in equally cryptic language: 'The situation in Berlin is increasingly tense. If we should fall in Berlin, the traitors of 23 April must be exterminated. Men, do your duty! Your life and honour depend on it!'

That was clear enough. Without actually saying so in print, Bormann was telling them to shoot Göring for his telegram of 23 April, asking if he was supposed to take over as Führer. Bormann had always hated Göring. Now was his chance to eliminate his rival once and for all.

But the SS weren't so sure. For one thing, they heartily despised Bormann. For another, they wanted to be on the winning side when the dust settled. Shooting Göring might not be a good idea if they were called to account for it later. They decided to cover their backs instead.

A copy of the telegram was delivered to Berchtesgaden and shown to General Karl Koller, the Luftwaffe's chief of staff. He had just sent a Luftwaffe signal unit to Mauterndorf to establish a force loyal to Göring in the town. The unit was small, but its numbers had been greatly exaggerated to the SS, making it clear to them that they would not escape unscathed if they tried to murder the Luftwaffe's former chief.

Koller's first thought on seeing the telegram was that perhaps he was one of the traitors to be exterminated, since he had helped draft Göring's signal of 23 April. He was relieved to learn from the SS officer who brought it that they had no intention of carrying out their orders. They weren't in a position to let Göring go, but they weren't prepared to kill him either.

Later, another SS officer arrived from Mauterndorf. Standartenführer Krause shared the general reluctance to kill Göring, but wouldn't set him free without proper authority. He wanted the Luftwaffe to take the decision out of his hands.

'Why don't you liberate Göring by force?' he asked Koller. 'You have more troops than I have.'

'I don't want to risk liberating a corpse.'[3]

Krause conceded the point. It couldn't be denied that some of the SS under his command might prefer to shoot Göring rather than let him go. 'I can't guarantee every one of my men, if we're attacked,' he admitted, after some thought. 'But if you decide not to act, Herr General, I promise that nothing will happen to Göring. But please make sure that his arrest is lifted soon.'

—

Back at Plön, Albert Speer had decided to stay the night at Dönitz's headquarters, rather than return to his trailer at Lake Eutin. With a bag packed by his secretary, he had been given a small room to himself in the naval barracks. He was mentally and physically exhausted as he went to bed after a day of drafting signals for Dönitz and bottling his emotions about the death of Hitler. Closing the door of his room after one of the worst days of his life, Speer was glad to be on his own at last.

> When I unpacked my overnight bag, I saw that Annemarie Kempf had put in the red leather case with Hitler's portrait, which he had signed for me on my fortieth birthday six weeks before. I was quite all right until – I don't know why – I opened the case and stood the photograph up on the night table next to the bed. And then suddenly, standing there, I began to cry. I couldn't stop. It just went on and on until I fell asleep, still fully dressed, on the bed.[4]

CHAPTER 18: MAY DAY IN RUSSIA

There were no tears for Hitler in Moscow. It was May Day, the greatest day of the year in the Soviet calendar. Stalin was up again, after a few hours' sleep, and everyone was gathering in Red Square for the parade. Troops of the Moscow garrison were taking their places, smart in their best uniforms as they formed up in front of Lenin's mausoleum. Diplomats and other invited guests were finding their seats on the stand beneath the Kremlin walls. Ordinary people were not allowed into the square without a pass, but they were thronging the surrounding streets in hundreds of thousands, waiting to cheer on the troops as they passed. Wartime regulations had been relaxed for the day to allow people from outside Moscow to come in and enjoy the fun. They had responded willingly, lining the streets in happy, excited crowds as they came to celebrate not only May Day but also the imminent end of the Great Patriotic War.

Stalin took the salute after the speeches. From the balcony of Lenin's mausoleum, he presented a benign figure as he beamed down on the troops, bayonets flashing as they goosestepped past. The troops were followed by jeeps and trucks, speeding tanks and heavy artillery, all the military might of a country at war. Fighter aircraft roared overhead. Stalin watched happily, knowing that the forces were his to command, knowing that the enemy was beaten and that a truly terrible conflict had been won against what had once seemed impossible odds. He said as much in his order of the day to the Russian armed forces:

> Comrades. This year, the peoples of our Motherland are celebrating May Day at the same time as the victorious termination of the Great Patriotic War.

The Red Army has captured East Prussia, home of German imperialism, Pomerania, the greater part of Brandenburg and the main districts of Germany's capital Berlin, having hoisted the banner of victory over Berlin…

The world war unleashed by the German imperialists is drawing to a close. The collapse of Hitlerite Germany is imminent. The Hitlerite ringleaders, who imagined themselves rulers of the world, have found themselves ruined. The mortally wounded Fascist beast is breathing its last. One thing still remains – to deal the death blow to the Fascist beast.

Fighting men of the Red Army and Navy! The last storming of the Hitlerite lair is on. Set new examples of military skill and gallantry in the concluding battles. Smite the enemy harder, skilfully break up his defence, pursue and surround the German invaders, give them no respite until they cease resistance![1]

There could have been more. Stalin could have had it announced over the loudspeakers that Hitler was dead and the Germans were suing for peace. Moscow would have erupted if he had. But Stalin held his tongue. He still didn't know for sure that Hitler was dead. All he had for certain was the unsubstantiated word of a German general, claiming that Hitler had been cremated and no corpse was available for inspection. Hitler could be on his way to South America for all Stalin knew. Much as he would have loved to announce it, he had decided to wait on events before going public with the news that all of Russia was longing to hear.

———

As part of the celebrations, Stalin had decreed that a gun salute was to be fired in all the important cities across the Soviet Union: Moscow, Leningrad, Stalingrad, Minsk, the capitals of the satellite republics and many others. The guns in Moscow duly sounded, twenty artillery salvoes reverberating around the city with a resonant boom. The noise penetrated everywhere, even as far as the walls of the Lubianka prison, where Aleksandr Solzhenitsyn, himself an artillery captain until his arrest, was being held in a cell with five others as he awaited sentencing for anti-Soviet activities.

In contrast to the rest of Moscow, it was a very quiet day at the Lubianka. The prison was normally very busy, full of noise and activity as prisoners were summoned from their cells and led away for interrogation. Sometimes they were beaten senseless, sometimes merely sent to the punishment block on reduced rations for being found asleep outside the permitted hours or some other trivial offence. But the prison was unnaturally silent that day. One prisoner was beaten up by warders, but nobody was summoned for interrogation, presumably because the interrogators had taken time off and gone to join the May Day celebrations. The Lubianka remained like the grave all day, so quiet by nightfall that the prisoners wondered at the silence and found it more than a little unnerving.

The blackout shade had just been removed from the window in Solzhenitsyn's cell. It was still impossible to see out, because the bulk of the window was permanently blocked from the outside by a sheet of metal known as a muzzle, but at least there was some daylight now that the blackout had gone. And maybe the war was over too, or soon would be, if the prison was no longer being kept in darkness.

Solzhenitsyn was in Cell No. 53. Among his cellmates were an engineer, a stool pigeon who relayed everything he heard to the interrogators, and a mentally ill mechanic who had once been chauffeur to Nikita Khrushchev, the rising star of the Communist Party. None of them was a boon companion, but it was a privilege for Solzhenitsyn to share a cell with other people, after so long in solitary confinement. He much preferred it to being on his own, cooped up in one of the punishment boxes with only himself for company.

Solzhenitsyn had been arrested early in February for criticising Stalin's conduct of the war. He had been in East Prussia, serving as a battery commander, when letters to a school friend had been found in which he had been less than respectful about 'the whiskered one's' military strategy. Solzhenitsyn had been careful not to mention Stalin by name and had been no more critical of the leadership than thousands of German and Allied officers in similar complaints to their friends. But the letters had been enough to see him relieved of his command and placed under arrest before being taken to the Lubianka.

Unfortunately, it was not only the letters. Solzhenitsyn's sergeant had gone through his possessions when he was arrested, hurriedly removing a looted German book containing a picture of Hitler before the investigators could find it. But they had found other pictures in his map case: stamp-sized portraits of German and Russian leaders taken from a book about World War One. The portraits had included Tsar Nicholas II and Leon Trotsky, clear evidence of subversive tendencies in Solzhenitsyn. There had been diaries too, four small notebooks containing the material for a novel about the war. Solzhenitsyn had noted down everything he had seen for himself in the war or heard from other soldiers, whether it was about the fighting at the front or the misery and famine that the Soviet collectivisation of the 1930s had visited on ordinary people. He had kept a note of the soldiers' names and the dates on which he had spoken to them. The material might not be enough to condemn him, particularly as his interrogators had not got around to reading it yet, but it was more than enough to prevent Solzhenitsyn from pleading his innocence. Bowing to the inevitable, he had decided to acknowledge his guilt in due course and accept his punishment, whatever it might be.

Solzhenitsyn had a good idea of what the punishment would be. A conviction under Article 58 of the Soviet criminal code meant penal servitude, many years of forced labour in a gulag somewhere, hard physical graft for the crime of saying what he thought in a letter to a friend. After serving his sentence he would not be allowed home. He would be sent into internal exile instead, banished thousands of miles away to spend the rest of his life in some godforsaken spot far from everything he held dear. It was how political prisoners had been treated in the bad old days under the Tsar. In his cell at the Lubianka, Aleksandr Solzhenitsyn was slowly beginning to realise that it was how they were treated under Communism too.

—

The guns boomed across Moscow. They boomed also in Kiev, capital of the Ukraine, where Lieutenant-General Nikita Khrushchev was Commissar. Twenty salvoes were fired, in accordance with Stalin's decree. The sound echoed noisily across the river Dnieper while Communist officials and local military commanders took the salute at the traditional May Day parade.

Khrushchev had had a good war. As a political officer at Stalingrad, he had been a pivotal link between Stalin and the front line generals in the increasingly bitter struggle to defend the city. He had led from the front, spending most of his time with the troops fighting the Germans rather than safely back at headquarters. He had taken a keen interest in their welfare, seeing to it that the fighting men's interests were paramount and they received all the food, weapons and training they needed. He had been promoted to his present rank as a result and had never looked back.

Stalingrad had taught Khrushchev two invaluable lessons for the future: that war was to be avoided at all costs and that Stalin himself was not infallible. Like Solzhenitsyn, Khrushchev had formed a poor opinion of Stalin's military capabilities as the war progressed. He also understood the shortcomings of collectivised farming, particularly amid the cornfields of the Ukraine. Unlike Solzhenitsyn though, Khrushchev had always been careful to keep his opinions to himself. As a career politician, he knew better than to say what he thought in a letter to a friend.

And now the war was all but over. With his services no longer needed at the front, Khrushchev had returned to Kiev earlier in the year to begin rebuilding the Ukraine while the rest of the army pushed on into Germany. He still kept in touch with the troops, particularly Marshal Zhukov. They had known each other before the war and continued to speak regularly on the phone. Zhukov had rung only the other day, full of enthusiasm now that his men were approaching Berlin. 'That bugger Hitler,' he had told Khrushchev. 'I'm going to put him in a cage soon and bring him to you. When I deliver him to Moscow, I'm going to come through Kiev first, so you can see him too.'[2] Khrushchev was rather looking forward to it. He recognised a photo opportunity when he saw one.

⁓

The guns also boomed in Odessa, the big Soviet port on the Black Sea. The May Day parade there was held in Kulikovo Square. It was normally a humdrum occasion, attended by local Communist leaders and party officials. That year, however, the *apparatchiks* were accompanied by a most distinguished guest from abroad: Clementine Churchill, wife of the British Prime Minister.

Mrs Churchill had been in the Soviet Union since 2 April. She was touring the country at Stalin's invitation to see the work being done with equipment provided by the British Red Cross. As patron of Britain's Aid to Russia Fund, she had raised enough money from voluntary contributions to re-equip two hospitals destroyed in the fighting and deliver ambulances, X-ray units, blankets and warm clothing on a grand scale. She had come to see the results for herself and also report back privately to her husband on the mood of the Russian people as the war came to an end.

It had been an exhausting few weeks. After flying in to Moscow with Mabel Johnson, secretary of the Aid to Russia Fund, she had gone by special train to Leningrad, still recovering from more than 800 days of German siege. From there, the two women and their staff had continued to Stalingrad, scene of the greatest single battle of the war. Clementine had had a distinct sense of déjà vu as they approached the ruins of the city:

> My first thought was, how like the centre of Coventry or the devastation around St Paul's, except that here the havoc and obliteration seems to spread out endlessly. One building that

caught my eye was a wreck that had been ingeniously patched and shored up. I learned that it was the building in whose cellar the Russians had captured von Paulus, the German commander. It was characteristic of them, I thought, to make every effort to preserve this ruin because of its symbolic value.[3]

After Stalingrad, Clementine had gone to the Crimea, where she had met the sister of the playwright Chekhov and stayed at the Vorontzov Palace, occupying the same room as her husband had during the Yalta conference. From there, she and Mabel Johnson had arrived eventually at Odessa, where they were spending two days before returning to Moscow and a flight home.

It was a busy day. After watching the parade, Clementine was taken to a holding camp to meet British prisoners of war who had been liberated by the Russians. There were about 250 of them, captured earlier by the Germans and now awaiting repatriation. A ship had just arrived to take them home. The prisoners were delighted to meet Winston Churchill's wife, knowing that the war was almost over and they were about to go home. She was pleased to see them too:

> It heightened for us the happy sense of liberation that filled the air, as the war news poured in, and made the pulses beat faster to see our own men going home, freed from the miseries of captivity and knowing that soon they would be with their families again after the long and bitter separation.
>
> We also went to a camp of one thousand French civilians who had been deported into Germany to do forced labour. These poor fellows were in sorry straits after years of hardship, slave work and poor rations. Many of them had been tattooed for identification purposes.[4]

Clementine was shocked to meet a Frenchwoman so brutalised by the Germans that she was no longer sure of her own name. 'I think I know it now,' she told Clementine, after some thought, 'but up to a week ago I used to think of myself by my number only.'[5] She showed Clementine her arm, with her camp number tattooed on it. Plenty of other women were in the same state, reduced to mere cyphers after years of slave labour for the Germans. As a major embarkation port, Odessa was full of such people as the war came to an end: Dutch and Belgian prisoners newly liberated from the Nazis, disparate Czechs and Slovaks, captured Hungarian and Romanian troops, Germans in ragged uniforms, Jews from Auschwitz. The camps were overflowing with displaced persons from all over Europe. Most were in a splendid mood that day, happy and cheerful as May Day was celebrated and the war was over and the news filtered through of Mrs Churchill's visit. All they needed now was a ship to take them home.

———

Otto Frank was not one of those who met Mrs Churchill, but he took great comfort from her arrival. Everyone in his camp was given thirty cigarettes in honour of her visit, and a double ration of chocolate. The cigarettes were particularly welcome, because they could be traded outside the camp for supplies of white bread.

Frank had been in Odessa since 24 April. After their arrest in Amsterdam the previous August, he and his family had been deported to Auschwitz, where they had been separated on arrival. His wife had later been selected for the gas chamber, but had managed to escape to another barrack block, dying eventually of disease. His two daughters had been sent to Bergen-Belsen. Frank himself had been lucky to escape execution. He had been in the camp hospital, weighing just over 100 pounds, when the Russians liberated Auschwitz in January.

The long journey home had begun in March. Frank had been taken initially to a refugee camp at Katowice, where he had had his first decent bath in months. There he had learned from another inmate of his wife's death. No one knew anything of his children, so he presumed they were still in Germany somewhere, perhaps already on their way home.

The onward journey to Odessa had taken three weeks by train, meandering past the Carpathians via Tarnow and Czernowitz. Frank had traded a shirt for bread at one point and a blanket for apples. At other times he had been well fed by local people, Jews and Gentiles alike, who had given him what they had and refused any payment. He had been irritated to learn on 17 April that he was not to proceed to Odessa with the other refugees because he was German-born (and had fought for the Kaiser on the Western Front). But the order had been rescinded a few days later and Frank had arrived in the port without further delay.

One of his shoes had split during the walk to the refugee camp, but Frank had taken it in his stride. With his bartering skills, he would soon find another from somewhere. He had had a bath and been deloused again when he arrived, and then fed by the Red Cross: 'Butter, meat, cheese, jam, soap, egg, salmon, chocolate, tea, milk, oatmeal.' It all seemed like a dream, after Auschwitz.

Best of all, though, better even than Mrs Churchill's visit or the chocolate or the cigarettes, was the news that Otto Frank was about to go home. A ship was sailing in two days' time and his name was on the list. Another forty-eight hours and he would be on the Black Sea. A few days after that, he would be back in Europe somewhere, liberated Europe, on his way to Amsterdam.

'I only hope to find my children back at home!' he had just told Swiss relations in a letter.[6] Still numb from the death of his wife, Otto Frank had nothing left now except his children. He missed them dreadfully, especially his younger daughter Anne. It was only the thought of Anne and Margot that had kept him going during the last, bitter months at Auschwitz. Frank was praying to his God and keeping his fingers crossed that they would both be there, waiting for him, when he got back to Amsterdam.

CHAPTER 19:
OPERATION *CHOWHOUND*

Over the North Sea, Operation *Chowhound* had just begun, the American version of Operation *Manna*. The sky was full of Flying Fortresses heading for Holland with a cargo of food for the Dutch. After waiting so long for the weather to improve, the Americans were raring to go. Like the RAF, they had had enough of dealing out death and destruction over Europe. Dropping food to starving people was much more to their taste.

There was still heavy cloud over East Anglia as they took off, but the operation couldn't be delayed any longer. Assured that the skies were clearer over Holland, the bombers formed up at low altitude and crossed the North Sea a few hundred feet above sea level. Their crews scanned the Dutch coast nervously as they approached, well aware that the Germans were still manning their anti-aircraft defences. As with the RAF, it had been arranged that a couple of bombers should fly ahead of the rest to test the Germans' reactions before giving the all clear. German guns tracked the aircraft closely to ensure that the Americans kept to the agreed route, but no shots were fired. Operation *Chowhound* went ahead as planned.

Flying from Snetterton Heath in Norfolk, Max Krell of the 96th Bomb Group found it an unnerving experience. His aircraft came in so low over the Dutch coast that he could see the German gunners staring up at him as he passed. They could almost have thrown rocks, let alone fired their guns. The aircraft was flying even lower by the time it reached the drop zone at Ypenburg, an airfield near The Hague. It had come down to 400 feet, lowering its wheels and wing flaps at the same time to bring the speed down to 130mph, about as slow as a Flying Fortress could go without stalling. The Dutch were pleased to see it, as Krell recalled:

Such signs of celebration we had never seen before nor since as the people hurried to retrieve their food from the sky. People waved at the planes, flags were everywhere and we had no doubt that the effort had been appreciated. Because of the unwieldy nature of the load, some packages didn't drop cleanly and had to be kicked out of the bomb bay by our crew. Each package seemed to have a recipient soon after it hit the ground, no matter where it landed. A few were even observed being recovered from canals.[1]

The Americans were dropping ten-in-one rations, boxes of military ration packs containing ten meals each for one man. Claude Hill, a member of the 390th ground crew, had persuaded the pilot of *Hotter 'n Hell* to take him along as a waist gunner on his first flight over enemy territory. He watched fascinated as the cardboard boxes fell into a canal, closely followed by the Dutch, who dived straight in after them. Others saw the boxes smashing into greenhouses or crashing through tiled roofs, a danger to life and limb. But the Dutch didn't mind. They were just happy to see the Americans, waving sheets and tablecloths, anything they could find, as the Fortresses roared overhead.

After flying his share of combat missions, turret gunner Bernie Behrman was happy in turn to see the Dutch. Everyone in his crew felt good about it as they opened the bomb bays over Valkenburg airfield and dropped food instead of high explosives:

> I could see German soldiers walking their station. We dropped the food. Because the food was in burlap bags, some got hung up on the shackles in the bay. This didn't cause trouble, however, so we closed the bay and returned to base with a good feeling. The crew that was on board was a combat crew and did its share of blowing up things. After all the destructive missions we all felt very good about this mission.[2]

Ralph DiSpirito, a waist gunner on the *Maiden Prayer*, shared their enthusiasm. Holland at low altitude had lived up to his every expectation: all canals, windmills and tulip fields on the way to Valkenburg. He remembered the tulips best, a wonderful sight from above.

THANKS, YANKS. The Dutch had spelled it out in flowers, clipping the fields of tulips into capital letters to show their appreciation. Some of the most hard-bitten airmen had tears in their eyes as they read the words and saw the waving crowds, so obviously glad to see them. But the most heartfelt response from the Dutch was spotted by a vigilant ball gunner, who immediately got onto his tail man over the intercom. 'Close your eyes,' he told him. 'You're much too young to see this.'[3] On the ground below, already vanishing into the distance, a young Dutch woman had lifted the front of her dress and was waving it cheerfully at the Americans. She wore nothing underneath.

———

Four hundred miles away, General George Patton was en route to the newly liberated prison camp at Moosburg, just north of Munich. Flying down from Nuremberg, he had landed at an airstrip behind the front line and was driving the rest of the way in a jeep. Moosburg was a prison camp for Allied officers and others, perhaps a hundred thousand in all, from a myriad of different nations. Thirty thousand of them were American.

The nearby town had been taken by the US Army on 29 April. The prisoners had watched ecstatically as what looked like US tanks appeared in the distance, checking the camp out before returning to their own lines. They had known for sure that liberation was at hand when Mustang fighters from the US Air Force flew low overhead, waggling their wings to let the prisoners know they were not forgotten. Cameron Garrett, a B-24 tail gunner before being shot down, was one of the American prisoners longing for their own people to arrive:

> All through the night we heard the sounds of loaded German trucks leaving the compound. They didn't get far before there was a single explosion. No one could sleep, there was an unmistakable air of expectancy among every one of the 110,000 prisoners. German SS troops moved under cover outside the city in an effort to set up a defensive perimeter against the American attack.
>
> Somewhere the German SS opened fire with small arms, the return volley comprised of heavy automatic weapons that dominated the confrontation. Having been ordered to stay in barracks, we needed no encouragement to remain low and keep our helmets on. Approximately one hour later, an eerie silence perforated the explosive air. I held my breath when I felt the vibration in the ground when our army tanks hit the ridge overlooking the camp and headed in our direction. Soon the sounds of the moving Sherman tanks could no longer be heard over the noise of screaming, cheering, crying and yelling in a dozen different languages.

The Sherman tanks of the Third Army came crashing through the fences of the compound. Every tank was immediately barraged by a ragged, emaciated, filthy multitude of POWs. When the German flag at the top of the Moosburg church was lowered, the men yelled at the top of their voices in jubilation. Just as quickly as they had begun, the entire mass fell silent when 'Old Glory' was hoisted in its place. The newly ex-POWs immediately came to attention and saluted the American flag, regardless of their nationality.[4]

Food had followed, showering down on the prisoners from the Sherman tanks. The crews had pitched K rations into the crowd like candy at a parade. It had been as good as a Thanksgiving feast to Garrett and his friends. The Germans had surrendered, the prisoners were free again, the war was almost over. And now here was General Patton, old Blood and Guts himself, striding around the camp in his famous silver-buckled belt with an ivory-handled six-gun on each hip.

He arrived at lunchtime, standing erect in his jeep as it drove in through the gate. The whole camp cheered and didn't stop until the old showman lowered his arms for silence. He gave them a short speech, the usual one about whipping the Germans all the way to Berlin. Then he descended from his jeep and set off on a tour of the camp, meeting the prisoners and seeing the conditions for himself.

What he found did not please him. Conditions at Moosburg were nowhere near as bad as Belsen or Buchenwald, but they weren't good either. The camp was horribly overcrowded and the only food in the past few weeks had come from American Red Cross parcels. Walking from hut to hut, stopping every now and then to talk to the men, Patton was not impressed. 'I'm going to kill those sons of bitches for this,' he told one group of prisoners.[5] He was sufficiently moved to shake hands with some of them, which he very rarely did.

Patton stayed for half an hour and then went back to the war. The last the prisoners saw of him, he was on his way to Landshut, where one of his staff officers had been a prisoner during World War One. From there, he was planning to push forward into Austria and Czechoslovakia if Eisenhower would let him, seeing how far he could take his conquering army before the final whistle blew and the greatest days of his military career and perhaps also of his life came to a triumphant end.

—

Twenty miles to the south, Lee Miller and Dave Scherman had arrived from Dachau to find that Munich had already surrendered to the Americans and the troops were busy settling in. There was no fighting to photograph, so they found their way instead to Prinzregentenplatz 16, a big old apartment building near the river. It was where Hitler had lived since the 1920s, whenever he was in Munich.

As Eisenhower had just said in a message of congratulation to the army, Prinzregentenplatz 16 was 'the lair of the beast', the place from which Hitler had built up the Nazi party before coming to power. It was also where his niece Geli Raubal had killed herself before the war. Overlooking a cobbled square, the building was comfortable, but nothing out of the ordinary. Hitler had occupied a single room at first, but had later acquired the entire building. He had established himself in a nine-room apartment on the second floor, with his SS guards on the ground floor, next to the entrance. The basement had been turned into kitchens for the staff with a bomb proof air raid shelter beneath.

Lee and Scherman arrived to discover that the whole place had been taken over by the 45th Division. The 179th Regiment had put a sentry on the door and was using the building as a command post. There was plenty of room to spare, so the two of them were invited in to stay the night.

They needed no urging. Where better in Munich? Scarcely believing their luck, they dumped their kit in Hitler's apartment and wandered from room to room, looking through his possessions, examining everything they found, searching for a glimpse of the real man behind the public mask. The library was full of leather-bound books, presentation volumes given to Hitler by admirers, but there were few books of his own, few signs of his personality at all beyond some mediocre paintings on the wall and a large globe of the world which had doubtless played its part in his deliberations.

Hitler's bedroom was scarcely more informative. It was hung with department store chintz and had a large, cream-coloured safe in the corner. The maid, valet and guard could all be summoned by pressing a button on the bedside table. The adjoining bathroom connected to a small room with a single bed where Eva Braun had slept when she was staying overnight.

At the other end of the apartment, there was a separate flat with a state of the art switchboard on the wall. Hitler had been able to dial straight through to Berlin, Berchtesgaden and similar places. Since Berchtesgaden had yet to fall to the Allies, Lieutenant-Colonel William Grace of the 179th had tried to telephone the Berghof when he arrived, on the off chance that Hitler might pick up the phone. An obliging German operator had put him through, but no one had answered. Berchtesgaden had still not recovered from the RAF bombing of a few days earlier.

Going downstairs again after they had looked around, Lee and Scherman found a German woman living in an apartment on the ground floor. Married to an Englishman named Gardner, she had British nationality and spoke excellent English. She told them about Hitler's mistress, Eva Braun, and showed them a jug shaped like King George VI's head, which played the British national anthem when lifted. A gift to Hitler from Neville Chamberlain when he visited Prinzregentenplatz, it had been passed on to her for safekeeping.

Outside, Lee and Scherman went to see the Hofbräuhaus, Munich's famous old beer hall, where Hitler had outlined the Nazis' twenty five-point manifesto at the beginning of his career. The roof had been blown in, but there was still beer in the cellar. The Hofbräuhaus was where Munich's university students celebrated May Day in happier times, but there were no celebrations that day, although a few drab civilians were drinking in the ground floor hall, which hadn't been destroyed. Lee had a beer too, just to say that she had drunk there.

Later, she and Scherman visited Eva Braun's house on Wasserburgerstrasse. It had already been looted when they arrived, given a thorough going over by refugees searching for something to eat. Curious to learn that Hitler had kept a mistress, Lee looked through Eva's scattered possessions with more than usual interest. The house was dull and nondescript, but she found some photographs of Hitler, affectionately inscribed to Eva and her sister Gretl. Most of Eva's clothes had gone, but the remaining accessories and scent bottles suggested a woman of considerable femininity. Among other things, there was a douche bag, lipstick from Milan and a supply of Elizabeth Arden cosmetics. From the array of products in the medicine cupboard, it was evident that the woman in Hitler's life had been a martyr to period pains.

Back in Hitler's apartment, Lee had a bath that night, the first proper bath she had had in weeks. Stripping off her clothes, she propped up a photograph of Hitler on the edge of the tub and soaped herself in the Führer's own bath while Scherman took photographs. He also photographed her at Hitler's desk and took a picture of Sergeant Arthur Peters lounging on Hitler's bed, reading a copy of *Mein Kampf*. Colonel Grace was photographed too, standing by the switchboard and holding the telephone to Berchtesgaden in his ear. If the Führer was in, he still wasn't answering.

South of Munich, the 36th Texas Division had reached Bad Tölz, a spa town on the River Isar. Learning from a prisoner that Field-Marshal Gerd von Rundstedt was waiting for them at a local sanatorium, 2nd Lieutenant Joe Burke of the 141st Infantry took a ten-man patrol from Company A and went to arrest him.

Rundstedt was no longer a serving soldier. Recalled to active service in 1939, he had led German armies into Poland, France and Russia, but had frequently clashed with Hitler about the conduct of the war. He had recognised the inevitable after D-Day, urging his superiors in Berlin to negotiate with the Allies rather than go on fighting a losing battle. 'Make peace, you idiots!' he had yelled, at one point. His advice had been ignored and Rundstedt had been quietly relieved of his command in March 1945.

Plagued with heart trouble and an arthritic leg, he had gone to Bad Tölz to take a cure. He was sitting by the fire with his wife and son when Burke arrived. Rundstedt was shocked, because he hadn't expected the Americans until next morning. Surrendering at once, he couldn't conceal his bitterness at the ignominious way in which his career had ended. 'It is a most disgraceful situation for a soldier to give himself up without resistance,' he told Burke, as he was led into captivity.[6] But he had been right about the Germans' conduct of the war. They should have made peace long ago.

—

Fifty miles to the west, Major Wernher von Braun of the SS was still waiting for the Americans to arrive, longing to be arrested as soon as they showed up. As Germany's leading rocket scientist, the man behind the attacks on London and Antwerp, Braun had no qualms about surrendering to the Americans. Rather than fall into the wrong hands, he wanted to give himself up to the Yanks and make his expertise available to them before anyone else could take him prisoner and hold him to ransom.

The last few weeks had been very difficult for Braun and his team. They had been at Peenemünde, the rocket base on the north German coast, until forced to retreat by the Russians. Fleeing south, Braun had been involved in a car crash which had left him with a broken shoulder and an arm still in plaster. Along with several hundred other rocket scientists and technicians, he had ended up in a Wehrmacht camp near Oberammergau, in the foothills of the Alps. The camp was surrounded by barbed wire and the scientists were prisoners, being held by their own people as bargaining counters for the peace negotiations with the Allies.

The man holding them hostage was Hans Kammler, an engineer turned SS general who had constructed Auschwitz and several other camps with the ruthless use of slave labour. Fearing that the Allies would hang him for war crimes, he intended to trade the scientists for his own life. Failing that, he planned to kill them all to prevent their expertise from being acquired by the enemy.

As if that wasn't enough, the camp was also under constant threat from Allied aircraft, bombing and strafing at will. Worried that his entire team could be wiped out in a single air raid, Braun had persuaded a junior SS officer to limit the danger by dispersing the more important scientists among the surrounding villages. The young major had been very reluctant, but Braun had managed to convince him that he would be held responsible if all the scientists were killed in a single attack.

Braun himself had been taken under escort to a skiing hotel at Oberjoch, a few miles west of Oberammergau. He was waiting there now with his brother and a few colleagues, hoping that the Americans would appear before the SS changed their minds and massacred the lot of them. There was a unit of the French Army not far away, but Braun didn't want to surrender to the French if it meant being separated from the rest of his team. And he certainly didn't want to surrender to the British. They would never accept his protestations that his rockets had been designed for space travel, rather than the destruction of London – particularly if they learned that his team had celebrated the first successful attack on London with champagne.

Braun was a scientist, before he was anything else. He wanted to deliver his entire team to the United States to ensure that their expertise was safely preserved for the benefit of all mankind. Nobody knew more about rockets than Braun and his men. They could go to the moon with their rockets, once the technical challenges had been overcome. But they could only do it with American help.

Conferring with his brother Magnus, Braun decided that they must go to the Americans, if the Americans weren't coming to them. Magnus spoke the best English of the party. If the Americans hadn't arrived by next day, it was agreed that he should go and fetch them on his bicycle. If he went down the mountain, he could surely find some American troops somewhere and bring them back to the hotel. The Americans would be delighted to arrest Braun and his team, once they realised that all the research and rocket data from Peenemünde had been hidden in a mine shaft in the Harz mountains, and only Braun knew where.

Further east, the trickle of soldiers deserting from the Wehrmacht was threatening to turn into a flood as the remaining forces in Bavaria joined the retreat towards the mountains. With Munich gone and the war obviously lost, there seemed little point in continuing the fight any longer. Soldiers were voting with their feet instead, abandoning their units and slipping quietly away, shedding their uniforms and heading for home to be reunited with their families.

Among them was Josef Ratzinger. As an eighteen-year-old conscript, small and distinctly unmilitary, Private Ratzinger had been against the war from the very beginning. He came from a family of devout Catholics who had had to move house before the war because of his policeman father's anti-Nazi outbursts. The Ratzingers had never wanted anything to do with German militarism.

Ratzinger himself had been in a seminary, training for the priesthood, when he was called up. He had served initially in an anti-aircraft battery, defending the BMW works north of Munich at first and then the Dornier factory west of the city. The battery itself had been attacked once, with a man killed and others wounded. With no stomach for the war, Ratzinger had been delighted to hear of the Allied invasion of Normandy, if it meant a quick end to the fighting. He lived only for getting back to the seminary and catching up on his Latin and Greek.

He had been released from the flak battery late in 1944, when he became old enough to join the real army. The SS had held a recruiting session soon afterwards, hauling the young men out of bed one night and calling on them to volunteer in front of their peers. Quite a few had obliged, too sleepy and malleable to say no. Ratzinger had refused, pointing out that he was going to be a Catholic priest after the war. The SS had sneered at that, sending him out of the room to a chorus of abuse. Ratzinger hadn't minded. He had seen slave labourers from Dachau and had watched Hungarian Jews being transported to their death. He didn't want to be in the SS.

Sent home instead to Traunstein, near Berchtesgaden, Ratzinger had done his basic training at the local barracks, marching through the streets with his platoon, singing military songs to reassure the local population. But his heart had never been in it. He was just waiting for the war to stop so that he could go back to the seminary and become a priest.

And now his wish was coming true. The war was almost over. Ratzinger's family lived in a farmhouse on the outskirts of Traunstein. He could be there in an hour, if he was prepared to slip away from his barracks.

It was still dangerous, of course. Deserters were still being hanged if they were caught, or shot against the nearest wall. But the risk seemed

worth it to Ratzinger as the Wehrmacht began to disintegrate. He decided
to try his luck:

> I knew that the town was surrounded by soldiers who had orders
> to shoot deserters on the spot. For this reason I used a little-
> known back road out of the town, hoping to get through
> unmolested. But, as I walked out of a railway underpass, two
> soldiers were standing at their posts, and for a moment the
> situation was extremely critical for me. Thank God that they, too,
> had had enough of war and did not want to become murderers.
> Nevertheless, they still needed an excuse to let me go. Because of
> an injury I had my arm in a sling, and so they said: 'Comrade,
> you are wounded. Move on!'[7]

Ratzinger needed no urging. Putting the war behind him, he set off for
home without a backward glance.

———

On the other side of the Alps, Leni Riefenstahl was on her way to
Mayrhofen. After completing the dubbing of her latest film *Tiefland*, she had
abandoned her studio at Kitzbühel and was heading for the mountains to
stay with an old lover until the war was over. As a public figure indelibly
linked to Hitler, she did not want to be in Kitzbühel when the Allies
arrived. She would feel a lot safer with Hans Schneeberger, keeping a low
profile at his cousin's boarding house in the mountains.

Leni had moved to Kitzbühel in 1943 to escape the bombing. She had
set up a makeshift studio in the town, storing her film archive in an old castle
at first to protect it from air raids. Changing her mind as the fighting came
closer, she had sent the originals of some of her most important films to
German HQ in Italy for safekeeping. Three metal boxes containing the
negatives of *Triumph of the Will* and other Nazi films had been taken by car
to Bolzano in April, but Leni had heard nothing since. With all the chaos on
the roads, she didn't even know if the car had reached its destination.

She was leaving Kitzbühel with reluctance. Her mother was still there,
and her film crew. Leni had wanted to stay with them, sticking together as
the enemy arrived, but they had all been adamant that she should go. They
didn't want to be associated with her when the Allies came, particularly if
the Russians got there first. The Riefenstahl name would jeopardise them
all if she stayed. Even Leni's mother had begged her to go.

She was all alone as she set out. Her brother was dead, killed by a grenade on the Eastern Front. Her husband was in the army somewhere, possibly Berlin, since that was where she had last heard from him. As Hitler's most talented film maker, she had once had everyone at her beck and call, senior Nazis falling over themselves to accommodate her wishes and provide her with everything she needed. But they had all melted away as Hitler's star faded. Even the Nazis in Kitzbühel, shameless sycophants in the past, were tearing up their party cards and reinventing themselves as resistance fighters. Nobody knew whether it would be the Russians or the Americans who reached the town first, but there were already banners across the street welcoming the liberators, whoever they might be. The only certainty was that nobody wanted Leni.

Adolf Galland, the air ace, had managed to procure twenty litres of petrol for her car. It was just enough to get to Mayrhofen. Leni was full of gloom as she started, wondering if she was ever going to see her mother again, or her husband, wondering if she would ever make another film. She was taking all her remaining valuables with her, including her most cherished possession, the original negative of *Olympia*, her prizewinning account of the 1936 Olympic Games. It was one of the most admired films of all time, not least for Leni's nude dancing in the prologue and the Olympic torch run into the stadium, an idea she had dreamed up with one of the officials to add drama to the opening ceremony. She was just hoping that she would be able to hang on to it in the days ahead and then continue her film career uninterrupted once the war was finally over.

CHAPTER 20:
DÖNITZ SPEAKS
TO THE NATION

Back in Berlin, Magda Göbbels was about to kill her children. She had six by Göbbels: a son and five daughters. Kind Dr Stumpfegger was waiting with sedatives to send them to sleep, after which their mother was going to poison them with cyanide. Rochus Misch, the bunker's switchboard operator, was one of the last to see them alive:

> All of the children were now wearing white nightgowns. This was their usual time for bed. Five were sitting in chairs; Heidi had scrambled up onto the table. She was still suffering from tonsillitis and had a scarf around her neck. Helga, the tallest, oldest and brightest, was sobbing quietly. I think she dimly suspected the mayhem about to come. She was most definitely Daddy's girl, with no great fondness for her mother.[1]

Misch squirmed as Magda Göbbels made a great play of combing the children's hair and kissing each of them affectionately, as she had every evening for the past week.

'I watched all of this with apprehension. I was appalled. I still have it on my conscience today that I did nothing but sit there on my backside, because I sensed what was about to happen. At the same time, watching the mother. I just couldn't believe it. I suppose I didn't *want* to believe it.'[2]

Without a word to anyone, Magda took the children upstairs to their room. Heidi, the youngest, turned back to Misch for a moment before climbing the stairs. 'Misch, Misch, du bist ein Fisch,' she giggled. Misch watched miserably as she disappeared, then began to say his rosary for them, praying that even at this late stage Magda might still relent and let the children go.

It was an hour before she reappeared. Accounts vary as to how the children died. They may have been injected with morphine or drugged with chocolates laced with Finodin 'to prevent air sickness'. From the bruises on her body, twelve-year-old Helga may have woken up and struggled as her mother forced a cyanide capsule between her teeth. Whatever the manner of their death, Magda Göbbels was red-eyed with weeping when she came downstairs again. Misch couldn't help but notice that she didn't have the children with her:

'At first she just stood there, wringing her hands. Then she pulled herself together and lit a cigarette. She did not speak or even nod to me, though she was only a few feet away as she passed by.'[3]

There was a small champagne bottle, a *piccolo*, which someone had left on the long table in the main corridor. Misch watched as Magda took it into the little room that Göbbels had been using as a study. 'She had left his door open. I got up, walked past, and could see that she had taken out a pack of small cards and had begun to play patience (solitaire). Instinctively, I knew that her children were no longer of this world. Another ten minutes or so passed. Then she got up and stalked out. Again, we didn't speak to each other. What was there to say?'[4]

Magda went to join her husband. Göbbels had completed the last entry in his diary, the seven-page summary of his life's work for posterity. Entrusting it to Werner Naumann, his ministry secretary, for safekeeping, he sat with Magda and Bormann for a while, drinking champagne and chain-smoking as they reminisced over old times. Various people drifted in and out, coming to say goodbye. The Göbbels withdrew for some private time together and then reappeared just before eight thirty that evening. General Mohnke and two junior officers, Schwägermann and Olds, were the only ones still present. Mohnke watched as Göbbels gave Schwägermann an autographed picture of the Führer as a farewell gift and then set off to commit suicide:

> Going over to the coat-rack in the small room that had served as his study, he donned his hat, his scarf, his long uniform overcoat. Slowly, he drew on his kid gloves, making each finger snug. Then, like a cavalier, he offered his right arm to his wife. They were wordless now. So were we three spectators. Slowly but steadily, leaning a bit on each other, they headed up the stairs to the courtyard.[5]

They passed Misch as they went. 'I don't need you any more,' Göbbels told him. '*Les jeux sont faits*.'[6] Continuing upstairs, he and Magda paused for a moment at the exit of the bunker, then stepped out together into the Chancellery garden.

Shots followed. As soon as he heard them, Schwägermann went out with some SS men to burn the bodies. As Göbbels had earlier requested, one of the men fired a bullet into each corpse to make sure they were dead. Then they sprinkled petrol over them and set the bodies alight. The flames burned for a few minutes and then went out, leaving the charred remains of Göbbels and his wife still perfectly recognisable amid the rubble. But nobody took any notice. They had already forgotten about Göbbels and were thinking only of saving themselves as night deepened and they prepared to make their breakout from the bunker.

———

Traudl Junge was in the first group to escape. She had watched in dismay as a nurse and a man in a white coat emerged from the children's room in the upper bunker, lugging a heavy crate between them. The crate had been followed by another, both of them the right size for a child's body. Shocked, Traudl was glad to leave the bunker soon afterwards. Passing Hitler's door as she went, she saw that his grey overcoat was still hanging on the coat stand, with his cap above it, his pale suede gloves and a dog leash. The stand looked like a gallows to her.

Hans Baur, one of Hitler's pilots, had taken the Führer's portrait of Frederick the Great out of its frame and rolled it up, claiming that Hitler had left it to him as a souvenir. Traudl thought of taking one of Hitler's gloves, but although she reached for it, she couldn't quite bring herself to. She wasn't taking Eva Braun's fur coat either. All she had as she left the bunker for the last time was her pistol and the cyanide capsule that Hitler had given her as a farewell present, apologising that it wasn't anything nicer.

Otto Günsche led the way to the new Chancellery. Traudl and Konstanze Manziarly followed, keeping close behind him as he pushed through the crowds with his broad shoulders. Some women packed a bag before they made their escape, but Traudl had decided to take very little with her when they left: no money, clothes or food, just a few treasured photographs and a supply of cigarettes. She had already destroyed her identity papers. In boots and steel helmet, she was ready and waiting when the order was given for everyone to assemble in the garage underneath the

Chancellery's Hall of Honour, facing the Wilhelmstrasse and the U-Bahn station beyond.

The vehicles in the garage had been pushed aside to make room for the escape. Ernst-Günther Schenck watched quietly as people began to appear:

> From the dark gangways, they kept arriving, in small groups, both the fighting troops being pulled in from the outside, then the officers and men of the Reich Chancellery group. The troops, many very young, were already street fighting veterans. Other soldiers had stubble beards, blackened faces. They wore sweaty, torn, field-grey uniforms, which most had worn and slept in, without change, for almost a fortnight.
>
> The situation was heroic; the mood was not. The official announcement of Hitler's suicide had not yet reached the lower ranks. But they guessed as much – from the silence of their officers. There was little talk now of 'Führer, Folk and Fatherland'. To a man, each German soldier was silently calculating his own chance of survival. For all the discipline, what was now building up was less a military operation in the classic sense than what I imagine happens at sea when the cry goes out to man the lifeboats.[7]

General Mohnke was in command. He was carrying copies of Hitler's testaments for delivery to Dönitz and had a bagful of diamonds in his underwear, the kind used for decorating the Knight's Cross. The escape was to be made in ten groups, leaving the Chancellery at twenty minute intervals. The first group was to consist mainly of those who had been in the bunker with Hitler, including the three female secretaries and Konstanze Manziarly, his cook. They waited as troops broke open the bricked-up window looking on to the Wilhelmstrasse. Pistol in hand, Mohnke was first through, checking the street for Russians. Seeing none, he gave the all clear and the rest of the first group followed him in rapid succession, scrambling through the window and hurrying frantically along the street towards the U-Bahn station a hundred yards away across the square.

Traudl Junge remembered it thus:

> We clamber over half-wrecked staircases, through holes in walls and rubble, always going further up and out. At last the Wilhelmsplatz stretches ahead, shining in the moonlight. The

dead horse is still lying there on the paving stones, but only the remains of it now. Hungry people have come out of the U-Bahn tunnels to slice off pieces of meat.

Soundlessly, we cross the square. There's sporadic shooting, but the gunfire is worse further away. Reaching the U-Bahn tunnel outside the ruins of the Kaiserhof, we go down and make our way forward in the darkness, climbing over the wounded and the homeless, past resting soldiers…'[8]

It wasn't quite as simple as that. The stairs down to the U-Bahn had been shot away, forcing Traudl and the others to scramble over the wreckage as best they could. They were reluctant to use their flashlights in case the Russians were waiting for them at the bottom. Stumbling towards the station platform, they stood listening for a moment, wondering if they were about to be attacked. There were certainly people on the platform, because they could hear them moving about in the darkness.

The people were German. The platform was packed with civilians and wounded soldiers, some of whom had been there for a week. As one of them explained to Mohnke: 'We kept as quiet as mice, putting out all our candles and hushing the babies. We thought you were all Ivans.'

Pushing through, the bunker party jumped down onto the railway track. The next station was Stadtmitte, to the east. From there, they intended to turn north and head along the tunnel under the Russian lines, aiming for Friedrichstrasse, the main line station on the banks of the Spree. If they reached Friedrichstrasse without mishap, they planned to cross the river and link up with other German units believed to be still fighting in the northern outskirts of the city.

It was a terrifying experience. Worried that they might bump into Russian soldiers at any moment, Mohnke forbade the use of flashlights as they set off. In fact, the Russians were very wary of the subway system, fearing that the Germans intended to flood it, but Mohnke didn't know that. Nor did he know if the third rail was still electrified. An attempt to short circuit it by stringing field telephone wires across the other two rails had suggested not, but the power plant was now in Russian hands and there was nothing to stop them reconnecting the supply at any moment.

Mohnke and Günsche went first. The rest followed, strung out over a hundred yards along the tunnel. Schenck put himself in charge of the women, patting their behinds every so often to keep them moving. They reached Stadtmitte without any trouble and found the platform crowded with refugees, just as the Kaiserhof had been. An abandoned subway car had been turned into a makeshift operating theatre, with several surgeons working nonstop by candlelight.

After a brief cigarette break, they continued north towards Freidrichstrasse. Several members of the group had dropped out by the time they arrived. There was an artillery barrage overhead, shaking the tunnel with every salvo, sometimes even making the rails tremble. Fearing that the roof might collapse, Mohnke hurried on, leading Traudl and the others past Friedrichstrasse station into the tunnel that led under the River Spree towards the north of the city.

They hadn't gone more than a hundred yards when they came to a giant steel barrier across the track. It was a waterproof bulkhead, closed every night after the last train had left to seal the tunnel under the river and prevent an accidental flood. No trains had run for the past week, but the nightly ritual continued. Two officials of the Berlin transport company had just closed the barrier and were surrounded by an angry group of civilians urging them to open it again.

Mohnke joined them, telling the officials to open it at once. They refused, citing a regulation that dated from 1923. They had the regulations with them and showed Mohnke the relevant section. Standing orders were quite clear. The barrier was to be kept shut at night.

Mohnke was a brigadier-general with a gun. He had come straight from Hitler's Chancellery. The officials were no-account employees of the U-Bahn company. But they were all German and orders were orders, there to be obeyed. Against his better judgement, Mohnke backed down. The barrier remained shut.

Retracing their steps, the group headed back to Friedrichstrasse station. While the others waited below, Mohnke climbed what remained of the stairs to reconnoitre the situation above ground. The river was only a hundred yards from the station. If they could only find a way across, they might discover friendly faces the other side.

Emerging from the U-Bahn, Mohnke was shocked at what he saw:

> For the first time since fleeing the Reich Chancellery, I now had a panoramic view of the Berlin night time battlefield. It was unlike any previous one I had ever seen. It looked more like a painting, something apocalyptic by Hieronymous Bosch. Even to a hardened soldier, it was most unreal, phantasmagoric. Most of the great city was pitch dark. The moon was hiding, but flares, shell bursts, the burning buildings, all these reflected on a low-lying, blackish-yellow cloud of sulphur-like smoke. I couldn't make out anything remotely resembling a clear battle line. But I spotted the

launch sites of the Katyusha rockets and I calculated they were
only about a mile away from us, in the direction of the Tiergarten.[9]

The River Spree lay immediately in front of them. They had to cross
somehow. There were Russians on the upper Freidrichstrasse, three or four
blocks ahead, and the Weidendammer Bridge was blocked by a German
anti-tank trap. Mohnke looked for another way across.

> Fortunately, after some reconnaissance, we found a narrow
> catwalk or swinging bridge just north of us and to our left. It was
> less than two yards wide. The way was blocked by concertina
> barbed wire, but we quickly cleared it with our wire cutters. My
> group – which had now dwindled to twelve – all scurried across
> at the double, knowing that our silhouettes were casting long
> dancing shadows on the water below. We made excellent moving
> targets, like dummies in a shooting gallery. But we all got across.
> No shots rang out.[10]

Traudl Junge was still in the group, sticking close to Konstanze Manziarly
and Gerda Christian as they scuttled across the bridge. She remembered an
inferno behind them as snipers opened up on others trying to follow them.
The plan had been for all the groups breaking out of the Chancellery to
keep together after they had left, maintaining contact as they tried to rejoin
their own lines. It quickly proved unworkable. Even people in the same
group had trouble keeping together in the chaos. It was every man for
himself as they raced across the bridge and threw themselves down in the
rubble the other side.

They still had a long way to go. They were in No Man's Land now, an
endless vista of blocked streets and ruined buildings, cellars full of frightened
civilians waiting for the Russians to appear. There was safety somewhere,
but nobody knew where. After resting in a cellar for a few minutes,
Mohnke's group picked themselves up again and set off uncertainly for the
north of the city. They had no real plan, as they started out. They all knew,
without saying so, that they would be lucky to get through the night alive,
let alone return safely to their own lines.

———

While Traudl and the others prepared to escape from the Chancellery,
Hildegard Knef and Ewald von Demandowsky were on Albrecht

Achillesstrasse, waiting to be executed. 'You deserted your company,' an officer had told them curtly, when they were brought in. He had ordered them to join a line of similar offenders awaiting sentence. They had all been herded together under the cold eye of a guard, who walked up and down the line telling everyone to keep quiet as they braced themselves to hear their fate.

'They're going to hang us,'[11] whispered the elderly private next to Hildegard. She didn't doubt it for a moment. They had already hanged plenty of others on the streets outside.

But fate intervened. As they stood waiting, a Russian shell burst through the door, killing several people and wounding others as it spewed shrapnel everywhere. Hildegard hit the floor at once. Grabbing some of Demandowsky's cigarettes, she rolled over to the guard and thrust them at him in the confusion, telling him that she was a woman and Demandowsky was her husband. 'Take these and let us go,' she pleaded. 'Please let us go.'

The guard stared at her uncomprehendingly. Hildegard shook him in exasperation when he didn't reply. Then she saw that he was dead. Seizing the moment, she and Demandowsky ran for their lives. They didn't look back as they scrambled over arms and legs and rushed for the door just as the wall buckled and the building began to collapse.

Outside, an old man from the Volkssturm was kneeling in despair with his head between his knees. His wife was buried beneath the rubble in a house that had just collapsed. Slipping past him, Hildegard and Demandowsky ran down an alley, only to be stopped at gunpoint by a lieutenant. Hildegard removed her helmet to show that she was a woman. Grinning, the lieutenant tossed them a bar of chocolate and sent them on their way.

They found shelter in a crater with three soldiers. 'Put your lid on!' one of them yelled at Hildegard as she and Demandowsky joined them. She felt much more comfortable without a helmet, but there were Russians in a nearby house, sniping at anything that moved. Putting it back on, she crouched down in the hole as bullets whizzed past. Demandowsky produced his cigarettes and passed them round. They all sat smoking and keeping watch while they waited for night to fall.

Once it was safely dark, the soldiers took lengths of rope from their pouches and tied themselves together, like mountaineers. They tied Hildegard and Demandowsky too. Emerging cautiously from their foxhole, they set off along the street, keeping a wary eye out for Russians as they probed forward in the gloom. But there were no Russians around. They found only Germans, happy and excited Germans, Germans who had been cheered by some very welcome news:

Two tanks have collided at the corner. There are soldiers sitting on them, others standing around. 'Hitler's dead!' they shout. 'Hitler's dead, the war's over!' Someone down the street repeats it, it echoes through the ruins, over the bridge, up and down the canals. They crawl out of their holes and doorways, surge together into a trampling, stamping swelling herd. The rope between us breaks, we shout our names, clutch each other, and are swept forward by an endless torrent.[12]

The news was official at last. It had been formally announced on the radio from Hamburg. Solemn music from Wagner and Bruckner had presaged 'a serious and important message' for the German people. The music had been interrupted by a roll of drums at three minutes past ten that evening, followed by the sombre tones of the radio announcer:

Our Führer, Adolf Hitler, fighting to the last breath against Bolshevism, fell for Germany this afternoon at his operational headquarters in the Reich Chancellery. On April 30 the Führer appointed Grand Admiral Dönitz his successor. The Grand Admiral and successor to the Führer now speaks to the German people.

Dönitz's address was equally apocalyptic:

German men and women, soldiers of the German armed forces! Our Führer, Adolf Hitler, has fallen. The German people bow in deepest sorrow and respect. He was quick to recognise the terrible danger of Bolshevism and dedicated his life to the struggle against it. At the end of the struggle he died a hero's death in the capital of the German Reich, after having followed an unswervingly straight path through life. It was a unique service for Germany. His mission in the battle against the Bolshevik storm-flood was undertaken on behalf of Europe and the entire civilised world.

The Führer has appointed me as his successor. Fully conscious of the responsibility, I assume the leadership of the German people at this fateful hour…

Dönitz's primary task was to save the Germans in the East from the advancing Bolsheviks. The war had to go on for that reason alone, he told his listeners. It had to go on against the British and Americans too, since they were hindering the fight against Bolshevism. Calling on all Germans to maintain order and discipline in the difficult days ahead, Dönitz urged them to do everything they could to stave off collapse. 'If we do all that is in our power to do,' he assured them, 'God will not abandon us after so much suffering and sacrifice.' In an afterword to the Wehrmacht, he added that the oath they had sworn to Hitler was now owed to him, as Hitler's successor. Any soldier who shirked his responsibilities and thereby brought death and enslavement to German women and children was a coward and a traitor. 'German soldiers!' he ended sternly. 'Do your duty! The lives of our people depend on it!'

In the barracks at Ruhleben, Helmut Altner could not conceal his dismay at Dönitz's words. There had been no mention of peace in the broadcast, no talk of the war coming to an end. Only of holding on and continuing the fight. But for what, when Germany was already overrun and Himmler was rumoured to be negotiating with the Western Allies? To Altner, a little drunk on the schnapps that had been distributed earlier in the day, Dönitz sounded just the same as Hitler, ranting about the Bolsheviks and ordering everyone else to keep fighting when it was obvious the war was lost and further resistance was useless. It made little sense to him.

> I go back across to the sleeping room. With the effects of the alcohol, everyone is merry and having a good time. Then somebody says what he is going to do when peace comes. The general feeling is that Dönitz will not continue the fight. Meanwhile, the can is being refilled again and again. Everyone is drinking as much as possible, and the company sergeant major, the lieutenant and the other officers are looking on quietly. It occurs to me that they are letting us do this because not many of us will survive tomorrow.
>
> Suddenly the company commander enters the room and waves down those who start to get up. He sits down and takes a drink of schnapps with us. Then he speaks about the order of the day from the new head of state and tries to explain to us why the fighting has to go on. 'We will have peace with the western powers within the next few days,' he says. 'Then it will only be against the Bolsheviks, and that won't go on much longer, only until the summer, and then you can all go home. And the oath to

our glorious Führer is transferred to his successor. Anybody wanting to desert will be shot. The war goes on!'[13]

An unhappy silence followed the company commander's speech. If the war was to go on, then the dying would continue too. Peace had been dangled in front of everyone, then cruelly snatched away again, as far out of reach as ever. Turning back to the schnapps as the company commander left, the soldiers poured more drinks and consoled themselves with alcohol as they contemplated a dismal future.

In the next room, the SS girls could be seen through the open door. Some were sitting at the table, but others were lying on beds alongside the soldiers. Two of the girls came through to Altner's room, draped in a blanket. Throwing it dramatically aside, they stood stark naked for a moment, while everyone roared with laughter. Then the girls returned to their own room 'like sheepish poodles' and went back to the war.

—

Leni Riefenstahl was in Mayrhofen. She had arrived after a long drive to find the streets crowded with soldiers retreating from the Russians. Heading for the hotel where she had arranged to meet Hans Schneeberger, she had taken a room and fallen asleep at once, exhausted after her journey. She awoke later that evening to find Schneeberger's wife Gisela standing over her.

Gisela was half-Jewish, an attractive redhead who worked for Leni in the photo lab at the film studio. She had recently been in prison, facing almost certain death for complaining about Hitler on a railway train. She had been saved by Leni, who had used her influence with the Gestapo to get her out. Leni had put a lot of effort into it in the hope that doing something for a Jew might count in her favour when the day of reckoning came.

Gisela had been grateful at the time, but seemed less so now. There was a distinct chill in her voice as she contemplated Leni's luggage and asked, perhaps sarcastically, if that was all there was. Leni was puzzled.

> Amazed at her attitude, I was about to ask her what had happened, when suddenly there was uproar in the restaurant underneath us. Gisela ran downstairs and returned an instant later, did a dance of joy and shouted 'Hitler is dead – he's dead!' What we had been expecting for a long time had finally come, and I cannot describe what I felt at that moment. A chaos of emotions raged in me. I threw myself on the bed and wept all night.[14]

Emmy Göring was in bed too. Plagued with heart problems and sciatica, she had gone to bed early in the gloomy castle at Mauterndorf, while the SS kept guard outside. Still worried that his telegram of 23 April had been interpreted as disloyalty to the Führer, Hermann Göring had learned of Hitler's death from their doctor's radio. He went at once to tell Emmy.

> My husband came to my bed and said simply: 'Adolf Hitler is dead.' I immediately felt an indescribable relief. I thought I should make some reply but I could find absolutely nothing to say. After a fairly long pause, Hermann said: 'Now I'll never be able to justify myself to him, to tell him to his face that he's slandered me and that I've always been faithful to him!' He repeated these words several times.[15]

Göring was so upset that Emmy wondered if he was losing his mind. She knew he was on heavy medication, not thinking straight. Worried that the shock of Hitler's death might push him over the edge and cause him to do something rash, she decided to divert Göring's attention to her own problems.

> I suddenly cried: 'Hermann, I don't feel well! I've got a terrible pain in my heart!' It was obviously a rather childish device in the circumstances, but I had instinctively found the words that saved the situation.
> 'I'll go and get the doctor,' Göring said at once.

Willy Brandt was in Sweden, attending a May Day rally in Stockholm. He was walking to the platform to say a few words on behalf of the International Workers Council when a note was thrust into his hand, telling him that Hitler was dead. He was to announce it in his speech.

The news could hardly have been better timed. Brandt had been an enemy of the Nazis from the very beginning, from long before their rise to power. Born illegitimate under another name, he had been a left-wing activist since his teens, bitterly opposed to everything the Nazis stood for and actively involved in street fighting against their thugs. He had fled Germany in 1933, when Hitler became Chancellor, bribing a fisherman to take him to Denmark with a copy of Karl Marx's *Das Kapital* in his luggage.

From Denmark, Brandt had gone to Norway, applying later for citizenship, after the Nazis revoked his passport. He had been forced to flee again in 1940, when the country was occupied by the Wehrmacht. Brandt had spent the rest of the war in Stockholm, one of many like-minded Germans in the Swedish capital. They had formed a centre of opposition to Hitler, an essential link between the resistance movement in Germany and the outside world. Brandt and his friends had known about the gas chambers earlier than most and had been in close touch with the July 1944 conspirators, seeking to assassinate Hitler and bring the war to a quick end.

And now the man was dead at last, perhaps by his own hand. Brandt wasted no time letting his listeners know. He was puzzled by their muted response: 'When I announced it to the audience, a deep silence was the answer, no applause, no joyful shouts. It was as if the people simply couldn't believe that the end had actually come. And at the same time a question stood almost physically in the room: Hitler's dreadful challenge to all mankind – had it really ended in this way?'[16]

Only time would tell. But Hitler had certainly gone and wouldn't be coming back. Brandt knew he would be able to go home as soon as the war was over. Yet where was home now? It was Norway for the moment, the country of which he was happy to be a naturalised citizen. In the longer term, though, Germany was the country of his birth and the land he still loved, despite all the shame of the past twelve years. There was a future for him in Germany, now that the Nazis no longer held sway. A future for millions like him too, now that ordinary Germans were free to return to their towns and villages to pick up the pieces and begin rebuilding their lives and their country from the ground up.

PART FIVE:
WEDNESDAY, 2 MAY

'I could hear the din outside and running footsteps, but I was strangely quiet... How do you handle the end of a campaign? I wanted to cry. Was it really over? Thirty one thousand Allied troops had died – a city of the dead. Is a war ever really over?'

Spike Milligan

CHAPTER 21:
THE NEWS IS OUT

Winston Churchill was at dinner when he learned of Hitler's death. After returning to London from Chequers, he had gone to the House of Commons that afternoon for Prime Minister's question time. The House had been packed with members hoping to hear that the war was over, but Churchill had been unable to oblige them. 'I have no special statement to make about the war position in Europe,' he had apologised, 'except that it is definitely more satisfactory than it was this time five years ago!'[1]

Back at No. 10, he had held a series of afternoon meetings before hosting a late-night dinner party for senior Conservative colleagues. They were discussing tactics for the post-war general election when Jock Colville, Churchill's private secretary, burst in with the radio transcript from Hamburg. Learning that Hitler had died fighting Bolshevism, Churchill took the announcement literally.

'Well,' he told his guests, 'I must say I think he was perfectly right to die like that.'[2]

Lord Beaverbrook was more cynical, replying that Hitler 'obviously did not'. It was welcome news, all the same. The dinner party continued until three am, after which Churchill worked on his telegrams until four. Then he went to bed, leaving Colville to sit up a little longer with a red box full of important-looking papers that nobody had yet had time to read.

—

Harold Nicolson took his son to dinner at his London club after listening to Churchill at the Commons. He was disappointed that the war still hadn't ended, yet glad to know at least that Mussolini had been caught and killed. The first pictures of the Duce's body had just been released in London:

> We had really dreadful photographs of his corpse and that of his mistress hanging upside down and side by side. They looked like turkeys hanging outside a poulterer's: the slim legs of the mistress and the huge stomach of Mussolini could both be detected. It was a most unpleasant sight and caused a grave reaction in his favour...
>
> I dined at Pratt's. Lionel Berry was there (the son of Lord Kemsley) who told us that the German wireless had been putting out *Achtungs* about an *ernste wichtige Meldung*, and playing dirges in between. So we tried and failed to get the German wireless stations with the horrible little set which is all that Pratt's can produce. Having failed to do this, we asked Lionel to go upstairs to telephone to one of his numerous newspapers, and he came running down again (it was 10.40) to say that Hitler was dead and Dönitz had been appointed his successor. Then Ben and I returned to King's Bench Walk and listened to the German midnight news. It was all too true. '*Unser Führer, Adolf Hitler, ist...*' – and then a long digression about heroism and the ruins of Berlin – '... *gefallen.*' So that was Mussolini and Hitler within two days. Not a bad bag as bags go.[3]

BBC radio was quick to pick up the story. Music on the Home Service was interrupted at half past ten that evening with an urgent announcement by the news reader Stuart Hibberd. 'This is London calling. Here is a newsflash. The German radio has just announced that Hitler is dead. I repeat, the German radio has just announced that Hitler is dead.'

That was all. The BBC knew no more. Normal service resumed with Evening Prayers on the wireless while those who had still been up for the newsflash wondered if it was true as they prepared for bed. With her husband serving in Germany, Elsie Brown was one of many who hoped it was as she made herself a cup of tea in London's East End:

> I was still warming the pot when I heard the news that Hitler was dead. At first I didn't believe it, then I thought, well, it's on the BBC so it must be true. I didn't know what to do. I wanted to tell

someone, but both the kids were asleep and I didn't want to wake them, so I decided to run next door. My neighbour, Vi, worked the late shift on the buses and was always up till after midnight so I went round and banged on her door and when she opened it I shouted something like 'He's dead, the old bugger's dead!' And she said, 'What old bugger? Alfie?' Alfie was an old bloke who lived at the end of our road and really was a miserable old bugger, always shouting at the kids. So I said, 'No, not Alfie, Adolf!'[4]

In Fleet Street, the newspapers hastily remade their pages with Hitler's death on the front page and a long-prepared obituary inside. In Germany, the few remaining papers did the same, struggling to produce an issue edged in black in time for distribution next morning. Elsewhere, though, there was little immediate reaction to the announcement of Hitler's death. Staff at Field-Marshal Montgomery's new headquarters at Lüneberg Heath had already gone to bed when the word came over the radio at ten thirty. They were in bed too at Reims, where General Eisenhower had his headquarters. The announcement had come too late at night for most people in Europe, particularly in Germany, where millions were on the move or no longer had access to electricity. It wasn't until well into the following day that most of them realised that Hitler was dead at last and Admiral Dönitz was Germany's new Führer.

Captain Charles Wheeler of the Royal Marines was among those who didn't hear the news until the Wednesday morning. He had just reached a prison camp outside Hamburg when Hitler's death was announced on the radio:

> I could speak pretty good German and I asked the army officer in charge of the camp if anyone had told the prisoners. He said no and so I asked if I could. There must have been about a thousand German prisoners standing there behind barbed wire in the rain. It was what they called a cage – basically just a gathering place enclosed by a couple of strands of barbed wire where prisoners could be held until they were properly sorted out.
>
> I got up on the roof of a truck, shouted for silence and then I told them, in German, that the Führer was dead. I'll never forget their reaction. First there was a long silence, probably about four seconds, then someone in the crowd started to clap slowly and

rather uncertainly. Then someone else joined him, then more, and then the whole lot started clapping together and cheering wildly.

Wheeler was surprised at the Germans' reaction. After thinking about it, he concluded that the prisoners were probably applauding the end of the war and a chance to go home at last, rather than taking any pleasure in their Führer's death. 'At that time the German Army was terribly demoralised, very much in retreat and surrendering in large numbers. Nevertheless the reaction was quite surprising. I think those prisoners were basically looking forward to the war ending and getting home.'

———

A few miles away, Lieutenant Robert Runcie of the Scots Guards was in Lüneberg when he heard the news. As a troop commander in charge of three Churchill tanks, he was sitting in a traffic jam that morning, stuck in a hopeless snarl-up of military vehicles heading north through the streets of the ancient town. Runcie's battalion was part of a force ordered forward to the Baltic to capture Lübeck before the Russians and prevent them sweeping on to Denmark. The Scots Guards had crossed their start line promptly at two am, only to find themselves stuck in Lüneberg at eight. With nothing to do until the military police had got the traffic flowing again, they were sitting in their tanks with their engines idling, listening to the wireless while they waited for the road to clear.

It had been a manic few months for Runcie. As a young subaltern before the invasion, he had thought he was living dangerously when he visited London's Bag O' Nails club in the company of officers more worldly than himself who didn't share his fear of clap and thought nothing of picking up a prostitute for the night. The invasion had taught him the real meaning of living dangerously. Runcie had come of age as his battalion pushed through Normandy and Belgium into Germany. He had seen twelve British tanks destroyed in his first action, watching helplessly as friends of his were blown to bits or burned to death before anyone could help them. He had killed Germans in his turn, often very young ones, despatching them without a moment's hesitation as his troop advanced. It was only afterwards, when he had a chance to contemplate his handiwork close up, that Runcie had come to think about what he had done:

'A German standing up bravely with a bazooka, and you training your gun on him, and just blowing him to smithereens as you went through. That was the first kind of "this is for real" feeling… When I'd been very successful in knocking out a German tank, I went up to it and saw four young men dead. I felt a bit sick. Well, I *was* sick, actually.'[5]

Runcie had found himself behind German lines more than once, surrounded by Wehrmacht troops as startled to see him as he was to see them. He had always proved equal to the challenge. His men knew him affectionately as 'Killer'. He had been recommended for the Military Cross in March, after an action in Holland in which his tanks had knocked out several German guns. Runcie was still waiting to hear if it had been awarded.

But the news that morning was about Hitler. As they sat in their traffic jam, the Scots Guards learned of his death from the wireless in their turrets. They lost no time sharing the information with Lüneberg's inhabitants. Hatches opened and heads popped up all along the line as the Scots cheerfully shouted to every German in sight that their leader was no more. Unlike Charles Wheeler's prisoners, the Germans in Lüneberg didn't seem pleased to hear it. In fact, they seemed 'very glum'. Their gloom was the only bright spot in a very tedious day as the Scots Guards inched forward through the town and spent the rest of the day in one traffic jam after another on their way to the River Elbe first and then the Baltic beyond.

―――

To the west, Lord Carrington's battalion of the Grenadier Guards had come to a stop at Mulsum, a few miles short of Hamburg. After liberating a minor concentration camp at Sandbostel, the battalion had just been sent to Mulsum to regroup and await further orders before continuing the advance.

It had been a long haul from Normandy. The Grenadiers had matched the Scots Guards' progress all the way from the Channel coast, keeping tidily abreast of their sister regiment as they pushed through Belgium into Holland. Carrington's squadron had done particularly well during the battle for Arnhem, when its tanks had rolled across the River Waal at Nijmegen before the Germans had time to blow the bridge. They had later taken pot shots at a motorised column that had included Heinrich Himmler, as they afterwards discovered.

Now they were at Mulsum, just short of the River Elbe. The way ahead led to Hamburg, still in German hands and heavily defended. But with Hitler's death on the radio and no orders forthcoming, it was beginning to look as if their war might be over. Carrington, for one, would be 'extremely relieved' if it was.[6] He had fought as well as anyone during the past few months, but he shared the general lack of enthusiasm for any more fighting, now that survival was beginning to look possible. All the Grenadiers wanted to do was sleep for the next few days before saddling up and moving forward again.

———

In Hamburg itself, the Germans were in two minds about what to do as the news of Hitler's death spread. Some wanted to lay down their weapons at once and surrender to the British. Others wanted to fight on, defending the city street by street. Gauleiter Kaufmann had declared Hamburg an open city on 1 May, but he had acted on his own initiative, without consulting Admiral Dönitz or the Wehrmacht. Hitler's death had only added to the confusion as ordinary citizens hunkered down in the rubble and braced themselves for whatever was going to happen next.

Among them was Sybil Falkenberg, an Englishwoman recently divorced from her German husband. While everyone else viewed the British arrival with gloom, she was longing for her countrymen to appear, counting the hours until Hamburg fell. After the last five years of hell, the British couldn't come too soon for her.

As Sybil Bannister, she had married a German gynaecologist before the war, taking his nationality and bearing him a German son. They had been in Danzig when the war came, wondering if the bombs falling on them were German or Polish. Her husband had been drafted and Sybil had found herself alone, trying to look after a child with no friends or family to call on in a very unfriendly environment. Most Germans had been polite, but a fair number had been thoroughly unpleasant, spying on the Engländerin behind her back and reporting her every move to the police.

Her marriage had collapsed under the strain. Sybil had retained custody of her son, only to see him taken away by order of the Gestapo. She had been bombed out of her flat as the air raids intensified, suffering third degree burns from phosphorus dropped by her own side. Making her way to Hamburg, she had found a room to let and was living like a troglodyte as the British halted outside the city. With nothing to barter for food, she had been reduced to setting snares for the rabbits that wandered freely among the ruins. She was so malnourished that she had stopped menstruating.

Sybil had been delighted when Kaufmann announced that Hamburg would not be defended. 'Oh, thank God! We shall live to see the end of the fighting after all. No more suspense! No more air raids! Every night will be undisturbed! The Russians will not come. Occupation by the English won't be so bad. This awful war will soon be over!'[7] The news of Hitler's death had only added to her delight that morning, coming so soon after Kaufmann's announcement.

But Sybil's excitement was premature. The Wehrmacht wasn't happy with Kaufmann's decision. Neither was Dönitz when he learned of it that lunchtime. The decision to surrender Germany's largest port and second largest city was his to take, not Kaufmann's. Dönitz was furious that Kaufmann had acted without authority and taken matters into his own hands.

Albert Speer knew Kaufmann. At Dönitz's request, he drove to Hamburg that afternoon to talk to the Gauleiter personally. He found him at his headquarters, surrounded by a bodyguard of students. Kaufmann was just as angry as Dönitz, pointing out that he had had an ultimatum from the British, threatening to bomb Hamburg into oblivion if he didn't surrender without a fight. 'Am I supposed to follow the example of Bremen's Gauleiter?' he demanded bitterly. 'He issued a proclamation calling on everyone to defend themselves to the last man, then escaped himself while Bremen was blown to bits in a terrible raid.'[8]

Speer took the point. He rang Dönitz, explaining the situation. He told him that Hamburg's Gauleiter was prepared to mobilise the city's population against the defending troops, if necessary, rather than fight on and see the city destroyed. There would be mutiny in Hamburg if the troops were ordered to fight on.

Dönitz asked for time to think it over. An hour later, he rang back giving permission for Hamburg to be surrendered without further ado. He did so because the situation had changed dramatically since lunchtime. The British had just broken through on their way to the Baltic and were unstoppable as they advanced on Lübeck. The Canadians were equally unstoppable as they advanced on Wismar, a few hours ahead of the Russians. With the escape route for the Germans in the East cut off, there was no reason for the Germans in the West to fight on any more.

Instead, Dönitz gave orders for Hamburg's commandant to contact the British under flag of truce next morning, agreeing to give the city up without a fight. He was also to warn the British that a delegation would shortly be on its way from Dönitz to begin the negotiations for a general surrender.

CHAPTER 22:
THE NAZIS CONSIDER
THEIR POSITIONS

Kaufmann began the preparations at once. Surrendering to the British was the only sensible option. Taking Speer aside, he proposed that Speer should surrender as well, the two of them giving themselves up together.

But Speer wasn't ready to surrender yet. Nor was he ready to escape, as his pilot friend Werner Baumbach had suggested. Baumbach had a seaplane standing by, a four-engined machine used for flying supplies from Norway to the German weather station in Greenland. It had already been loaded with books, medicine, writing materials, extra fuel tanks and enough paper for Speer to begin work on his memoirs. With rifles, skis, tents, a folding boat and hand grenades for fishing, they could live quietly in one of Greenland's many bays for a few months, until the fuss had died down and it was safe to fly to England to give themselves up.

Speer was tempted, but said no. As a minister in the new government, his duty lay with Dönitz. Leaving Hamburg, he headed back to Plön. He arrived late that night to find that the admiral had moved headquarters in his absence to escape the British advance. He had gone north to the naval cadet school at Mürwik, near Flensburg, on the Danish border. Keitel and Jodl were preparing to join him. They just had time for a quick word with Speer before they too headed north. After a brief visit to his trailer at Lake Eutin, Albert Speer went that way as well.

⁓

Himmler was going too. Wherever Dönitz's government went, he was sure to follow. Wearing a crash helmet, he was driving his own Mercedes at the head of a motorised column carrying his personal retinue, which still amounted to 150 people. They were approaching Kiel in the last hours of daylight when the RAF found them.

'Discipline, gentlemen, discipline!' Himmler yelled, as panic set in.[1] The column came to an abrupt halt as staff of both sexes dived for cover. The mud was so thick that it sucked the women's shoes from their feet. Picking themselves up after the aircraft had gone, Himmler's people regrouped in some disarray and withdrew to find a less dangerous route to Flensburg.

The roads were so disrupted that it was early next morning before they arrived. Himmler immediately arranged for the women on his staff to be taken across the border to Denmark, where they could wash in safety and have something to eat before returning to his headquarters. As for himself, he had no idea what to do next. Count Schwerin von Krosigk, the new Foreign Minister, thought he should shave off his moustache, disguise himself in a wig and dark glasses, and vanish before the Allies caught up with him. Either that, or shoot himself. Himmler didn't want to do either.

—

Rudolf Höss too was on his way to Flensburg, trying to avoid the RAF as he headed north for a final meeting with Himmler. As the former commandant of Auschwitz, he was one of several camp commanders who had been summoned to Flensburg for a conference next morning to receive their last orders from the Reichsführer SS.

It was not an easy journey. Höss had his wife and children with him as he went. They had been sheltering in a farmhouse along the road when they learned of Hitler's death. Höss's immediate reaction had been the same as his wife's: to kill himself immediately, now that his world had collapsed. 'Was there any point in going on living? We would be pursued and persecuted wherever we went. We wanted to take poison. I had obtained some for my wife, lest she and the children fell alive into the hands of the Russians.'[2]

Höss had good reason to be nervous. As commandant of Auschwitz for three and a half years, he had presided over the establishment of the gas chambers and the slaughter of innocent people on an industrial scale. He had left Auschwitz in December 1943, only to return the following May when the Jews from Hungary began to arrive. It had been all hands to the pump with so many new bodies to process. They had got the murder rate up to almost 10,000 a day at one point, a figure viewed by Höss with considerable satisfaction. A Jewish mother had berated him for driving her children to the slaughter, but she had evidently failed to realise that the children had to be killed too, in case they came looking for revenge when they grew up.

Höss had few qualms about what he had done, but he knew the Allies would see it differently if they found him. He had been at Ravensbrück with his family as the Russians approached. They had escaped with several other families, leaving by night in a convoy of unlit vehicles, bumper to bumper along a road crowded with refugees. Under regular attack from the air, they had travelled for days from one clump of trees to the next, desperate to keep together as Spitfires and Typhoons roared overhead. They had glimpsed Field-Marshal Keitel at Wismar, arresting deserters from a front that he himself had never visited. From there, they had turned west towards Lübeck and then Flensburg to the north.

The Höss children's old governess from Auschwitz lived at St Michaelisdonn, near the mouth of the Elbe. With nowhere else to go, Höss left his wife and four of his children there while he continued towards Flensburg with only his eldest son for company. The boy wanted to stay with his father, both of them hoping that there might yet be a part for them to play in the final hours of the Reich. Höss still had his poison with him, but he was very reluctant to use it with the children to think about. He preferred to believe that Himmler would know what to do next, when he reported to Flensburg. Himmler surely wouldn't have summoned the commandants to Flensburg, if he didn't know what they should all do next.

—

Joachim von Ribbentrop was going the other way. He saw no point in following Dönitz to Flensburg, if he was no longer in the government. Annoyed to learn that Schwerin von Krosigk had been given his job, he had decided to go to Hamburg instead to make contact with the British. He still had a duty to Hitler to pass on his message urging the Western Allies to join forces with Germany against Bolshevism.

Ribbentrop knew Hamburg well. He had business connections there from before the war. There was a wine merchant from his champagne-selling days who would give him shelter for a while, enabling him to remain out of sight until tempers had cooled and it was safe to show his face again. While in hiding, he could compose a letter explaining Hitler's reasons for wanting an alliance against the Bolsheviks and then present it to the British at a time and place of his own choosing. As the bearer of the Führer's last message to the British, he would surely be treated with all the respect and consideration that he deserved. Ribbentrop certainly hoped so, because Hitler's last message to the British was the only card he had left to play.

——

In the forest above Schliersee, south of Munich, Hans Frank and his adjutant were watching the Americans advance on the little village of Neuhaus. The village was not defended, but the Americans didn't know that as they probed cautiously forward. None of them wanted to be killed this close to the end of the war. Their Sherman tanks were advancing with the hatches closed, ready for immediate action as they pushed aside a tank trap composed of tree trunks and approached Neuhaus from the south end of the lake. Frank watched with contempt from the mountain path above.

'Just look at those scared rabbits,' he told his adjutant. 'They're frightened they've finally got a whiff of our impregnable Alpine fortress.'[3]

Frank was ready for the Americans. As the Governor General of Poland, he was expecting to be arrested when they reached the village. He had destroyed all his files after fleeing Krakow in January and had since attempted to rewrite his later speeches and diaries to present his time there in a better light. But he knew the Americans would want to talk to him about his time in Poland. They would demand to know about Auschwitz, the starvation, the slave labour, the hangings in the streets, the summary executions of intellectuals, the humiliation and murder of Jews in synagogues, the wholesale looting of art and property, much of it to Frank's own benefit. He had been a most efficient governor, by Nazi standards. The Americans would certainly want to talk to him about that, when they took control of the village.

Frank had been lord of all he surveyed when he ruled the Poles from Krakow's glorious castle. His empire since then had shrunk to a few secretaries and personal followers who had stuck with him because they didn't know what else to do. There had been a bad moment recently when his valet of many years had told him to 'kiss my ass' before walking out, leaving Frank to press his own uniforms from now on. What remained of the Governor's Poland secretariat had all been accommodated in Neuhaus at the Café Bergfrieden, No. 12 Josefstalerstrasse, with plenty of room to spare. Frank had been living at the Haus Bergfrieden since 3 April, waiting for the Americans to put in an appearance.

He had assembled his staff there as soon as he learned of Hitler's death. While the women of the village prepared white flags for surrender, Frank had privately ordered his staff to swear allegiance to Dönitz, their new Führer. They had all done so, although for what purpose, none could tell.

There seemed little point in swearing allegiance to Dönitz when their only remaining option now was to sit in the Haus Bergfrieden and wait for the Americans to come. Hans Frank joined them there after he had finished watching the American tanks from the path above the village.

———

On the other side of the mountains, Adolf Eichmann was on his way to the Austrian lake resort of Altaussee. A number of top Nazis had moved to Altaussee in recent weeks because the approaches were easy to defend and the steep sides of the mountain valley made attack difficult from the air.

As head of the SS's Jewish office, Eichmann had been the operations manager for the Final Solution, responsible, by his own estimate, for the efficient elimination of five million Jews, although the figures that came to him may have been exaggerated to meet their quotas.* He had been particularly efficient in Hungary, rooting out the bulk of the Jewish population at breakneck speed after the Wehrmacht moved in, then sending them on to Auschwitz for further processing.

Eichmann had left Berlin in mid-April after spending several days destroying all his department's files before the Russians could find them. He had gone from there to Prague and other places on a fool's errand for Himmler to arrange for a few hundred prominent Jewish prisoners to be transported to the Alps and held hostage. The task had proved impossible in the chaos, so Ernst Kaltenbrunner, Himmler's deputy in the SS, had ordered Eichmann to Altaussee instead to await further instructions.

Eichmann reported in as soon as he arrived. He found Kaltenbrunner playing patience at his mistress's villa on the outskirts of the town. Like everyone else in Altaussee, Kaltenbrunner was not pleased to see him. No one in the town wanted to be associated with a leading Jew-killer, now that retribution was at hand. Kaltenbrunner intended to get rid of him without delay.

Sending for cognac, he told him first that Hitler was dead.

Eichmann was shocked. It was terrible news. He had known the situation was bad in Berlin, but not that bad.

---

* By the end of the war almost six million Jews had perished, approximately two-thirds of the entire Jewish population of Europe. Romani Gypsies, Soviet prisoners of war, homosexuals, Jehovah's Witnesses, disabled people as well as other religious and political opponents were also sent to the death camps increasing the total to an estimated eleven to sixteen million.

Kaltenbrunner didn't discuss it any further. He hadn't yet decided what to do with Eichmann, but he certainly didn't want him around Altaussee. He was toying with the idea of giving him some of the valuables looted from the Jews and sending him into the mountains with a few other potential war criminals to make sure that they were nowhere near Altaussee when the Allies arrived. He wanted nothing more to do with Eichmann, even though they had grown up together in Linz, Hitler's home town.

'It's all a lot of crap,' Kaltenbrunner was heard to mutter, as he sent Eichmann away to await further instructions. 'The game is up.'[4]

Kaltenbrunner himself was going to hide in the mountains when the time came. There was a cabin on the Wildensee where he could hole up for a few days until he knew which way the wind was blowing. He had abandoned his hopes of negotiating a separate peace for Austria with the Allies. Like many Nazis, however, he remained convinced that the Allies would still appreciate his services in the continuing struggle against the Soviets.

Failing that, he had had a set of false papers prepared, in case he needed to disappear in a hurry. It was Ernst Kaltenbrunner, head of the Reich Security Main Office, who would set off for the mountains when the Allies arrived, but it was Josef Unterwogen, a doctor in the Wehrmacht, who would reappear in due course, ready to pick up the threads of his life and resume his place in a post-war world.

———

At Mauterndorf, Hermann Göring was in talks with the SS, urging them to let him go now that Hitler was dead. The SS were agreeable, but still wouldn't do so without proper authority.

At Mayrhofen, Leni Riefenstahl had spent the day looking for Hans and Gisela Schneeberger, her hosts for the next two weeks. She was supposed to be staying with them at Hans's cousin's boarding house higher up the mountain, but there had been no sign of Gisela when she woke that morning, no message either. Gisela had left without saying a word.

Leni was in a dilemma. She couldn't stay where she was, because her room had already been taken and every other hotel in Mayrhofen was full. She couldn't drive back to Kitzbühel either, because she had no petrol for the car. She decided to go up the mountain instead to find the Schneebergers and ask them what had gone wrong.

It was late afternoon by the time she managed to hitch a ride on a hay wagon. Darkness was falling as she reached the Hotel Lamm and rang the bell. The door was opened by an old man who eyed her without enthusiasm.

'I'm Frau Riefenstahl,' she told him. 'Herr Schneeberger asked me to come here.'

The man looked her up and down. 'You're not entering my house,' he said.

'Aren't you Hans's cousin? I'm supposed to stay here for a couple of weeks.'

'Sorry. You're not entering my house. Hans apparently didn't realise I don't take Nazis.'

Pushing him aside, Leni stormed into the house, looking for Hans. She found him in the kitchen with his wife.

'You here?' Gisela was shocked. 'Are you mad? Did you really think you could stay here with us?'

Hans said nothing. As well as being a colleague of Leni's, he had lived with her as her lover for four happy years. 'Help me!' she cried.

Hans stayed silent. Gisela stood protectively in front of him, yelling at Leni. 'You thought we'd help you? Nazi slut!'[5]

Leni was out in the cold. She still had her luggage with her, but the wagon had disappeared and there was far too much to carry. Dumping it where it was, she turned away uncertainly and set off down the mountain in the dark, hoping to find a barn somewhere to shelter for the night.

—

Paula Hitler was in her room at the Dietrich Eckart Hütte, a boarding house in Berchtesgaden. She was spending most of the time in her room, eating her meals there rather than in the dining room with the other guests. They knew her only as Frau Wolff and had no idea that she was the Führer's slow-witted younger sister.

Paula had been in Berchtesgaden since mid-April. She had been at home in Austria, at her house on the Linz–Vienna road, when a car had appeared outside with orders to take her to Berchtesgaden. She had been given two hours to pack, although she hadn't actually left until the following day.

Paula had been most reluctant to leave at all. She was looking after the vegetable garden at home and knew it would be neglected without her. But the men who came for her had insisted that she had to go with them to Berchtesgaden. It was only when they were halfway there that one of them had told her that they hadn't expected her to agree.

Paula knew nobody in Berchtesgaden. She was the Führer's younger sister by seven years and they had never been close. Even as a youth, her big brother had had strong views about what to do with the feeble-minded. As Führer, he had arranged for her to have a small allowance on condition that she called herself Paula Wolff and never told anyone they were related. But he had taken no interest in her. Like Alois Hitler, their scapegrace half-brother, like everyone in the family, she had never been invited to the Berghof, never set foot in her brother's house on the mountain.

She had last seen Adolf in March 1941, when they had had a brief meeting at the Imperial Hotel in Vienna. There had been no contact since then, although Hitler had just remembered her in his will. Her nearest living relation, now that Adolf was dead, was probably her nephew, William Patrick Hitler, a seaman in the US Navy. British by birth, he had tried to join the Royal Navy first, only to be told that the British wouldn't have any Hitlers in their fleet.

Paula had been devastated to learn of Adolf's death. Whatever others might think, he was still her big brother, the only full sibling she had. He had been too big to spend much time with her as a child, but he had enjoyed playing cops and robbers with other little boys. Their mother had spoiled him rotten, perhaps because their father had beaten him so often.

Adolf should never have been Führer, in Paula's view. He should have been an architect instead. If he had been an architect, none of this would have happened and he would still be alive today. But he wasn't alive any more. He was dead, and nothing could bring him back. Like any sister whose brother had been killed in the war, Paula Hitler in her room at Berchtesgaden felt only 'unspeakable sorrow' as she learned of Hitler's death at the same time as millions of other Germans across the country.[6]

Far away in his Welsh asylum, Rudolf Hess had been as shocked as Paula to learn that Hitler was dead. The *Times* that morning had devoted a whole page to his obituary. Hess had been careful to show no emotion when he read the newspapers, but his minders could see that he had been deeply affected. He sought comfort from a favourite passage of his in *Natural Life*, a book by Konrad Günther: 'The work of great men does not attain its full effect until its creator has passed on – the present day cannot comprehend it… Can there exist any being more heroic than the one who follows an undeviating path in pursuit of a preordained mission, however entangled that path might become, even if it becomes a path to martyrdom?'[7]

Hess's behaviour had become increasingly erratic in the past few days, as the news from Germany turned from bad to worse. Getting dressed on 29 April, he had smashed his underpants against the wardrobe for a full minute before putting them on. He had laughed like a maniac at Himmler's peace offer and had sniggered uncontrollably at photographs in the paper of Germany's new leaders. He had developed a new habit, first observed by his minders at about the time of Hitler's death, of repeatedly dropping a small key onto his writing paper, a ritual that seemed important to him, although it served no discernible purpose.

He had a request to make of his captors. According to the newspapers, films had been made of the concentration camps captured by the Allies, dreadful films of German atrocities. Hess had already seen some of the pictures in the papers. He wanted to see the films as well, if it could be arranged. He told his guards that he would greatly appreciate it if they would allow him to have a viewing.

His request was refused. There were no special favours for Maindiff Court's most notorious inmate.

CHAPTER 23:
SURRENDER IN ITALY

In Italy, the German High Command was still divided over whether to accept the surrender terms agreed at Caserta. Some generals had already passed the word to their troops, ordering them to cease fire at two o'clock that afternoon. Others were refusing to comply, arguing that there could be no surrender while the war continued against the Russians. Hitler's death had released them from their binding oaths, but they still wouldn't budge without a direct order from Field-Marshal Kesselring, who was nominally in command of the Wehrmacht forces in Italy. But Kesselring was in the field somewhere and couldn't be contacted by phone.

The situation was so tense that the generals at Bolzano had begun to arrest each other as they disagreed vehemently about what to do. General Karl Wolff of the SS had been in secret negotiations with the Allies for weeks and was determined to honour the agreement signed at Caserta. Sitting in Wehrmacht headquarters at about half past one that morning, he feared the worst as orders came for surrender-minded officers to be arrested at once. Sneaking out of the tunnel complex with a couple of other generals, Wolff hurried back to SS headquarters in the Duke of Pistoia's palace. There he learned that the Wehrmacht was about to surround the building with a tank unit.

Wolff had tanks of his own, which he quickly deployed around his command post. SS troops took up defensive positions while Wolff sent an urgent message to Field-Marshal Alexander, pleading for help from Allied paratroopers. The SS were crouching over their weapons, waiting for the Wehrmacht to attack, when the telephone rang. It was Field-Marshal Kesselring for Wolff.

Kesselring had just learned that the proposed surrender was going ahead without his authorisation. He rang at two am and over a bad line blasted Wolff for the next two hours, calling him every name under the sun as he lambasted him for his treachery in talking secretly to the Allies. Other officers joined in, discussing the situation over the phone and swearing at each other as they argued about what to do next. Wolff stood his ground, pointing out that surrender was not only inevitable but the best option still open to them, since there was nothing to be gained from fighting on. Unusually for an SS officer, he saw no point in fighting to the last man. He told Kesselring so quite bluntly:

> It is not only a military capitulation in order to avoid further destruction and shedding of blood. A ceasefire now will give the Anglo-Americans the potential to stop the Russian advance into the west, to counter the threat of Tito's forces to the port of Trieste and of a Communist uprising that will try to establish a Soviet republic in northern Italy… Since the Führer's death has released you from your oath of loyalty, I beg you as the most senior commander of the entire Alpine region devoutly and with the greatest sense of obedience to give your retroactive sanction to our independent action which our consciences impelled us to take.'[1]

Kesselring wasn't convinced, but could see Wolff's point. Ringing off at four am, he promised to think it over and get back to him. Half an hour later, another officer rang to say that Kesselring had reluctantly agreed to the surrender and was withdrawing the directive for various officers to be arrested.

Headquarters at Bolzano wasted no more time. The order to surrender went immediately to all the remaining units that hadn't already received it. The radio messages were sent *en clair*, since the Germans no longer had any need to disguise their intentions from the Allies. At two o'clock that afternoon, as agreed, German forces in Italy ceased all hostilities against the Allies. In the Italian theatre at least, the war was over.

—

Wolff was quite right about Trieste. The Allies were already on their way, aiming to take control of the port from the German garrison before Tito's Communists could seize it for Yugoslavia.

The charge was led by the New Zealanders. They left Monfalcone at eight thirty that morning, intending to complete the remaining seventeen miles to Trieste without delay. But the ceasefire did not come into effect until two that afternoon, and anyway did not apply east of the River Isonzo, where the Germans retained the right to defend themselves against partisans. There were still isolated pockets of resistance along the road as individual German units continued to put up a fight.

It wasn't until two thirty in the afternoon that the Kiwis reached Miramare, a peninsula with a white castle, across the bay from Trieste. The Germans defending it with 88mm guns and machine gun nests in pillboxes were quickly brushed aside. The New Zealanders' Sherman tanks pressed on to Trieste and were in the middle of the city by three pm, exchanging greetings with Tito's men, who had arrived earlier from the other direction.

But the fighting was far from over. Various strongpoints in the city were still in German hands, fiercely defended by troops determined to hang on until the Allies appeared, so that they could surrender to them rather than the Yugoslavs. The ancient castle was under siege as the New Zealanders arrived, the German garrison taking pot shots at the partisans and regular Yugoslav troops surrounding them. The Germans fired at the New Zealanders too, until they realised who they were. Then, to the irritation of the Yugoslavs, they opened the gate and allowed a company of Kiwis in to take their surrender.

The Yugoslavs were quick to retaliate. They continued to snipe from the rooftops, shooting at the New Zealanders in the castle as well as the Germans. The German commander offered to help with the defence if his men could have their weapons back, but was rebuffed. As night fell, the New Zealand defenders and their German prisoners pooled their rations and sat down to a meal together, sharing their food inside the castle while sentries kept a careful watch on the Yugoslavs outside.

At the Law Courts, the SS commander flatly refused to surrender to anyone. A New Zealand officer went forward under a white flag, but the SS man appeared too drunk for a rational discussion. The New Zealanders therefore joined forces with the Yugoslavs, using their tanks to blast holes in the walls of the building while Yugoslav infantry poured through. The fighting continued long into the night. It wasn't until next morning that the garrison finally agreed to lay down their weapons.

Elsewhere, only the Villa Opicina and a stretch of land along the northern edge of Trieste remained under German control by nightfall on 2 May. The rest of the city was occupied by a variety of different forces: New Zealanders, Tito Communists, Chetnik royalists, Slovenian home guards, Serb collaborators and the Italian nationals – some Fascist, some not – who formed the majority of the city's population. Many were armed to the teeth and ready to defend themselves if necessary. The New Zealanders had been cheered by the Italians as they raced towards Trieste, but there had been cheers for Tito too, signs along the road claiming the land for Yugoslavia. The Yugoslavs themselves were bitterly divided between royalists and Communists, united only in their desire to inflict atrocities on the Germans. The New Zealanders established their headquarters that night in Trieste's grandest hotel, but it was still anybody's city as sporadic shooting continued and Tito's Yugoslavs began the sinister business of rounding up and disarming anyone who didn't share their particular view of Trieste's future.

—

At Caserta, the staff at Allied headquarters spent the first part of the day wondering if the surrender was actually going to happen or not. Field-Marshal Alexander had set a deadline the previous night for a response from Wehrmacht HQ, allowing both sides time to give the necessary orders for a ceasefire. But with the Germans bickering among themselves and Field-Marshal Kesselring impossible to locate, the night had come and gone without any answer from Bolzano. It wasn't until later that morning, when the Allies learned that General von Vietinghoff had been restored to his command, that a surrender began to seem possible. It was confirmed at noon when Wolff sent Alexander a message from Kesselring promising that the surrender would go ahead at two that afternoon, as agreed.

Nevertheless, Alexander waited until late afternoon before going public with the news. The Germans had asked for it to remain secret for another twenty four hours, but the orders for a ceasefire had already gone out *en clair*. Alexander was adamant that the timetable agreed at Caserta must be adhered to. He was under pressure from Harold Macmillan, his political adviser, to confirm the surrender in time for Winston Churchill to announce it in Parliament that day. He didn't want to do so unless he was quite sure the surrender was actually happening.

It wasn't until five pm, therefore, with good reports from the front and the surrender going ahead as planned, that he and Macmillan felt able to make the announcement. They released the news at six thirty. An hour later Churchill stood up to give the details to a cheering House of Commons. The war in Italy really was over.

—

For 2nd Lieutenant Robert Dole of the US Army's 10th Mountain Division, it had been over for some time. Dole was in hospital at Pistoia, near Florence, when the surrender was announced. He heard the cheers from the GIs in the wards as the word came through, but was too badly injured to take much notice. He was so far gone that his doctors were expecting him to die within the next few days.

Dole's war had come to an abrupt end on 14 April, just over two weeks earlier. As a replacement platoon commander, he had only been with the 85th Regiment since February. They had been fighting in the Apennine mountains, south west of Bologna, when the order had come to capture Hill 913 as part of a drive towards the Po Valley. Dole's company had experienced heavy mortar fire as they advanced. One officer had been killed by a mine, another by a sniper. Dole himself had been hit by shell splinters, his shoulder ripped apart and his spinal column badly damaged. He had lain where he fell for six hours until the battle had moved on and the medics were able to come to his rescue.

It had been a further three hours before Dole reached the hospital. He had lost so much blood that the doctors had to wait until the next day to operate. Cutting him open from neck to shoulder, they had cleaned up his wounds, removing numerous bone fragments and doing what they could to stem the internal bleeding. Then they had stitched him up and sent him back to the base hospital at Pistoia, paralysed from the neck down.

The damage to Dole's spine was severe. The surgeons at Pistoia had opened him up again to see if anything was pressing against the spinal column, but had found nothing amiss. Dole was just paralysed, no feeling in his arms and legs, unable to do anything for himself, a prey to all sorts of infections if his body couldn't function properly. From a medical point of view, he was almost certainly a goner.

But he was also young and strong, with a burning desire to live. Bob Dole wasn't finished yet. Once the sedatives wore off, he had begun to feel pain again after several days, acute pain throbbing intensely throughout his body. He had welcomed every agonising moment of it, because if he could feel pain he couldn't be paralysed. His body was sending him a message and Bob Dole was responding. While the rest of the hospital cheered for the end of the war, he had noticed some feeling return to his legs and had already managed to wiggle his toes a little. The doctors still thought he was a goner, but where there was life, there was hope. Bob Dole was going to live to prove them all wrong.

—

Just outside Caserta, Lance-Bombardier Spike Milligan of the Royal Artillery was at Maddaloni when the surrender was announced. Like Bob Dole, he had been wounded by a mortar bomb during the Allied advance and had been taken out of the line to recover.

Temporarily unfit for active service, he had been working as a wine waiter in the mess at Portici before transferring to Maddaloni, an outpost of the Caserta GHQ, as a clerk/driver to the officers.

Milligan's war had begun in 1940 when he had sat in a Martello tower on the Sussex coast, listening to the sounds of Dunkirk across the Channel and wondering how he and the only other occupant of the tower were supposed to stop the Germans with a single rifle between the two of them. Sent to Algiers in 1943 to support the US landings, he had fought through the Western Desert before landing at Salerno in September. The fighting in Italy had been intense, taking an increasing toll on his mental health as the war progressed. By Milligan's reckoning, the longer he survived without a scratch, the greater the price to pay when his number came up, as it surely would, sooner or later.

Milligan had been hit in January 1944. The wound had been minimal, a two-inch gash to his right leg, so slight that he hadn't even noticed it at first. But the damage to his mind had been far worse. Diagnosed with battle fatigue, he had been examined by a psychiatrist who clearly thought him a malingerer and sent him back to his unit without delay. The first thing he had seen on his return was the graves of some comrades killed in a direct hit on their battery. The next time he heard gunfire, Milligan ran straight to his dugout and hid there, stammering with fear.

Reduced to the ranks, still stammering, he had been sent back to hospital with manic depression. At one point he had slashed his face with a razor to gain attention. After a long period of rehabilitation, he had been promoted to Lance-Bombardier again and had found his way eventually to Maddaloni, where he played trumpet in the dance band in his spare time.

Milligan had also begun to regain his sense of humour as time healed his mental wounds. Learning that the German Army in Italy was on its last legs, he had just written a sketch for the camp review in which Göbbels tried to explain to Hitler that the Wehrmacht was running out of legs. But humour was only a mask for the pain. In between recurring bouts of depression, Milligan had been horrified to learn of Mussolini's treatment after his death: 'Someone is worse off than me. Mussolini has been murdered; he and his mistress are hanging upside down in a garage in Milan. It was a barbaric act that puts the clock back. However, the natives seem happy. Nothing like an assassination to cheer the masses.'[2]

And now the war was over, in Italy at least. Milligan had been saving a bottle of Dom Perignon 1935 for the occasion, stolen from the officers' mess in Portici. The church bells were ringing in Maddaloni and Italians in the square were singing 'Finito, Benito, finito' as they celebrated the Duce's departure. Spike Milligan joined them for a while, but somehow couldn't share their enthusiasm as he contemplated an uncertain future now that the fighting was finished:

> I walked back through the milling streets, lay on my bed and lit up a Capstan. I could hear the din outside and running footsteps, but I was strangely quiet. Suddenly a complete change of direction. How do you handle the end of a campaign? I wanted to cry. Was it really over? Thirty one thousand Allied troops had died – a city of the dead. Is a war ever really over?[3]

—

In Milan, there was jubilation on the streets as the surrender was announced, but mayhem too as old scores continued to be settled. The Americans were tightening their grip, but Mussolini's followers were still being hunted down across the city. German troops were being hunted too. A few were still in hiding or refusing to surrender. Most were already in American hands, desperately hoping that their captors would continue to protect them from the mob.

For Herbert von Karajan, there was bitter irony in the situation as he remained indoors, too scared to show his face until the hunt for Fascists had subsided. A long time member of the Austrian Nazi party, he had fled to Italy at the beginning of the year to get away from the chaos in Berlin. The bombing of the capital's concert halls had been bad enough, but Karajan had also fallen foul of the Nazi leadership after marrying Anna Gütermann in 1942. Her Jewish grandfather had not commended her to the Nazis, although Josef Göbbels was said to have taken a fancy to her. Karajan's brilliance as a conductor had seen him through the war years, but he and his wife had decided to flee as the Russians approached. They had persuaded a friend to invite them to Milan for a series of radio concerts, using the invitation as a pretext to obtain exit visas from Germany more valuable than gold.

They had lived in a Milan hotel for the first few weeks, before joining friends in Como. Back in Milan on business, Karajan and his wife had found themselves trapped as the war ended, unable to go anywhere for fear of being attacked as Germans. According to Karajan, the lawyer they had been to see was keeping them hidden in his own home until it was safe to go out again. He had warned them that they risked being shot on sight if they ventured out before it was safe.

The present was bad enough, but the future looked even worse to Karajan. Other conductors had been careful to keep their distance from the Nazis during the war, but he had been closely associated with the party from the first. It was even said that he had joined the SS Security Service to avoid being drafted – a claim he always denied. Like everyone else, Karajan insisted he had only been a Nazi for professional reasons, but he feared retribution when prominent party members were hauled before the courts after the war. He would probably be blacklisted from conducting, perhaps banned from ever working again.

The only consolation was that Karajan's chief rival Wilhelm Furtwängler would probably be blacklisted too. Furtwängler had been even closer to the Nazis: the funeral march from the *Götterdämmerung*, broadcast on the radio at Hitler's death, had been conducted by him. But Furtwängler too had fallen foul of the regime. Suspected of complicity in the July 1944 bomb plot against Hitler, he had fled to Switzerland in February, urgently seeking asylum as a refugee from the Nazis. The Swiss had refused him sanctuary, but were allowing him temporary residence while he recovered from concussion after a fall. While Karajan laid low in Milan, Wilhelm Furtwängler was in a nursing home on Lake Geneva as the war ended. He was deeply unpopular with the local Swiss because of his Nazi past, yet terrified also that German agents were on their way to kill him as an enemy of the Reich.

———

Rachele Mussolini was on the road to Milan. Worn out with weeping for her dead husband, she was being taken back to the city where his bruised and battered body had been strung up for the amusement of the mob. She and her two children had been collected from Como at four thirty that afternoon and were being driven to Milan in an Alfa Romeo. They had no idea where they were going and were too frightened to ask what would happen to them when they arrived.

They reached Milan at six and were escorted to a building near the Castello Sforzesco, where they were to spend the night. Romano and Anna Maria were still in deep shock after the horrors of the past few days, distraught at the murder of their father and the mutilation of his body.

Rachele was desperately afraid that the same thing was about to happen to them, but took some comfort from the friendliness of their American guards. The men were so kind, so respectful towards her, that they seemed almost apologetic, hardly likely to throw her children to the mob. Italians were being kind too, perhaps appalled at the manner of her husband's death.

Mussolini himself was in the morgue, awaiting burial. He had always wanted to be buried in the family plot at Predappio, his home town, but the authorities had decided otherwise. Along with the other Fascist leaders from the garage, he was to be buried next day in Milan's municipal cemetery at Musocco. They were all going to be buried together, side by side in the same grave.

The grave was to be left unmarked, so that the bodies couldn't be dug up and desecrated. The bad news for Rachele, the news she really didn't want to hear, was that Clara Petacci was going to be buried beside Mussolini, lying next to him in death as she had in life. Rachele may have been the mother of Mussolini's children, the woman he claimed to have always loved, but it was the glamorous Clara, with her high heels and her makeup, who was going to be with him in death. Rachele's only consolation was that she was still alive and still had the children. She kept them very close as they were taken to their accommodation in Milan and settled down under American guard to a miserable night's sleep.

CHAPTER 24:
BERLIN FALLS

In Berlin, it was all over. The city had surrendered. There was still fighting in the suburbs, but the defenders in the centre were laying down their weapons and emerging sullenly from the rubble. Germany's capital had fallen and the Red flag flew undisputed all over the city.

The process had begun just before six that morning, when three German civilians from the Ministry of Propaganda presented themselves at Marshal Chuikov's headquarters and told him Göbbels was dead. They brought a letter from Hans Fritsche, the Ministry's deputy director. With a voice that sounded like Göbbels's, Fritsche had originally made his name as a radio announcer and still had a following across Germany. As 'the last responsible representative of the government',[1] he presented his compliments in writing to Chuikov and formally requested him to take the city of Berlin under his protection. He also offered to make an announcement on the radio, urging Germans everywhere to stop fighting and surrender.

The civilians were followed by General Weidling, commander of the Berlin garrison, who reached Russian headquarters just as they were leaving. The Germans were evidently speaking with different voices. Sensing chaos at the Chancellery, Chuikov asked Weidling why Krebs hadn't come instead and was told that he had probably committed suicide. Weidling himself was in a highly nervous state, breaking down uncontrollably at one point while the Russians pretended not to notice. He hadn't heard of Dönitz's broadcast on the radio and was surprised to learn that Hitler's death was public knowledge. He couldn't guarantee a general surrender either, because he had lost contact with some of his forces and had no control over the SS.

Chuikov told him not to worry about it. At his instigation, Weidling sat down and drafted an order for all German troops in Berlin to stop fighting at once. The order was typed up by Weidling's staffer, Major Knappe. Keeping the original for himself, Chuikov sent Knappe off with a Russian officer to tour the streets in a jeep, announcing the news to the troops and showing carbon copies of the surrender to senior commanders.

They went first to Russian divisional headquarters, where a German-speaking Russian tackled Knappe about Auschwitz. Knappe had no idea what he was talking about. He claimed not to have heard of Belsen, Treblinka or Buchenwald either. 'Don't pretend you don't understand!' yelled the Russian, storming angrily out of the room.[2]

There was still fighting at the Anhalter station when they arrived. From a group of German prisoners, Knappe selected a pair of sergeants to return to their own side under a white flag, risking SS fire to deliver Weidling's order to the German commanders. The same procedure was followed at several different places. Then Knappe and the Russian captain returned to Chuikov's headquarters for a celebratory lunch. They had champagne and caviar, tarts, meat, cheese, every conceivable kind of gourmet food. Knappe was well fuelled by the time he was sent to the rear to join a column of German prisoners. He had hardly arrived when a Russian guard tried to steal his boots.

—

The big prize was the Chancellery. Officially, it was captured after a fierce fight by Marshal Zhukov's troops, who stormed the building soon after three that afternoon. Major Anna Nikulina of the 9th Infantry Corps then had the honour of raising the Red banner on the roof.

Unofficially, the Chancellery had almost certainly been abandoned long before. There were still 300 wounded Germans in a makeshift hospital in the basement, but they were in no position to put up a fight. Russian troops from Koniev's division, ignoring orders to allow Zhukov's men in first, appear to have reached the building early that morning. Annoyed that their own advance had been halted to let Zhukov have all the glory, they had pushed ahead without permission to find that nothing stood between them and the open doors of the Chancellery.

Whatever the real story, it was certainly true that Hitler's bunker had been abandoned. The only person still there when the Russians arrived was Johannes Hentschel, a civilian mechanic, who had stayed behind to look after the generator that ventilated the building and pumped water to the wounded troops. His friend Rochus Misch had left at about ten to four that morning, joining one of the last groups to break out from the Chancellery. They had exchanged letters for their wives beforehand, in the hope that one at least would get through. After Misch's departure, Hentschel had been left all alone in the bunker, wishing that he could have gone too, yet knowing that the wounded soldiers in the hospital depended on him to keep them supplied with water until the Russians came.

The bunker was no place to be alone. Several of the occupants had committed suicide rather than join the breakout. Generals Krebs and Burgdorf had shot themselves after a mammoth drinking session. Others had followed suit. By Hentschel's calculation, there were at least nine bodies lying around unburied, either in the bunker itself or just outside the entrance. He wasn't sure of the exact number because some of the bodies lay behind closed doors, which he certainly wasn't going to open.

Terrified that some lunatic might have left a time bomb somewhere, primed to go off as the Russians appeared, Hentschel had made a thorough search for explosives as the bunker was evacuated. He had also checked the bunker's electric wiring with his volt metre. He had found nothing amiss, but he still wasn't happy being the only one to stay behind. The place seemed like a crypt to him, after everyone else had gone. A charnel house.

About five am, unable to stand it any longer, he went upstairs for a few minutes to get a breath of air. Stepping out into the Chancellery garden, he saw that dawn was just coming up over the ruins of Berlin:

> The garden looked like some cemetery where the gravediggers had gone on strike. There were eight or nine bodies sprawled about in awkward, ghoulish poses, heads off, bellies torn open, here and there stray arms and legs.
>
> When I strolled over towards the gazebo, I spotted both Göbbels bodies, still side by side. They weren't burned, only roasted. Göbbels's face was deep purple, like a mummy's. Frau Göbbels's face had been horribly consumed by fire. Her dress was only charred. Captain Schwägermann had not done a very efficient job of cremation.[3]

Back in the bunker, Hentschel switched the radio on and listened to the BBC news in German. It was not good. Dönitz had announced the Führer's death, 'fighting valiantly in front of his troops', if the admiral was to be believed. The United Nations were meeting in San Francisco and the

Americans had advanced well beyond Munich. Hentschel thought he heard something about the Red flag flying over the Reichstag, but after more than sixty hours without sleep couldn't remember for sure.

There was nothing to do now except wait for the Russians to come. He occupied the time by checking his machinery again, making his rounds of the bunker to ensure that everything was working as it should. He was terrified of what would happen when the Russians did arrive. They might throw grenades down the stairs or blast the place with a flamethrower. If they used high explosive, his lungs might be ripped apart by the air pressure. Whatever they did, his chances of survival did not look good.

By Hentschel's account, it was just after nine that morning when he heard the first Russian voices. They were female, a lot of chattering and giggling coming from the tunnel that led to the Chancellery. Bracing himself, he put his hands up as a group of about twelve uniformed women appeared. They seemed to be doctors, or trainee medics, carrying satchels and duffel bags. The senior one spoke German in a fluent Berlin accent.

After asking what Hentschel was doing there, they inquired about Hitler. He explained what had happened and was then questioned about Hitler's woman. Her clothes, her glad rags. Where were they?

Sensing the purpose of the duffel bags, Hentschel led them to Eva Hitler's room. She had always loved clothes, changing her outfit five times a day in the bunker in an attempt to cheer everyone up. According to bunker gossip, she had a lot of exotic underwear and frilly stuff that was hard to come by in wartime. The women went to work, pulling open the drawers and stuffing everything they found into their bags.

They took lamps as well, helmets, bottles, photographs, SS dress daggers, carpets, crystal, Hitler's monogrammed silver, an accordion, a table cloth and a copy of *Mein Kampf*. They were hard at it when two Russian officers emerged from the tunnel. Some of the women broke off what they were doing and brushed guiltily past them, hurrying back towards the Chancellery with their loot. The rest continued rummaging while the two officers confronted Hentschel and put a pistol to his head.

In fractured German, spoken with a Yiddish accent, the senior officer demanded to know where Hitler's body was. Hentschel had not seen it burned and couldn't say for sure. He showed them Göbbels's children instead, lying in pairs on bunks that folded down from the wall. They had evidently not been removed, as Traudl Junge had thought, but were covered in white sheets, only their bare legs visible. The Russians took one look and quickly closed the door again.

More Russians arrived, about twenty young officers in battle dress. They had liberated the bunker's champagne and were knocking the tops off with their bayonets. Cheerfully offering some to Hentschel, they began to sing a drinking song and danced around him as if he was King of the May.

Unused to champagne, Hentschel was soon squatting dizzily on the floor while the Russians poured another bottle over his head. He was delivered eventually to the military police, who stole his rucksack and wrist watch before taking him away. They were passing the emergency exit to the bunker when it suddenly opened and the remaining Russian women burst into the garden, 'whooping like Indian squaws in a Western movie. Above their heads, one in each hand, they were gaily waving at least a dozen brassieres, all black satin trimmed with lace.'[4]

Exhausted, Hentschel fell asleep in the garden for a few minutes while waiting for other prisoners to be collected. At about midday, they were all herded together and marched out of the Chancellery towards a waiting truck. It was the first time in almost a fortnight that Hentschel had left the building. He never forgot the sight that met them on the Vossstrasse:

> Dangling bodies of some six or seven German soldiers were suspended from lamp posts. They had been hanged. Each had a crude German placard pinned or tied to his limp body – *traitor, deserter, coward, enemy of the people.*
>
> They were all so young. The oldest may have been twenty, the others in their mid-teens. Half of them wore Volkssturm armbands or Hitlerjugend uniforms.
>
> As we were shoved into our truck, prodded in the buttocks by bayonets, I saw that I could almost reach out and touch one of those lifeless boys. He looked about sixteen. His wild, bulging, porcelain blue eyeballs stared down at me, blankly, unblinking. I shuddered, looked away. I was ashamed in front of those Russian soldiers, peasant boys. Their stoic, stern silence was reproof enough.[5]

While Hentschel was taken away, the first of several Russian search teams was hurrying towards the Chancellery to begin the hunt for Hitler's body. The Russians were not convinced that he had been cremated, or even that he was dead at all. *Pravda* had voiced its doubts in an article that morning. But if he was dead, the gold star of a Hero of the Soviet Union had been promised to whoever found the body. Ignoring the protests of the soldiers, the search team from SMERSH (Death to Spies) sealed the garden and bunker to all unauthorised personnel and went to work to unearth the corpse.

It was a thankless task. There were body parts all over the place, most of them impossible to identify. There was a danger too that the Germans might have left booby-traps behind, as Hentschel had feared, bombs primed to explode hours or even days after their departure. The SMERSH team waited while their engineers checked the bunker and declared it safe. Then they rolled up their sleeves and began the painstaking business of picking through the rubble in search of something – anything – that would show beyond dispute what had happened to the Führer.

Göbbels was easy enough to identify. With an orthopaedic boot and a calliper on one leg, he had already been pointed out by Hentschel. Next to him, Magda Göbbels may still have been wearing the golden Nazi party badge given to her by Hitler. Krebs and Burgdorf could be identified from the contents of their pockets. But of Hitler himself there was no sign, no evidence that his body had ever been taken out and burned, as the few Germans they had found so far kept insisting.

Marshal Zhukov visited the Chancellery later, coming to view the scene for himself. He was not allowed down into the bunker, ostensibly because it still hadn't been cleared, but perhaps also because Stalin's agents had orders to report their findings only to their master. Instead, Zhukov spoke to some wounded prisoners who were adamant that they knew nothing about Hitler or the Nazi leadership, didn't know anybody more senior than their company commander. Zhukov was inclined to believe them, since they were only rank and file soldiers, nothing to do with the hierarchy.

> We began to look for the bonfires on which Hitler and Göbbels were supposed to have been burned, but couldn't find them. We did see the ashes of some fires, but they were obviously too small. German soldiers had probably been boiling water on them.
>
> After a while, when we had almost finished inspecting the Chancellery, it was reported to me that the bodies of Göbbels's six children had been found in an underground room. I have to confess that I didn't have the heart to go down and look at the children ruthlessly killed by their mother and father.[6]

The search continued after Zhukov had gone. Several more corpses were discovered in a water tank and fished out. One of them bore a faint resemblance to Hitler. There was talk of murdered body doubles, perhaps even a corpse made up after death to look like the Führer. But there were no obvious answers, no quick solution to the mystery. With an NKVD team of security police on its way to join the investigation, the immediate priority was to interrogate all the bunker survivors in depth and then go through the garden again, sifting methodically through the earth to analyse every scrap of cloth and bone fragment for clues as to how the Führer met his end. It would take time, several days, but there was no alternative with Stalin pressing for an answer and the whole world demanding to know exactly what had happened to Adolf Hitler.

—

At the Reichstag, Russian graffiti was already beginning to appear on the walls as the troops scratched their names into the brickwork and listed all the battles they had fought in before Berlin. Soldiers were cooking in the ruined hall, warming themselves on indoor bonfires and opening cans of condensed milk with their bayonets. Others outside were firing guns and rockets into the air, singing and dancing as they celebrated victory. Some were drunk on industrial alcohol that they had looted, not realising that it would kill them within a couple of days.

A few SS were still holding out in a building nearby, but nobody paid much attention as artillery reduced it to rubble. On the roof of the Reichstag, the raising of the Red banner was being re-enacted for the cameras. Several photographers had attempted to recreate the scene. The most successful was Lieutenant Yevgeny Khaldei, a Jewish cameraman in the Soviet Navy, who had seen his father and three of his four sisters murdered by the Germans.

Khaldei had brought a Red flag with him, a home-made effort sewn together from three table cloths. Shoving it into the hands of a young soldier, he persuaded him to pose on the roof, waving the flag aloft while two others hung on to him to stop him falling. Khaldei snapped furiously as the soldier clambered out past the statues on the edge of the roof, wobbling precariously over a sheer drop. Khaldei used a whole roll of film, composing his pictures carefully to include the Brandenburg Gate in the middle distance and the government area beyond, with the Chancellery and Hitler's bunker.

The shots weren't perfect. One of the supporting soldiers had two wrist watches on the same arm, clear evidence of looting and a poor advertisement for the Soviet Army. The flag didn't look right either. But the problems could all be sorted out later, in the dark room. Scratch out one of the watches with a needle, add another flag and some smoke in the distance to create atmosphere, and Khaldei would have the picture his country wanted. Packing his camera after he had finished, he went straight to the airfield and was on the plane back to Moscow that same night.

———

While the Russians celebrated at the Reichstag, Traudl Junge was hiding in the cellar of a brewery on the Schönhauserallee, three miles to the north east. After a terrifying night, many of the people from the bunker had managed to rendezvous there, seeking safety in numbers as they waited for the Russians to come. Beer was flowing and complete strangers were enjoying group sex on the top floor, but for Traudl's party there was only fear and exhaustion as they lay in the cellar and wondered what would happen when the Russians did arrive.

There had been an ugly incident during the night when a naked woman had leapt from a rooftop, falling five or six storeys to certain death to avoid the Russians coming after her. Traudl had stayed close to Gerda Christian and Konstanze Manziarly as they crept through the streets. Together with Else Krüger, Martin Bormann's secretary, they were all hoping the same wouldn't happen to them when their turn came to meet the enemy.

General Mohnke had just announced Hitler's death to those who didn't already know. Many of the civilian women in the brewery had burst into tears when they heard that he had fallen in battle. Others had turned on the soldiers, cursing them for cowards who should be fighting to the last man like the Führer instead of allowing women to be raped. But Mohnke had quietly released the men from their oath to Hitler, now that he was dead. Abandoning any hope of reaching German lines, he had also sent a Wehrmacht colonel to find the Russians and negotiate a peaceful surrender.

Mohnke still hoped to get a message through to Dönitz, reporting on the situation in Berlin. His eye fell on Traudl and the other women. 'You must help us now,' he told them. 'We're all in uniform, none of us will get out of here. But you can try to get through, make your way to Dönitz and give him this last report.'[7]

Traudl wasn't at all keen, but was persuaded by the other women, who kept badgering her until at last she agreed to accompany them. Escorted by a Luftwaffe sergeant who came from Berlin, they took Mohnke's report and emerged reluctantly from the brewery:

We leave our steel helmets and pistols there. We take our military jackets off too. Then we shake hands with the men and go.

An SS company is standing by its vehicles in the brewery yard, stony-faced and motionless, waiting for the order for the last attack. The Volkssturm, the Organisation Todt men and the soldiers are throwing their weapons down in a heap and going out to the Russians. At the far end of the yard Russian soldiers are already handing out schnapps and cigarettes to German soldiers, telling them to surrender, celebrating fraternisation. We pass through them as if we were invisible. Then we are outside the encircling ring, among wild hordes of Russian victors, and at last I can weep.

Where were we to turn? If I'd never seen dead people before, I saw them now everywhere. No one was taking any notice of them. A little sporadic firing was still going on. Sometimes the Russians set buildings on fire and searched for soldiers in hiding. We were threatened on every corner.[8]

They managed to stay together until nightfall. Konstanze Manziarly was still wearing her Wehrmacht jacket, but decided that civilian clothing would be less conspicuous. She went off to find something suitable while Gerda and Else looked around for a place to hide for the night. They all lost contact after that. The last Traudl saw of Konstanze Manziarly, she had reappeared in the company of two Russian soldiers, who were leading her down towards the entrance of a U-Bahn tunnel.

'They want to see my papers,' she yelled over her shoulder, as she disappeared into the gloom.[9]

She was never seen again.

—

While Traudl emerged nervously from the brewery, Martin Bormann lay dead and unrecognised near the Lehrter railway station, across the river from the Reichstag. He had Hitler's last will and testament with him, unless he had lost it during the night.

Bormann had been with the third group to break out from the bunker. The plan had been for him to slip through the Russian lines and then fly north with the pilot Hans Baur to deliver the will to Dönitz. Following the first two groups, they had set off along the U-Bahn tunnel from the Kaiserhof station, but had taken a wrong turn somewhere and got lost. Surfacing at Stadtmitte, they had headed along the street instead, aiming for the Weidendammer bridge across the river. The tank trap that had prevented Traudl's group from crossing had just been blown to pieces by Tiger tanks from the SS. Baur and Bormann lost touch as they hurried across, but linked up again on Friedrichstrasse, where Baur found Bormann on the steps of a bombed-out house with a dead Russian sprawled in front of him.

The way north was blocked by the enemy, so they turned west instead, heading past the Reichstag towards the Lehrter station. According to Baur, they had taken shelter in a ruined tenement when they spotted twenty Russians in the back yard. With only an hour left to daybreak, they made a hurried exit, keeping the river to their left as they continued towards the station.

Snipers soon spotted them. Baur lost sight of Bormann again as they dived for cover behind the railway embankment. He was next seen by Artur Axmann, the Reich youth leader who had lost an arm on the Russian front. Axmann's group joined forces with Bormann and Dr Stumpfegger and crept forward with them along the bridge towards the station:

> Several of us jumped down from the bridge and found, to our dismay, that there was a whole Russian infantry platoon camped underneath. They promptly surrounded us. But to our joy and amazement they simply kept announcing in a boisterous chorus: '*Hitler kaputt, Krieg aus!*'
>
> They then chatted very pleasantly to us in broken German. They all seemed fascinated by my artificial arm. I kept showing it to them as if it was the latest product from some Nuremberg toy factory. Then they graciously offered us *papirosi* – cigarettes with paper tips. Apparently they thought we were simple Volkssturm men returning from a long, hard evening at the front.
>
> What spoiled this little fraternisation was a psychologically inept move by the drunken Bormann and Dr Stumpfegger. They began to edge away and finally ran off. This put the Russians on their guard, but Weltzin and I were able to shuffle off as casually as possible without being noticed.[10]

Continuing on their way, Axmann and his aide Günther Weltzin ran into more Russians, prompting them to retrace their steps and try a different route. They had reached a bridge over the railway lines leading to the Lehrter station when:

We now came across the bodies of Martin Bormann and Dr Stumpfegger, lying very close together. I leaned over and could see the moonlight playing on their faces. There was no visible evidence that they had been shot or hit by shellfire. At first, they looked as if they were unconscious or asleep. But they weren't breathing. I assumed then, and I am sure today, that both men had taken poison. Weltzin and I didn't hang around to take their pulses. We were in danger ourselves, hardly interested in the historical significance.[11]

Axmann was right about the poison. Accidentally unearthed near the Lehrter in 1972, Bormann's skull was found to have glass splinters from a cyanide capsule embedded in its teeth. Tested later, his DNA matched too.

—

Hildegard Knef was in Spandau, the suburb north west of Berlin. From the window of an apartment block, she and Ewald von Demandowsky were watching the old town burn across the river. After walking all night, both were exhausted as they ate the last of their rations and waited for the order to break through the Russian lines.

The aim was to get through somehow and then head across country to find the Americans. They would much rather surrender to the Western Allies than the Russians. The soldiers around Hildegard had managed to convince themselves that the Americans would never leave Berlin to the Russians. They must surely be out there somewhere, coming to save the city.

The breakout was made by tanks, fifty men with each vehicle. Hildegard and Demandowsky went with the second, sticking close but not too close as they followed it over the bridge into Spandau. They had barely crossed the river when the tank blew up, hit by Russian fire. Hildegard was hit too, whisked through the air by the force of the explosion, then smashing her head against something hard.

Her clothes were ripped and blood was trickling from her hairline as she and Demandowsky picked themselves up and ran for cover. They took shelter in a ruined shop, hunkering down as Russian flamethrowers gushed past the windows. They could hear Russian voices outside and the urgent sound of Russian boots and machine guns. There were mortars too, and dead bodies everywhere. But there were also ploughed fields not far away and darkness was fast approaching. If they could just hang on for a bit longer, stick it out until nightfall, they might still manage to get through and make their escape.

———

Helmut Altner was in Spandau too. His unit had left Ruhleben at dawn to link up with Wenck's army at Potsdam. They had joined a long column heading west: men, women, children, guns, tanks, horse-drawn artillery, farm carts, prams piled high with possessions, staff cars carrying suitcases and expensive mistresses in fur coats. Altner had struggled to keep in touch with the rest of his company as they all crowded along the road together.

The town hall was in flames when they reached Spandau. Ammunition was exploding from a burning tank and machine guns were chattering ahead. They were also under fire from low flying aircraft. When mortars opened up as well, Altner and the others ran for cover in a ditch. An SS officer ordered them out at gunpoint, but was ignored. They weren't obeying orders any more.

Pressing on when the firing had eased, they pushed through Spandau and turned south towards Staaken and then west again towards Döberitz. Their lieutenant had told them that Wenck's army was waiting for them beyond Döberitz. He had promised that they would be given several weeks' rest when they arrived, in huts that Wenck's army had already set up for them. Dönitz would come to see them, their new Führer, to brief them about the next phase of the war.

Altner hitched a ride for part of the way, clinging to the wing of a truck for the wounded and refusing to let go. They were driving along a country road, in full view of the Russians, when a vehicle ahead got stuck on a bend and the traffic came to a halt:

> Suddenly shells explode close to the road and a truck in front of us bursts into flames. The passengers jump off and run into the field with their clothes on fire. Another truck is hit and torn bodies with their limbs ripped off are hurled into the air and fall around, blood spurting everywhere. The car in front of us can't move because a mangled corpse is stuck between its wheels. Then the explosions start all around us, slamming into the tangle of vehicles that have run into each other, throwing bits of metal and bodies around.
>
> The next shell could hit our truck, so I jump off the wing and go over to the right, where a trench runs under the fence

into the field. Suddenly something hits me, knocking me down.
I look at it with horror. It is a bloody something without either
head, hands or feet, just a bloody, smashed torso.[12]

Drenched in blood, almost crippled by a shell splinter in his right foot,
Altner stumbled on for hours, hobbling across country until he reached
Döberitz. There was no sign of Wenck's army when he arrived, no sign
either of the huts the lieutenant had promised. No one had even heard of
Wenck in Döberitz. Potsdam had been Russian for days. All the talk of a
relief army for Berlin, all the talk of hanging on by their fingertips until help
arrived to deliver them from the Red menace, all of that had all been a lie
from the very beginning.

CHAPTER 25: NOW THAT THE FÜHRER HAS GONE

While Martin Bormann lay dead in Berlin, his eldest son was in a village near Salzburg, wondering if he too should kill himself now that Hitler was dead. Martin Bormann junior was only fifteen, innocent of any crime, but he could see no future for himself with the Führer gone and his father probably dead as well. The people around him were taking their own lives. He was trying to pluck up the courage to do the same.

Bormann junior had been a pupil at Feldafing, the school near Munich for the sons of the Nazi elite, until its closure on 23 April. The other boys had been given 100 Reichsmarks each and told to make their own way home, but Bormann had been issued with false papers in the name of Martin Bergmann and driven to Salzburg. His father's staff from Berchtesgaden had regrouped there after the bombing of Hitler's mountain retreat.

They were in the Gaststube at the village inn when they learned of Hitler's death. It was two o'clock in the morning, as Bormann recalled. The room was small and they were packed tightly together on the benches when the announcement came over the radio. Like everyone else, Bormann sat stunned, unwilling to believe that his godfather was dead:

> I can't describe the stillness of that instant, which seemed to last for hours. Nobody said anything, but very soon afterwards people began to go outside, first one – then there was a shot. Then another, and yet another. Not a word inside, no other sound except those shots from outside, but one felt that that was all there was, that all of us would have to die.[1]

Bormann didn't want to die. At fifteen, his whole life lay in front of him. But his family had been very close to Hitler. They had had a special edition of *Mein Kampf* printed on human skin, until his mother had got rid of it. If his father's staff were killing themselves, he saw little option but to do the same.

A gun was put into his hands. Reluctantly, desperately wishing that there was an alternative, Bormann accepted the inevitable. Getting to his feet after a long period of introspection, he took the weapon and went outside to shoot himself.

> My world was shattered. I couldn't see any future at all. But then, out there, in the back of that inn, where bodies were already lying all over the small garden, there was another boy, older than I – he was eighteen. He was sitting on a log and told me to come and sit with him. The air smelled good, the birds sang, and we talked ourselves out of it. If we hadn't had each other at that moment, both of us would have gone – I know it.[2]

———

In Marienbad, far to the north, Private Günter Grass of the Waffen-SS accepted Hitler's passing with far more equanimity. Lying wounded in a hospital bed, he wasn't in the least surprised to be told that Hitler had fallen in Berlin. Something of the sort had long been inevitable, nothing to get upset about. At the very least, they could all joke about him now, and that had to be good for something.

Grass was seventeen, old enough to be a tank gunner in the SS but not old enough to have participated in the atrocities on the Eastern Front. There had been no mention of atrocities during his training. Drafted into the SS at sixteen, he had been happy to join an elite unit in the fight against Bolshevism. It was only later, after being advised to ditch his SS markings for his own safety, that he had had to admit to himself what kind of unit he was in.

On his way to the front he had passed through the ruins of Dresden, seeing what might have been dead bodies lying in charred bundles beside the track. The first bodies he had seen for sure had been Wehrmacht soldiers, old men and young boys hanging from trees with placards of cowardice around their necks. He had wet himself when he first came under fire, urinating uncontrollably as Stalin's organs, the Katyusha rockets, whistled overhead. Picking himself up afterwards, he had turned to see the tangled intestines of the young man he had just been talking to.

Later, caught in another fire fight behind Russian lines, Grass had played dead as the rest of his patrol scattered in the darkness. He had retreated with a Wehrmacht lance corporal, only for both to be arrested as deserters since they had no written orders to explain their absence from their units. Locked in a farmhouse to await summary court martial, they had taken advantage of a Russian attack to make their escape, joining a column of refugees along the road to Spremberg.

The corporal had advised Grass to change his SS jacket for a Wehrmacht one from a dead man. Bribing a sergeant to give them official marching orders, they had continued on their way, only to come under fire again from Russian tanks. Grass had been hit in the right thigh and left shoulder. The corporal had been hit in both legs. On the way to the dressing station, he had asked Grass to check his balls for him to make sure they were still okay.

It was all good material for the novel Grass was hoping to write one day. The corporal's legs had been amputated while Grass had been evacuated to a rear hospital in Marienbad. Strafed en route by an American fighter-bomber, he had just managed to roll into a ditch before his truck went up in flames. He had eventually reached Marienbad days later, unconscious, on the back of a military policeman's motor bike.

Grass was glad to be in hospital. The bed was freshly made and the nurses were solicitous as they bandaged his thigh and probed the splinter in his shoulder. Their light touch meant much more to him than the announcement of Hitler's death in faraway Berlin. It was May outside and the lilacs were in bloom. The war was almost over and Grass was out of it for good. Like millions of German soldiers, he couldn't get too upset about the death of Adolf Hitler if it meant an end to all the fighting.

In Odette Sansom's camp, the prisoners had tried to escape that morning, making a concerted rush for the gates in full view of the guards. The SS had opened up at once, raking the compound with machine gun fire. Odette had watched in horror as the prisoners crumpled and fell, pathetic bundles of blue and white lying dead or dying while the SS looked on without concern.

As soon as it was over, Odette went to complain to the commandant. As Frau Churchill, she demanded to see Fritz Sühren. The radio was playing while they fetched him. Quietly eavesdropping, Odette learned that Berlin had fallen and the British were in Lübeck. The German Army in Italy had surrendered. It was no surprise that Sühren was in tears when he appeared.

'Why don't you open the gates of the camp?' Odette demanded. 'The war's over. It's useless murder to keep people here.'

'They'd die on the roads.'

'Better to die on the roads than be killed here.'

But Sühren wasn't interested in the prisoners. 'Adolf Hitler is dead,' he told Odette despondently. 'He died a hero in the forefront of battle.'

'Really?' Odette managed to suppress her grief. 'Are you going to do the same, die a hero?'

'Go back to your hut. I haven't finished with you yet.'

'Will you open the gates? I've never asked a favour of you in my life. I do now. For God's sake!'

'No. The war isn't over.'[3]

Odette returned to her hut. There was no food. Towards evening, those prisoners who still had the strength formed a working party to make a pile of the bodies in the compound. After dark, they made bonfires of doors and bed boards from the huts and danced hysterically around them, half-mad with fear and loathing as they waited to be set free. The gates were still shut, and the SS were still there with machine guns, but their release couldn't be much longer now.

—

At Mauthausen, near Linz, the prisoners were only a day or two away from freedom as Patton's army swept into Austria. They too were counting the hours, because they badly needed the Americans to come. Malnutrition had reduced the camp to cannibalism when an Allied bomb had killed some of them by mistake.

Mauthausen was a work camp attached to a stone quarry. The prisoners hewed rock all day for the rebuilding of German cities. By order of Himmler, every block they hewed had to weigh at least 110 pounds, which was heavier than most of them. They then had to carry it above their heads up 186 steps to the surface of the quarry. Prisoners lacking the strength were routinely thrown over the cliff for the amusement of the guards. They called it 'parachute jumping' as they watched the prisoners tumble to their deaths.

Peter van Pels, the Jewish teenager arrested with Anne Frank, may have been in Mauthausen, if the records claiming that he had reached the camp from Auschwitz were correct. Simon Wiesenthal was certainly there, lying sick in Block VI as the news of Hitler's death circulated. Block VI was the death block, where prisoners were left to expire when they were no longer able to work.

Son of an Austrian officer killed in World War One, Wiesenthal had been an architect in Poland until the Red Army invasion of 1939. He had escaped a Russian pogrom only to be arrested later by the Germans. An SS man had installed a Polish prostitute in his apartment, while Wiesenthal had been sent to a labour camp to paint swastika-and-eagle shields on captured Russian locomotives.

He had been well treated by some of the German guards, closet anti-Nazis who bore Jews no ill will. Others had been less humane. According to Wiesenthal, he had narrowly escaped death in 1943 when a group of drunken SS had decided to shoot a few Jews to celebrate Hitler's birthday. Wiesenthal had been stark naked, waiting to be executed, when a friendly German had insisted that he was needed to finish painting the signs for the birthday celebrations.

Later, as the casualties at the front mounted, the SS had become much more solicitous towards their Jewish prisoners, keeping them all alive in the hope of avoiding active service by having someone to guard. It had been six SS guards to every prisoner at one point. Then normal service had resumed as Wiesenthal arrived at Mauthausen. Dropping out of the four-mile march from the station, he had been shot at by an SS man as he lay helpless in the snow. It was only next morning, when the prisoners were carrying his body to the crematorium, that someone had noticed that he was still alive.

Wiesenthal was a story-teller, prone to exaggerate his escapades. Yet his sufferings had been real enough as he lay in Block VI, waiting for the Americans to come. A friendly prisoner had supplied him with pencils and paper and he was whiling away the time by making sketches of the Nazi leaders – using his skills as an architectural draughtsman to produce grim caricatures of a monster Himmler and a death's head Hitler behind a mask.

He had also made a sketch of Franz Ziereis, Mauthausen's commandant. Ziereis was a cold-blooded murderer who had once given his son a birthday present of fifty Jews for target practice. Wiesenthal had captured his features perfectly on paper: a useful guide for the Allies, if Ziereis tried to disappear in the next few hours, rather than wait to be hanged for his crimes. The Allies would know exactly what he looked like as they hunted for him after the war – and thousands of other Nazis too, if Simon Wiesenthal had anything to do with it.

In Unterbernbach, it had been snowing as Victor Klemperer set off for Kühbach to see his first American soldiers. He was cold and ragged as he walked, but he had a full stomach for the first time in months, because the Germans in the village had just slaughtered all their pigs rather than let the Americans have them. Klemperer was feeling well fed and happy as he went forward to search for provisions and meet his liberators.

The shops were closed when he reached Kühbach, but the village was full of American troops. The first ones he saw were black, the crew of a vehicle recovery team, making friends with the village children in the square. Slipping down a side street, Klemperer approached a young blonde woman and asked why the shops were shut. She replied that the Americans had looted everything when they arrived, but had otherwise been well-behaved.

'The blacks too?'

'They're even friendlier than the others,' the woman beamed. 'There's nothing to be afraid of.'

Back in the square, Klemperer asked two old ladies the same question and received the same answer:

> Exactly the same beam of delight because the negroes were the especially good-natured enemies. (I thought of all the black children's nurses, policemen and chauffeurs in our life.) And what had been said about the cruelty of these enemies – that had all been nothing but slogans, that was only rabble-rousing. How the populace is being enlightened![4]

There was a woman in the back streets who could sell Klemperer a loaf of bread for ninety pfennigs. He went that way with a spring in his step.

———

At Brünnlitz, in the Czech Sudetenland, the Jews of Oskar Schindler's metalworking factory had learned of Hitler's death from radios that their employer had illegally installed in the offices of key personnel. He had also arranged for one of his car radios to be permanently under repair, so that the repairman could plug his earpiece into the BBC and pass the news on to prisoners in another part of the camp.

Schindler's Jewish workers had been at Brünnlitz since leaving Krakow to escape the Russians. There were more than 1,000 in all, including wives, children and some with physical handicaps. He had saved them from almost certain death by placing their names on an official list, insisting to the Nazis that they were all skilled workers, essential for the war effort. He had also spent a fortune in bribes, using all the profits from the factory and what was left of his own money to grease the right palms and make sure that none of the Jews under his protection were harmed.

He had been afraid, nevertheless, that the SS would massacre the lot as the war came to an end. Josef Leipold, the SS commandant, was perfectly capable of giving the order. To forestall him, Schindler had filed an official complaint against Leipold in mid-April, protesting that he wanted to kill 'sophisticated technicians engaged in the manufacture of secret weapons'. By some accounts, he had then plied Leipold with alcohol before getting him to sign an order for the liquidation of the Jews that was actually a request to be sent to the front. Whatever the truth, Leipold had been transferred to a front line unit soon afterwards. Schindler had driven him there just as Hitler died.

The rest of Leipold's troops had gone with him, to be replaced by older, meeker men who looked to Schindler for orders. Now that Hitler was dead, they were very keen for the Jews to know that they had only recently been drafted into the SS for guard duty and had no intention of harming anyone.

The Jews remained sceptical. They were ready to defend themselves if they had to. With Schindler's help, they had been stockpiling weapons for weeks: rifles, machine guns, a few pistols and hand grenades. The weapons were hidden under bales of wire and other innocent-looking places around the camp. They were available at a moment's notice, if need be.

Schindler himself was preparing to flee the camp before the Russians came. A Czech-born German and paid-up Nazi, he could expect short shrift from the Czechs and Russians when they took over. He was very reluctant to abandon his Jewish workers at such a critical time, but they were adamant that he must for his own safety.

Unknown to Schindler, they were also making a farewell gift to present to him before he left. Gold teeth had been sacrificed to produce a small ring in the metalworking shop. The ring was to be a present from them all, engraved with a saying from the Talmud. It put into words what every Jew in the camp felt about Oskar Schindler:

'Whoever saves one life saves the world entire.'

———

Schindler's Jews had been lucky to escape from Krakow. Most of the city's Jewish population had been rounded up and liquidated during the German occupation. The survivors had only recently begun to trickle back, emerging from their hiding places after the Germans' departure in January. There were precious few of them. The Jewish quarter seemed like a ghost town as they wandered the cobbled streets, desperately searching for a face they knew.

Eleven-year-old Roman Polanski had been one of the lucky ones. He didn't look Jewish, for one thing, passing himself off as an ordinary Polish boy, so long as no one saw that he was circumcised. Son of a metalworker, he had sometimes slipped out of the ghetto in the early days, removing his Star of David and roaming the streets without his parents' knowledge. He had once seen a German officer shoot a Jewish woman simply because she was too old to keep up with the others.

His own mother had followed, taken away one day while Polanski was out and never seen again. The rest of the ghetto had been liquidated in March 1943. Polanski had managed to escape through a hole in the barbed wire, trailing after his father as the Germans marched him away. He had then been looked after by Poles, who had sent him into the country to stay with a peasant family so poor that they had no electricity and had never seen a motor car.

Back in Krakow as the Germans withdrew, Polanski had seen German prisoners beaten and spat on, and had watched Poles defecating on German corpses. He had lived on the streets with other little boys, picking up the discarded weapons of war – signal flares and explosives – and making fireworks out of them. One gang of boys had killed themselves blowing up a supply of cordite. Polanski had nearly done the same with a German grenade.

He had also looted some toys from a deserted garret, trading them for a magic lantern that could project picture postcards onto the wall. The lantern was a simple epidiascope, a cardboard box with a lens and a bulb holder, but it meant the world to Polanski. He loved the idea of projecting images onto a wall. It was a way of forgetting the horrors all around him.

He was living with his uncle when the news came of Hitler's death. They had just bumped into each other on the street, neither aware that the other was still alive. After years of a feral, school-free existence, the illiterate boy was living in a real apartment again, on the sixth floor of a block overlooking the town.

He was also hoping to be reunited with his parents now that Hitler was gone. People were beginning to return from the camps, flinging their arms around each other as they arrived in prison garb at the railway station. Polanski had often been to the station to see if his own parents might come, but they never had. Instead, he had had to watch bitterly as the lucky few celebrated while he remained out in the cold.

But at least he had his magic lantern. As long as he could make pictures and project them on the wall, Polanski could forget about everything else. The pictures on the wall were all that really mattered to him, now that the war was over.

———

While Polanski grieved and the rest of Krakow celebrated Hitler's death, Karol Wojtyla was quietly rebuilding the life he had had before the war. He had been nineteen on the first day of the war, saying his prayers in the cathedral as the Luftwaffe roared overhead to attack the city. The Jagellonian University had been shut down as soon as Krakow had fallen. Many of its staff had been sent to concentration camps, but Wojtyla had continued his studies regardless, attending clandestine classes throughout the German occupation.

He had worked in a quarry for much of the war, blasting rocks with dynamite by day, continuing his studies by night. Every stick of explosive had had to be scrupulously accounted for, on pain of death if even a few ounces found their way to the Resistance. Wojtyla had been arrested in a café once, pulled in by the Gestapo in a mass roundup of suspects. Most of the arrested men had been sent to Auschwitz, where twenty five had soon been shot. Wojtyla had escaped because he had an Ausweiss identifying him as a vital worker. The card had been given to him by his employer, a friendly Pole who used Ausweisses to protect intellectuals and members of the Resistance from Nazi persecution.

Wojtyla had helped others in turn, hiding Jews from the Germans, arranging new identities for them, providing them with baptism certificates to show that they were Christian. His mentor, Archbishop Sapieha, had made repeated pleas to the Pope on behalf of Poland's Jews, but there had been no meaningful response from the Vatican. Wojtyla wondered what kind of Pope they had in Rome who had sat back and done nothing while the Jews suffered all over Europe. It wasn't Christian charity as he understood the term.

He had been hiding in the Archbishop's palace when the Germans left Krakow, sheltering in the cellar from Russian artillery fire. Tiles had been shattered and all the windows blown out, but the palace had survived. Wojtyla and his colleagues had prayed and sung hymns as they waited for the Russians to come. The first ones had arrived late at night, to be greeted with bread and tea, which was all the Poles had to offer.

That had been in January, but there was still plenty to do before life returned to normal. Wojtyla and a few others had volunteered to restore the theological seminary after the Germans' departure. The building had been occupied by the SS and then almost destroyed by a nearby explosion. Every window pane had been smashed, every roof tile blown off. The lavatories had been piled high with frozen excrement which had to be chopped into smaller pieces before it could be taken away. Wojtyla had flung himself into the work, breathing only through his mouth to avoid retching. The stink had been horrendous.

But the seminary was restored now and the Germans were gone and Hitler was dead. Wojtyla had just found a proper job as well, one that might have been tailor-made for him. He had been appointed assistant theology lecturer at the university. Another few months and he would be ordained a Roman Catholic priest, free to devote the rest of his life to the mother church. His cup could hardly have been fuller.

—

The French politician Pierre Laval was in Spain. He had just flown in after a frantic search for a country prepared to admit him. As a Vichy Frenchman, formerly head of the government and arch-collaborator with the Germans, he was persona non grata all over Europe. Nobody wanted to give him shelter, if it meant offending the victorious Allies.

The Vichy government had been transported to Germany in September 1944, but had been left to its own devices as the Allies approached. Marshal Pétain had decided to return to France to face trial for treason, but Laval knew he would be executed if he went back. Determined to escape to a neutral country, he had approached Switzerland and Liechtenstein first, only to be refused permission for a stay of anything longer than twenty four hours. He had tried to cross the Swiss frontier every day for a week, only to be turned back every time. Bursting into tears, he had complained to unsympathetic Swiss officials that they were condemning him to death.

The Spanish didn't want him either. A colonel was waiting at Barcelona airfield as Laval's Junkers 88 touched down. The colonel told him bluntly that Spain was not prepared to give him asylum. He suggested that Laval should take another plane immediately, either to Portugal, where a day of mourning had just been announced for Hitler's death, or to southern Ireland, which had not signed the international convention on war crimes and therefore would not extradite him.

Laval was a collaborator, but he did not see himself as a war criminal. He tried to go over the colonel's head by telephoning Spain's Foreign Minister, formerly the Ambassador to the Vichy government, to plead his case. But the minister declined to come to the phone. It could not have been clearer that Laval had no friends in Spain.

He had none in Portugal or Ireland either. When he refused to leave for either country, the colonel told him that he had orders to intern him instead, while the Spanish government decided what to do with him. Without further ado, Laval and his wife were taken by car to the citadel of Monjuich, high above the port, where accommodation had quietly been prepared for them in the newly built officers' mess.

—

While Laval drove to Monjuich, Irish Prime Minister Eamon de Valera was on his way to Dun Laoghaire to see the German Ambassador. He was going to offer his condolences on the death of Adolf Hitler.

The German embassy was in Ballsbridge, a smart Dublin suburb, but de Valera was visiting the Ambassador in his private home. The Germans still had no official confirmation of Hitler's death beyond what they had heard on the radio, but the embassy swastika was flying at half-mast and people from Ireland's tiny German community had been calling all day to pay their respects. De Valera may have decided to avoid the embassy to escape the unwelcome publicity that might have come with it.

The Ambassador was at home when de Valera arrived. Eduard Hempel was an old-style Prussian officer who had been in the post since 1937. The Irish had stipulated that the German minister in Dublin should not be a Nazi, so he had waited until after his arrival before quietly joining the party. He had had an active war, making contact with the IRA and sending thousands of reports back to Berlin by radio or telegraph. He had transmitted weather forecasts for the Luftwaffe and had recorded the effects of their bombing raids on Britain. It was said that his reporting of Canadian troop movements along the south coast had doomed the Dieppe raid of 1942 to failure. The Americans had become so incensed at his activities that they had persuaded the Irish government to seize the embassy's radio transmitter in 1943.

Hempel was visibly distressed as de Valera's car drew up, wringing his hands and complaining repeatedly that it was all so humiliating. Whether he was referring to Germany's defeat or de Valera's visit was not clear. Hempel's wife insisted later that he hadn't been wringing his hands, merely chafing at the eczema between his fingers. But he was not a happy man as he received the Irish Prime Minister in his own home on the occasion of Adolf Hitler's death.

They didn't discuss Hitler for long. The conversation soon turned to other matters: the safety of the Hempels' relations in Germany and the question of asylum for himself and his family. Hempel was hoping to remain in Dublin after the war, rather than return to Germany. He was afraid, though, that anti-German feeling might make his life difficult if he tried to set up in business. If all else failed, his wife was prepared to sell home-made cakes and buns to make ends meet.

De Valera was surprised to find Hempel so abject. He knew the man well and thought he was made of sterner stuff. But Germany's collapse had unmanned him. Without the Nazis behind him, Hempel was just a middle-aged official wondering how to survive with his salary cut off and no other visible means of support. His career as a diplomat was over.

De Valera himself was riding into a storm, although he had yet to realise the full extent of it. He had taken advice before offering his condolences on Hitler's death. Some people had agreed with him that it was the correct protocol for a neutral Prime Minister, implying no approval of Hitler or his regime. Others had begged him not to go, arguing that the visit would be misconstrued, that he would be seen as a Nazi-lover bringing great shame on Ireland if he did anything so stupid. Bloody-minded as ever, de Valera had decided to go ahead.

The Irish were not pleased, as the implications sank in. They had remained studiously neutral during the war to avoid occupation by either Britain or Germany, but there had never been any doubt whose side they were on. They had seen the pictures from the camps. They had flocked to Britain in tens of thousands to fight for the Allies. They didn't want their Prime Minister commiserating with the Nazis now that Hitler was dead. As the news of de Valera's visit went out over the wires that night, the rest of the free world shared their outrage. De Valera had scored a spectacular own goal, one that was to haunt him for the rest of his life.

—

Yet de Valera's visit was only a sideshow. With Hitler dead and Berlin in Russian hands, the real story that night was that the war in Europe was all but over. Even as de Valera was being driven back to Dublin, the Germans had accepted the inevitable and were preparing to surrender. Led by General Hans Kinzel and Admiral Hans-Georg von Friedeburg, a four-man delegation was on its way to British Army headquarters at Lüneberg Heath to meet Field-Marshal Montgomery and ask for terms.

CHAPTER 26:
GERMANY SURRENDERS

The German delegation arrived at Lüneberg at eleven thirty am on 3 May. Their welcome from Montgomery was frosty. 'Who are these men?' he demanded, when they presented themselves at his headquarters . 'What do they want?'[1] He was using the words traditional since medieval times for the opening of a parley.

Kinzel and Friedeburg offered to surrender to the British all the German forces in Holland, Denmark and northern Germany, including those fighting the Russians. Montgomery refused, insisting that the Germans fighting the Russians must surrender to the Russians. He warned that the fighting would continue to the bitter end if the Germans did not agree. 'I shall go on with the war, and will be delighted to do so, and am ready. All your soldiers will be killed.'[2]

Chastened, two of the Germans returned to their own side to consult Dönitz and Keitel. They were back again next day to agree Montgomery's conditions. Leonard Mosley was with a party of war correspondents who watched them arrive:

> Montgomery kept the German delegates waiting, standing miserably about in the rain, first while he told us of the events which had led up to the armistice, and later while he conferred with his aides inside the caravan. With their backs towards us, von Friedeburg and his three companions stood there, on the spot where all of them must, at some time in their careers, have watched German armies manoeuvring on the plain below in the exercises of pre-war days, and where now unending convoys of British troops

were moving. Montgomery kept them standing there, letting them watch and think, letting the rain splash over them, until he judged the moment right; and then he sent Colonel Ewart clattering down the steps to round the Nazi generals up and shepherd them to the tiny army tent on the lip of Lüneberg tor, where the klieg lights were ready, and the microphones, for photographs to be taken and records made of the signing ceremony.[3]

The Germans were shown to a plain trestle table covered by an army blanket. They sat in glum silence as Montgomery put on his spectacles and read the terms of the surrender to them. He was loving every minute of it:

'You will now sign,' he said, and, meekly, one by one, they came. The Post Office pen scraped on the paper; the delegates sat down again, expressionless, and waited. There was a moment, while the last photographs were being taken, when von Friedeburg turned his full face into the lights, an expression of tremendous anguish in his eyes as he posed for the pictures; and then the flap of the tent dropped and it was over.[4]

Almost. Friedeburg went to Eisenhower's headquarters next day to negotiate the surrender of the remaining forces in southern Germany and elsewhere. He repeated his plea for a separate peace, but the Americans proved no more receptive than the British. Chief of Staff Bedell Smith told Friedeburg coldly that the surrender was unconditional and had to be simultaneous on all fronts. In desperation, Dönitz tried to buy more time for the Germans fleeing the Russians by sending Jodl to Reims to argue their case. Jodl had no more success than Friedeburg. Dönitz finally accepted defeat in the early hours of 7 May, when he authorised the surrender of all Germans everywhere on the terms stated.

Jodl signed on his behalf at 1.41 am, Bedell Smith signed for the Allied Expeditionary Force and General Ivan Susloparov for the Soviet High Command. The surrender was to come into effect at midnight on 8 May. After the brief ceremony was over, Jodl stood up and made a short speech, beginning in English and continuing in German: 'Sir, with this signature, the German nation and the German armed forces are at the mercy of the victors. Throughout this war, which has lasted for five years, both have performed more, and perhaps suffered more, than any other nation on earth. At this hour, we can only hope that the victors will be generous.'[5]

He was greeted with stunned silence. The suffering of the German people had not been uppermost in anyone's thoughts as they watched the surrender being signed. When no answer came, Jodl snapped to attention, saluted and left the room. The war in Europe was over.

PART SIX

'Sir, with this signature, the German nation and the German armed forces are at the mercy of the victors... At this hour, we can only hope that the victors will be generous.'
Alfred Jodl

EPILOGUE

Rachele Mussolini was in Montecatini as the Germans surrendered, staying at the Hotel Italo-Argentine. She and her children were on their way to a British internment camp, where they remained until the end of July. They were then taken to the island of Ischia, in the bay of Naples, and set free to resume their lives.

Mussolini's body was stolen by Fascist supporters in 1946 and spent several months in a trunk before reappearing at a Franciscan monastery in Pavia. It was secretly reburied in another monastery at Cerro Maggiore until 1957, when it was handed over to Rachele. It lies now in a crypt at Predappio, Mussolini's home town, where it enjoys a steady stream of visitors.

The sliver of Mussolini's brain taken to America for further examination was returned to Rachele in 1966. The American consul in Florence was happy to report that they had found nothing wrong with it. In 2009, Mussolini's granddaughter Alessandra complained that samples of his blood and brains were for sale on eBay.

———

Alessandra's aunt, Sophia Villani Scicolone, outgrew her dismal childhood in Naples. Changing her name to Sophia Loren, she pursued her mother's dream and became one of the world's most beautiful film stars.

Audrey Hepburn and her mother left for London after the war, living in genteel poverty while Audrey trained as a ballerina. Her height and wartime diet would have prevented her from reaching the top, so she turned to acting instead. She too became a much-loved star.

Hildegard Knef was captured by the Russians and had a fraught time as a prisoner of war before eventually making her way back to Berlin, where she starred in many films. As Hildegard Neff she played opposite Gregory Peck in *The Snows of Kilimanjaro*, but her German background – she refused to reinvent herself as an Austrian named Gilda Christian – meant that her Hollywood career never took off.

Leni Riefenstahl tried to get back into mainstream cinema after the war, but was blacklisted because of her Nazi past. Like the headless horse in *The Godfather*, she never worked again.

Reunited with his father after the war, Roman Polanski pursued his fascination with light shows on the wall, first in Poland, later in France and the United States. He became one of the finest film directors of his generation, but his personal life continued to be deeply troubled.

Spike Milligan acted occasionally in films, but was happiest performing his own material on British radio and TV. With Michael Bentine, Peter Sellers and Harry Secombe, he starred in *The Goon Show*, one of the funniest radio comedies of the 1950s, but always remained at the mercy of his mental health.

———

Ezra Pound was arrested by the US Army at the end of May and taken to America to stand trial for treason. His plea of insanity was accepted and he spent twelve years at St Elizabeth's psychiatric hospital in Washington, where Mussolini's brain was already under examination. Released in 1958, he too returned to Italy.

Kurt Vonnegut was released from prison camp in May and repatriated to the United States. His Dresden experiences later inspired his novel *Slaughterhouse Five*. Joseph Heller was a Fulbright scholar at Oxford after the war and then wrote *Catch-22*, a thinly disguised account of his own service in the Mediterranean, borrowing part of his friend Yohannon's name for the main character Yossarian. Both novels were masterly indictments of the idiocy of war.

Aleksandr Solzhenitsyn was sentenced to eight years in a labour camp, followed by exile for life to Kazakhstan. The experience gave him the material for some remarkable books, including *Cancer Ward*, *The Gulag Archipelago* and *One Day in the Life of Ivan Denisovich*, none of which he expected to see published in his lifetime. Exonerated in 1956, after Nikita Khrushchev had succeeded Stalin, he later won the Nobel Prize for literature.

Günter Grass was captured by the Americans and spent some time in a prison camp at Bad Aibling, where he made friends with the deserter

Josef Ratzinger. He too became a writer and put his wartime experiences to good use, most notably in *The Tin Drum*. He won the Nobel Prize in Literature in 1999.

—

Josef Ratzinger got home safely after escaping from the Wehrmacht, but was picked up later by the Americans. Released in June, he became a priest and spent much of his career in Rome. His Polish colleague Karol Wojtyla became Pope John Paul II in 1978. Ratzinger succeeded him as Pope Benedict XVI in 2005.

Lieutenant Robert Runcie, MC, later became Archbishop of Canterbury and officiated at the wedding of the Prince of Wales and Lady Diana Spencer in 1981.

Army life had taught Runcie's brother officer Willie Whitelaw that he was best suited to be a second-in-command. He became deputy Prime Minister to Margaret Thatcher. Peter Carrington served in the same government before becoming Secretary General of Nato.

Spain was admitted to the United Nations in 1955. General Franco remained head of state until 1974 and died a year later.

Jack Kennedy won the US presidency in 1960 and established a close personal rapport with British Prime Minister Harold Macmillan.

Willy Brandt became mayor of West Berlin and then chancellor of West Germany. He was standing at Kennedy's side in 1963 when the President declared himself to be a Berliner.

Bob Dole recovered from his wounds but was never able to lift his right hand above his head again. Long a Republican senator for Kansas, he ran for the Presidency in 1996 but lost to Bill Clinton.

While serving with the British Army, Chaim Herzog enjoyed a brief glimpse of Himmler after his capture and later became President of Israel.

Henry Kissinger was secretary of state and foreign policy adviser to President Richard Nixon. Despite a controversial role in the Vietnam War, he was awarded the Nobel Peace Prize in 1973.

—

Victor Klemperer and his wife returned on foot to the ruins of Dresden as soon as the war ended, to find that their house had been 'Aryanised' in their absence. Klemperer reclaimed it and resumed his life as a university professor, becoming a significant figure in post-war East Germany.

Simon Wiesenthal devoted the rest of his life to tracking down Nazi war criminals and bringing them to justice. He was never as successful as he claimed, but thousands of Nazis slept less easily in their beds, knowing that he had their details on file and was actively looking for them.

Otto Frank returned to Amsterdam to be told that both of his daughters had died in Belsen. All that remained of them was Anne's diary of their time in hiding, kept safe for him by his friend Miep Gies.

Oskar Schindler's story was told in the award-winning movie *Schindler's List*. He ran into financial difficulties after the war and was helped out several times by the Jewish workers from the factory. Named by Israel as one of the Righteous among the Nations, he is the only former member of the Nazi party to be buried in Jerusalem's Roman Catholic cemetery.

Wernher von Braun became an American citizen and played a leading role in the United States' efforts to land a man on the moon.

Lee Miller married an Englishman and spent the rest of her life in the United Kingdom. Badly traumatised by her wartime experiences, she took refuge in alcohol and went into a downward spiral for many years.

Odette Sansom married an Englishman too, but not before bringing the commandant of Ravensbrück to justice. He released her from prison camp on 3 May and drove her to the American lines in his black Mercedes. 'This is Frau Churchill,' he told them, when they arrived. 'She has been a prisoner. She is a relation of Winston Churchill.'[1] Sühren was hoping to save his skin by delivering such an important figure, but Odette confiscated his pistol at once and denounced him as the commandant of Ravensbrück. He was executed by the French in 1950.

———

Josef Kramer, the ex-commandant of Belsen, and Irma Grese, his onetime lover, were hanged with nine others at Hameln prison on 13 December 1945. Kramer appealed for clemency to Field-Marshal Montgomery but was turned down. Fritz Klein, another of the condemned men, refused to appeal, accepting that he deserved to die for what he had done.

Rudolf Höss obeyed Himmler's last order to him and disappeared into the armed forces at the end of the war. Disguised as a bosun's mate, he found work on a farm near Flensburg and lived there anonymously until March 1946, when a tipoff led to his arrest. He was executed at the scene of his crimes on 16 April 1947. An open air gallows was specially constructed for the purpose behind Auschwitz's first, experimental gas chamber. Gallows and chamber are both still there.

'Small, ill-looking and shabbily dressed' after a week of sleeping rough, Heinrich Himmler had shaved off his moustache and was wearing a false eye-patch when the British picked him up at a check point. He soon identified himself and demanded to be taken to Field-Marshal Montgomery at Lüneberg. A doctor was about to examine his mouth when Himmler crunched on a cyanide capsule hidden in a hollow tooth. Despite frantic attempts to prevent him from swallowing, he was dead within a quarter of an hour.

Pierre Laval tried to remain in Spain until tempers had cooled, but was flown back to Austria in July and delivered to the Americans, who handed him over to the French. The jury at his show trial heckled him and the presiding judge demanded a verdict before France's forthcoming general election. Sentenced to death by firing squad, Laval took poison instead, only to discover that the poison was old and had lost its strength. His stomach was pumped and he was placed in front of a wall at Fresnes prison on 15 October 1945. He died bravely, crying 'Vive la France!' as he was shot. The election was held six days later.

Vidkun Quisling sent a telegram to Dönitz on 2 May, expressing the Norwegian people's condolences on the death of Adolf Hitler, but knew that he had backed the wrong horse. Like Laval, he was hoping that his countrymen would come to share his view that collaboration was the most sensible course in a country under military occupation. Sentenced to death instead, he was shot at Oslo's Akershus Fortress on 24 October 1945.

Unable to find a boat to Sweden, William Joyce was hiding in Flensburg when the British arrived. He foolishly spoke to a couple of officers and was recognised at once from his voice. The officers shot him through the thighs when he reached unexpectedly for his false identity card. After a controversial trial, Joyce was hanged for treason at Wandsworth prison on 3 January 1946. It was said that an old street-fighting scar running from his mouth to his cheek burst wide open under the impact of the drop.

Adolf Eichmann escaped from captivity in 1945 and lived anonymously in Germany before emigrating to Argentina in 1950. Israeli agents tracked him down ten years later and spirited him back to Israel. After a sensational trial, Eichmann was found guilty of crimes against humanity and hanged at Ramla prison on 31 May 1962. His body was cremated and the ashes scattered at sea, outside Israeli waters.

⁓

After escaping from Berlin, Helmut Altner was captured by the Russians on 3 May and held prisoner for the next eighteen months. With American permission, he published a book of his experiences in 1948 and later worked as the Paris correspondent for several German newspapers.

Martin Bormann never escaped from his father's shadow. He became a Roman Catholic priest for a while and worked as a missionary in the Congo. He also toured German schools, talking about the evils of Nazism and visiting Israel to apologise to Holocaust survivors. But his name followed him everywhere, blighting his career and making it impossible for him to enjoy a normal life.

Paula Hitler was interrogated by the Americans in July 1945 and broke down in tears at the thought of her brother's death. She returned to Vienna after the war and worked in an arts and crafts shop before retiring quietly to Berchtesgaden, where she was looked after by former members of Hitler's entourage. She died in 1960.

Traudl Junge was captured by the Russians and questioned closely about the last days in the bunker. She resumed work as a secretary after the war and was often pestered by people wanting to shake the hand that had shaken Hitler's. She tried to emigrate to Australia at one point, but was refused permission.

Else Krüger, Martin Bormann's secretary in the bunker, was questioned by the British after the war and fell in love with her interrogator. They married in 1947 and moved to Cheshire.

———

The rest of the top Nazis were brought to trial at Nuremberg in the autumn of 1945. Most were sentenced to death, but some received only prison sentences and three were acquitted of all charges, although they too were later imprisoned by German denazification courts.

Admiral Dönitz was sentenced to ten years. Along with the others, he served his time at Spandau prison in Berlin. He was released in 1956 and died in 1980. His funeral was attended by a number of elderly U–Boat commanders illegally wearing their wartime caps.

Albert Speer freely admitted his guilt in court. Sentenced to twenty years, he wrote several books on his release and is said to have contributed most of the royalties anonymously to Jewish charities. In London to appear on a television programme, he died of a stroke in 1981.

Rudolf Hess got life. There was doubt about his state of mind during the trial. Some people thought he was faking insanity to avoid execution, but his behaviour in prison grew steadily more bizarre. He was Spandau's only remaining inmate when he hanged himself in 1987.

The other top-ranking Nazis were hanged at Nuremberg in the early hours of 16 October 1946. Three black-painted gallows were erected in the prison gymnasium, thirty yards from the cells. Working through the previous night, the carpenters tried hard to keep quiet, but the prisoners all heard the sound of banging as the gallows were constructed on what had formerly been the basketball court.

It had been agreed that the prisoners should be executed in the same order as their indictments at the trial. Göring should have gone first, but he had cheated the gallows by taking poison, either concealed during numerous body searches or obtained by bribing a guard. The remaining prisoners were immediately handcuffed to American soldiers to prevent them from following suit. Wearing black silk pyjamas under a blue shirt, Göring's body was placed on a stretcher and laid to one side until the hangings were over.

In his absence, it fell to Ribbentrop to hang first. Dressed in a dark suit, he entered the gym at eleven minutes past one and climbed the thirteen steps to the platform without hesitation. 'My last wish is that Germany realise its entity and that an understanding be reached between east and west,' he announced, as he stood on the trap. 'I wish peace to the world.'[2] He looked straight ahead as a black hood was pulled over his face and the trap gave way.

Keitel went next, the first soldier to be condemned under the new international doctrine that obeying orders was no defence. He burst into tears as he prayed with the chaplain in his cell, but pulled himself together by the time he reached the scaffold. He mounted it in military uniform as if reviewing a parade. 'I call on God almighty to have mercy on the German people,' he declared, as he stood on the second trap. 'More than two million German soldiers died for the Fatherland before me. I now follow my sons – all for Germany.'[3]

There was a pause while American and Russian doctors disappeared behind the curtain concealing Ribbentrop and Keitel's bodies to confirm that they were dead. The watching reporters were allowed to smoke as the bodies were removed and Kaltenbrunner replaced them on the trap. 'I am sorry my people were led by men who were not soldiers and that crimes were committed of which I had no knowledge,'[4] Kaltenbrunner announced. 'Germany, good luck.'

Hans Frank, the Governor of Poland, had converted to Roman Catholicism after his arrest. 'A thousand years will pass and still this guilt of Germany will not have been erased,'[5] he had told the court at his trial, repenting of his sins a little too late. Nervous, swallowing frequently, he expressed thanks for his kind treatment during captivity and called on God to accept him with mercy as he died.

With the collar of his Wehrmacht uniform half turned up, Jodl was visibly scared as he climbed the steps to the scaffold. 'My greetings to you, my Germany,'[6] he said miserably, as the hood went over his head. He was later granted a posthumous pardon by a German denazification court.

The last to die was Seyss-Inquart. With a club foot, he had to be helped up the steps by the guards. 'I hope this execution is the last act of the tragedy of the Second World War,' he told his audience, 'and that the lesson taken from this world war will be that peace and understanding should exist between peoples. I believe in Germany.'[7]

Jodl and Seyss-Inquart were still dangling from their ropes when Göring's body was brought in to show that he was dead. Once Jodl and Seyss-Inquart's deaths had been confirmed as well, the bodies were all laid out in an adjacent room and photographed by a volunteer from the Signal Corps. Several of the hangings had been botched by the hangman. Perhaps overwhelmed by the numbers, Master Sergeant John Woods and his two assistants, one of them German, had not always calculated the drop correctly to produce a clean snap of the neck. Woods left the country later to avoid German retribution.

St Elizabeth's hospital in Washington had asked for the Nazis' brains to add to its collection, but the request had been refused. Instead, the bodies were driven to the concentration camp at Dachau and cremated soon after dawn. That evening, after the ashes had cooled, they were taken to the outskirts of Munich and thrown into a tributary of the River Isar to ensure that Hitler's henchmen should have no final resting place.

—

The Russians spent several days looking for Hitler's body in the ruins of the Chancellery. They thought they had him when a mischievous German identified the wrong corpse for them. They eventually took away a jawbone and several other bits and pieces, but were never able to identify them beyond dispute. Some of the fragments went to the Kremlin. The rest were buried at a Soviet base near Magdeburg until 1970, when they were dug up and thrown into the River Biederitz.

The balance of probability is that very little of Hitler survived his cremation in the Chancellery garden. His ashes were almost certainly scattered to the wind in the hours that followed. Assertions to the contrary are rarely supported by established fact.

The Chancellery remained under Russian control after the war and was soon razed to the ground. The site was a wasteland for many years, but has now been rebuilt as a modern apartment block. There are parking spaces, a playground and a Chinese restaurant where Hitler once strutted. The exact site of his cremation is surrounded by street furniture to prevent large crowds from gathering.

'I shall never leave this place,' Hitler had told his people grandly, when they begged him to flee the bunker. 'I shall stand watch here for ever, in sacred ground.'

Dogs do their business on the spot.

ENDNOTES

Chapter 1: The death of Mussolini

1. Christopher Hibbert, *Benito Mussolini*, p.328
2. Rachele Mussolini, *My Life with Mussolini*, p.176
3. Ibid., p.179

Chapter 2: In Berlin

1. H. R. Trevor-Roper, *The Last Days of Hitler*, p.180
2. Helmut Altner, *Berlin Dance of Death*, p.62
3. Ibid., p.146
4. Ibid., p.151
5. Hildegard Knef, *The Gift Horse*, p.82
6. Ibid., p.83

Chapter 3: Himmler sues for peace

1. Count Folke Bernadotte, *The Fall of the Curtain*, p.61
2. Walter Schellenberg, *The Schellenberg Memoirs*, p.452
3. Wilhelm Wulff, *Zodiac and Swastika*, p.177
4. Count Folke Bernadotte, *The Fall of the Curtain*, p.62
5. Ewan Butler, *Amateur Agent*, p.193
6. Ibid., p.199
7. Gitta Sereny, *Albert Speer*, p.535

Chapter 4: Nazis on the run

1. Albert Speer, *Inside the Third Reich*, p.484
2. Ibid., p.469
3. Roger Manvell, *Hermann Göring*, p.302
4. Edwin Hoyt, *Göring's War*, p.186

5. Willi Frischauer, *Göring*, p.265. The telegram did not survive, but eyewitnesses recalled it from memory.
6. Emmy Göring, *My Life with Göring*, p.123
7. Quoted in David Irving, *Hess*, p.270

Chapter 5: Chaos in Italy
1. Christopher Hibbert, *Benito Mussolini*, p.333
2. James E. Roper, *UPI Archives*
3. Philip Hamburger, *The New Yorker*, 19 May 1945
4. Rachele Mussolini, *My Life with Mussolini*, p.180
5. Ibid.
6. Ibid., p.181
7. Allen Dulles, *The Secret Surrender*, p.206
8. A. E. Hotchner, *Sophia*, p.33
9. Ibid., p.41
10. Ibid., p.50
11. Ibid., p.47
12. Harold Macmillan, *The Blast of War*, p.702
13. Ibid., p.703
14. Joseph Heller, *Now and Then*, p.181

Chapter 6: Himmler looks to the stars
1. Wilhelm Wulff, *Zodiac and Swastika*, p.185
2. Ibid., p.186
3. H. R. Trevor-Roper, *The Last Days of Hitler*, p.195
4. Traudl Junge, *Until the Final Hour*, p.184
5. Ibid.
6. William Shirer, *The Rise and Fall of the Third Reich*, p.1,128
7. Helmut Altner, *Berlin Dance of Death*, p.160
8. Ibid., p.161
9. Cornelius Ryan, *The Last Battle*, p.363
10. Ibid, p.362

Chapter 7: Belsen
1. Michael Bentine, *The Long Banana Skin*, p.132
2. Ben Shepherd, *After Daybreak*, p.76
3. Leslie Hardman, *The Survivors*, p.46
4. Chaim Herzog, *Living History*, p.61
5. Jo Reilly, *Belsen in History and Memory*, p.212
6. Alan Moorhead, *Eclipse*, p.221

7. William Whitelaw, *The Whitelaw Memoirs*, p.22
8. Mollie Panter-Downes, *London War Notes*, p.371

Chapter 8: Operation *Manna*
1. Operationmanna.secondworldwar.nl
2. Ibid.
3. Martyn Ford-Jones, *Bomber Squadron*, p.212
4. Desmond Hawkins, *War Report*, p.338
5. Henri van der Zee, *The Hunger Winter*, p.253
6. Barry Turner, *Countdown to Victory*, p.241
7. BBC Archives, *WW2 People's War – Netherlands*
8. Walter Cronkite, *A Reporter's Life*, p.123
9. Barry Paris, *Audrey Hepburn*, p.20
10. Ibid., p.30
11. Ibid., p.31

Chapter 9: Dachau
1. Interview, G. Petrone and M. Skinner, 25 February 2000
2. Flint Whitlock, *The Rock of Anzio*, p.359
3. Ibid., p.362
4. Ibid., p.365
5. Marguerite Higgins, *New York Herald Tribune*, 29 April 1945
6. Flint Whitlock, *The Rock of Anzio*, p.373
7. Ibid., p.377
8. Interview, G. Petrone and M. Skinner, 25 February 2000
9. Sam Dann, *Dachau 29 April 1945*
10. Flint Whitlock, *The Rock of Anzio*, p.384
11. Sigismund Payne Best, *The Venlo Incident*, p.231

Chapter 10: The United Nations
1. W. H. Thompson, *I was Churchill's Shadow*, p.155
2. Winston Churchill, *The Second World War Vol. VI*, p.442
3. Martin Gilbert, *Winston S. Churchill Vol. VII*, p.1,322
4. J. C. Smuts, *Jan Christian Smuts*, p.471
5. Ibid., p.478
6. Herbert Parmet, *Jack*, p.132
7. Simon Callow, *Orson Welles*, p.239
8. Ibid., p.240
9. H. Franklin Knudsen, *I was Quisling's Secretary*, p.160

Chapter 11: Assault on the Reichstag

1. Siegfried Knappe, *Soldat*, p.50
2. Anton Joachimsthaler, *The Last Days of Hitler*, p.140
3. Traudl Junge, *Until the Final Hour*, p.186
4. Ibid., p.186
5. Anton Joachimsthaler, *The Last Days of Hitler*, p.141
6. Ibid., p.144
7. Helmut Altner, *Berlin Dance of Death*, p.175
8. Ibid., p.177
9. Hildegard Knef, *The Gift Horse*, p.87
10. Ibid., p.88
11. Vasili Chuikov, *The End of the Third Reich*, p.206
12. James O'Donnell, *The Berlin Bunker*, p.177
13. Ibid., p.177
14. Traudl Junge, *Until the Final Hour*, p.186

Chapter 12: Curtain call for Lord Haw Haw

1. Admiral Dönitz, *Memoirs*, p.441
2. Ibid., p.441
3. Ibid., p.443
4. Nigel Farndale, *Haw-Haw*, p.269
5. Francis Selwyn, *Hitler's Englishman*, p.154
6. Wanda Poltawska, *And I am afraid of my dreams*, p.146
7. Jerrard Tickell, *Odette*, p.325
8. Jürgen Thorwald, *Flight in the Winter*, p.190
9. Ibid., p.191
10. Micheline Maurel, *Ravensbrück*, p.116
11. Ibid., p.116

Chapter 13: The Americans take Munich

1. Francis de Guingand, *Operation Victory*, p.452
2. Charles MacDonald, *The Last Offensive*, p.437
3. Charles Hawley, *Spiegelonline International*, 29 April 2005
4. Ibid.
5. Lee Miller, *Lee Miller's War*, p.182

Chapter 14: Italy

1. Allen Dulles, *The Secret Surrender*, p.214
2. Kurt von Schuschnigg, *Austrian Requiem*, p.241
3. Geoffrey Cox, *The Road to Trieste*, p.182

4. James Lucas, *Last Days of the Reich*, p.164
5. Mussolini's autopsy report
6. Rachele Mussolini, *My Life with Mussolini*, p.182

Chapter 15: Hitler goes to Valhalla

1. James O'Donnell, The Berlin Bunker, p.131
2. Traudl Junge, *Until the Final Hour*, p.187
3. Gitta Sereny, *Albert Speer*, p.539
4. Traudl Junge, *Until the Final Hour*, p.187
5. Ibid.
6. Anton Joachimsthaler, *The Last Days of Hitler*, p.154
7. Ibid., p.155
8. Ibid., p.156
9. James O'Donnell, *The Berlin Bunker*, p.187
10. Anton Joachimsthaler, *The Last Days of Hitler*, p.193
11. Ibid., p.197
12. Traudl Junge, *Until the Final Hour*, p.188
13. Anton Joachimsthaler, *The Last Days of Hitler*, p.213
14. Ibid., p.214

Chapter 16: The Germans want to talk

1. Vasili Chuikov, *The End of the Third Reich*, p.217
2. Marshal Zhukov, *The Memoirs of Marshal Zhukov*, p.622
3. Vasili Chuikov, *The End of the Third Reich*, p.231
4. Helmut Altner, *Berlin Dance of Death*, p.184
5. Hildegard Knef, *The Gift Horse*, p.91
6. Ibid., p.91
7. Joachim Fest, *Inside Hitler's Bunker*, p.137
8. Traudl Junge, *Until the Final Hour*, p.175

Chapter 17: The Nazis regroup

1. Albert Speer, *Inside the Third Reich*, p.488
2. Wilhelm Keitel, *The Memoirs of Field-Marshal Keitel*, p.225
3. Willi Frischauer, *Göring*, p.272
4. Gitta Sereny, *Albert Speer*, p.544

Chapter 18: May Day in Russia

1. Josef Stalin, *Order of the Day No 20*, 1 May 1945
2. Nikita Khrushchev, *Memoirs Vol. I,* p.633
3. Clementine Churchill, *My Visit to Russia*, p.28

4. Ibid., p.45
5. Ibid., p.46
6. Carol Ann Lee, *The Hidden Life of Otto Frank*, p.132

Chapter 19: Operation *Chowhound*
1. Operationmanna.secondworldwar.nl/maxkrell
2. Ibid., /chowhound2
3. Harry Crosby, *A Wing and a Prayer*, p.317
4. Cameron Garrett, *Stalag VIIIA*, Oral History
5. Ibid.
6. Charles Messenger, *The Last Prussian*, p.231
7. Joseph Ratzinger, *Milestones*, p.36

Chapter 20: Dönitz speaks to the nation
1. James O'Donnell, *The Berlin Bunker*, p.207
2. Ibid.
3. Ibid., p.208
4. Ibid.
5. Ibid., p.211
6. Joachim Fest, *Inside Hitler's Bunker*, p.144
7. James O'Donnell, *The Berlin Bunker*, p.220
8. Traudl Junge, *Until the Final Hour*, p.193
9. James O'Donnell, *The Berlin Bunker*, p.226
10. Ibid., p.227
11. Hildegard Knef, *The Gift Horse*, p.91
12. Ibid., p.92
13. Helmut Altner, *Berlin Dance of Death*, p.188
14. Leni Riefenstahl, *The Sieve of Time*, p.304
15. Emmy Göring, *My Life with Göring*, p.130
16. Willy Brandt, *My Road to Berlin*, p.136

Chapter 21: The news is out
1. *Hansard*, 1 May 1945, col 1239
2. John Colville, *The Fringes of Power*, p.596
3. Harold Nicolson, *Diaries and Letters*, p.453
4. *The Day the War ended*, p.22
5. Humphrey Carpenter, *Robert Runcie*, p.76
6. Letter to the author, 19 February 2009
7. Sybil Bannister, *I lived under Hitler*, p.232
8. Albert Speer, *Inside the Third Reich*, p.494

Chapter 22: The Nazis consider their positions

1. Roger Manvell and Heinrich Fränkel, *Heinrich Himmler*, p.240
2. Rudolf Höss, *Commandant of Auschwitz*, p.172
3. Niklas Frank, *Hans Frank's Son*, p.316
4. Neil Bascomb, *Hunting Eichmann*, p.22
5. Leni Riefenstahl, *The Sieve of Time*, p.305
6. US Army interview with Paula Hitler, 12 July 1945. Original transcript now in the University of Pennsylvania library
7. Quoted in David Irving, *Hess*, p.271

Chapter 23: Surrender in Italy

1. Allen Dulles, *The Secret Surrender*, p.236
2. Spike Milligan, *Milligan's War*, p.217
3. Ibid., p.219

Chapter 24: Berlin falls

1. Vasili Chuikov, *The End of the Third Reich*, p.257
2. Siegfried Knappe, *Soldat*, p.61
3. James O'Donnell, *The Berlin Bunker*, p.283
4. Ibid., p.290
5. Ibid., p.291
6. Marshal Zhukov, *The Memoirs of Marshal Zhukov*, p.625
7. Traudl Junge, *Until the Final Hour*, p.194
8. Ibid., p.194
9. Ibid., p.219
10. James O'Donnell, *The Berlin Bunker*, p.248
11. Ibid., p.249
12. Helmut Altner, *Berlin Dance of Death*, p.202

Chapter 25: Now that the Führer has gone

1. Gitta Sereny, *Albert Speer*, p.543
2. Ibid., p.543
3. Jerrard Tickell, *Odette*, p.329
4. Victor Klemperer, *To the Bitter End*, p.451

Chapter 26: Germany surrenders

1. Field-Marshal Montgomery, *Memoirs*, p.335
2. Martin Gilbert, *The Second World War*, p.684
3. Barry Turner, *Countdown to Victory*, p.417

4. Ibid.
5. Ibid., p.418

Epilogue
1. Jerrard Tickell, *Odette*, p.332
2. John Carey, *Faber Book of Reportage*, p.643
3. Ibid., p.643
4. Ibid., p.644
5. Robert Conot, *Justice at Nuremberg*, p.380
6. John Carey, *Faber Book of Reportage*, p.647
7. Ibid., p.647

BIBLIOGRAPHY

Alexander, Harold, *The Alexander Memoirs* (London, Cassell, 1962)

Altner, Helmut, *Berlin Dance of Death* (Staplehurst, Spellmount, 2002)

Avon, Earl of, *The Eden Memoirs* (London, Cassell, 1965)

Bach, Steven, *Marlene Dietrich* (London, HarperCollins, 1992)

Bannister, Sybil, *I lived under Hitler* (London, Rockliff, 1957)

Bardgett, Suzanne and David Cesarini, *Belsen 1945* (Portland, Or, Valentine Mitchell, 2007)

Bascomb, Neal, *Hunting Eichmann* (London, Quercus, 2009)

Beevor, Antony, *Berlin* (London, Viking, 2002)

Bentine, Michael, *The Long Banana Skin* (London, Wolfe, 1976)

Bergaust, Erik, *Wernher von Braun* (Washington, DC, National Space Institute, 1981)

Bernadotte, Count Folke, *The Fall of the Curtain* (London, Cassell, 1946)

Black, Peter, *Ernst Kaltenbrunner* (Princeton: Princeton University Press, 1985)

Bloch, Michael, *Ribbentrop* (London, Bantam Press, 1993)

Boldt, Gerhardt, *Hitler's Last Days* (London, Arthur Barker, 1973)

Bradley, Omar, *A Soldier's Story* (London, Eyre & Spottiswoode, 1951)

Brandt, Willy, *In Exile* (London, Oswald Wolff, 1971)

Brandt, Willy, *My Road to Berlin* (London, Peter Davies, 1960)

Bromage, Bernard, *Molotov* (London, Peter Owen, 1950)

Burke, Carolyn, *Lee Miller* (New York, Knopf, 2006)

Butler, Ewan, *Amateur Agent* (London, George Harrap, 1963)

Callow, Simon, *Orson Welles* (London, Jonathan Cape, 2006)

Carey, John, *The Faber Book of Reportage* (London, Faber and Faber, 1987)

Carlton, David, *Anthony Eden* (London, Allen Lane, 1981)

Carpenter, Humphrey, *Robert Runcie* (London, Hodder & Stoughton, 1996)

Carrington, Peter, *Reflect on Things Past* (London, Collins, 1988)

Chaney, Otto, *Zhukov* (London, University of Oklahoma Press, 1999)

Chuikov, Vasili, *The End of the Third Reich* (London, Macgibbon & Kee, 1969)

Churchill, Clementine, *My Visit to Russia* (London, Hutchinson & Co., 1945)

Churchill, Peter, *The Spirit in the Cage* (London, Hodder and Stoughton, 1954)

Cole, Hubert, *Laval* (London, Heinemann, 1963)

Colville, John, *The Fringes of Power* (London, Hodder and Stoughton, 1985)

Conot, Robert, *Justice at Nuremberg* (London, Weidenfeld and Nicolson, 1983)

Coogan, Tim Pat, *De Valera* (London, Hutchinson, 1995)

Cox, Geoffrey, *The Race for Trieste* (London, William Kimber, 1977)

Cronkite, Walter, *A Reporter's Life* (New York, Knopf, 2001)

Crosby, Harry, *A Wing and a Prayer* (London, Robson Books, 1993)

Crowe, David, *Oskar Schindler* (Cambridge, Mass, Westview Press, 2005)

Crozier, Brian, *Franco* (London, Eyre & Spottiswoode, 1967)

Dahl, Hans Fredrik, *Quisling* (Cambridge: Cambridge University Press, 1999)

Dann, Sam, *Dachau 29 April 1945* (Texas Tech University Press, 1998)

De Guingand, Sir Francis, *Operation Victory* (London, Hodder and Stoughton, 1947)

Dimbleby, Jonathan, *Richard Dimbleby* (London, Hodder and Stoughton, 1975)

Dombrowski, Roman, *Mussolini* (London, William Heinemann, 1956)

Dönitz, Admiral, *Memoirs* (London, Weidenfeld and Nicolson, 1959)

Drath, Viola Herms, *Willy Brandt* (Radnor, Pennsylvania, Chilton, 1978)

Duggan, John, *Neutral Ireland and the Third Reich* (Dublin, Lilliput Press, 1989)

Dulles, Allen, *The Secret Surrender* (London, Weidenfeld and Nicolson, 1967)

Elath, Eliahu, *Zionism at the UN* (Philadelphia, Jewish Publication Society of America, 1976)

Ellwood, Sheelagh, *Franco* (New York, Longman, 1993)

Endler, Fritz, *Herbert von Karajan* (London, Sidgwick and Jackson, 1989)

Erskine, David, *The Scots Guards* (London, William Clowes, 1956)

Farndale, Nigel, *Haw-Haw* (London, Macmillan, 2005)

Ferrell, Robert, *Harry S. Truman* (Missouri: University of Missouri Press, 1996)

Fest, Joachim, *Inside Hitler's Bunker* (London, Pan, 2005)

Fest, Joachim, *Speer* (London, Weidenfeld and Nicolson, 2002)

Fishman, Jack, *My Darling Clementine* (London, W. H. Allen, 1966)

Ford-Jones, Martyn, *Bomber Squadron* (London, William Kimber, 1987)

Frank, Niklas, *In the Shadow of the Reich* (New York, Knopf, 1991)

Frankland, Mark, *Khrushchev* (London, Penguin, 1966)

Frischauer, Willi, *Göring* (London, Odhams Press, 1951)

Frischauer, Willi, *Himmler* (London, Odhams, 1953)

Gilbert, Martin, *The Day the War ended* (London, HarperCollins, 1995)

Gilbert, Martin, *The Second World War* (London, Phoenix, 2009)

Gilbert, Martin, *Winston S. Churchill* (London, Heinemann, 1986)

Gjelsvik, Tore, *Norwegian Resistance* (London, C. Hurst, 1979)

Goodman, Cecily and Leslie Hardman, *The Survivors* (London, Valentine, Mitchell, 1958)

Göring, Emmy, *My Life with Göring* (London, David Bruce & Watson, 1972)

Grass, Günter, *Peeling the Onion* (London, Harvill Secker, 2007)

Grossman, Vasily, *A Writer at War* (London, Harvill, 2005)

Hastings, Adrian, *Robert Runcie* (London, Mowbray, 1991)

Hawkins, Desmond, *War Report* (London, BBC Books, 1995)

Heller, Joseph, *Now and Then* (New York, Simon & Schuster, 1996)

Herzog, Chaim, *Living History* (London, Weidenfeld and Nicolson, 1997)

Hewins, Ralph, *Quisling* (London, W. H. Allen, 1965)

Hibbert, Christopher, *Benito Mussolini* (London, Longmans, 1962)

Higham, Charles, *Marlene* (London, Granada, 1978)

Hillson, Norman, *Alexander of Tunis* (London, W. H. Allen, 1952)

Hoidal, Oddvar, *Quisling* (Oslo, Norwegian University Press, c.1989)

Höss, Rudolf, *Commandant of Auschwitz* (London, Phoenix, 2000)

Hotchner, A. E., *Sophia* (London, Michael Joseph, 1979)

Hoyt, Edwin, *Göring's War* (London, Robert Hale, 1990)

Hyde, H. Montgomery, *Stalin* (London, Rupert Hart-Davis, 1971)

Irving, David, *Hess* (London, Macmillan, 1987)

Isaacson, Walter, *Kissinger* (Boston, Faber and Faber, 1992)

Joachimsthaler, Anton, *The Last Days of Hitler* (London, Arms and Armour, c.1996)

Johnson, Frank, *RAAF over Europe* (London, Eyre & Spottiswoode, 1947)

Junge, Traudl, *Until the Final Hour* (London, Phoenix, 2005)

Kalb, Marvin and Bernard, *Kissinger* (London, Hutchinson, 1975)

Keitel, Wilhelm, *The Memoirs of Field-Marshal Keitel* (London, William Kimber, 1965)

Kesselring, Field-Marshal, *The Memoirs of Field-Marshal Kesselring* (London, William Kimber, 1954)

Khrushchev, Nikita, *Commissar* (Pennsylvania: Pennsylvania State University Press, 2005)

Kirby, Norman, *1100 Miles with Monty* (London, Alan Sutton, 1989)

Kirkpatrick, Sir Ivone, *Mussolini* (London, Odhams, 1964)

Klemperer, Victor, *The Diaries of Victor Klemperer* (London, Weidenfeld & Nicolson, 2000)

Knappe, Siegfried, *Soldat* (New York, Orion, 1992)

Knef, Hildegard, *The Gift Horse* (London, Granada, 1980)

Knudsen, Franklin, *I was Quisling's Secretary* (London, Britons, 1967)

Kurz, Evi, *The Kissinger Saga* (London, Weidenfeld & Nicolson, 2009)

Lang, Jochen von, *Eichmann Interrogated* (London, Bodley Head, 1983)

Langer, Walter, *The Mind of Adolf Hitler* (London, Secker & Warburg, 1973)

Le Tissier, Tony, *Race for the Reichstag* (Portland, Oregon. Frank Cass, 1999)

Lee, Carol Ann, *The Hidden Life of Otto Frank* (London, Penguin Books, 2003)

Levy, Alan, *Forever Sophia* (London, Robert Hale, 1980)

Levy, Alan, *The Wiesenthal File* (London, Constable, 1993)

Lindwer, Willy, *Anne Frank* (London, Macmillan, 2000)

Lloyd, Alan, *Franco* (London, Longman, 1970)

Lomax, Judy, *Hanna Reitsch* (London, John Murray, 1988)

Longford, Earl of, *Eamon de Valera* (London, Hutchinson, 1971)

Lucas, James, *Last Days of the Reich* (London, Cassell, 2002)

Lüdde-Neurath, Walter, *Regierung Dönitz* (Leoni am Starnberger See, Druffel, 1985)

Lynn, Vera, *The Day the War Ended* (London, Weidenfeld and Nicolson, 2005)

MacDonald, Charles, *The Last Offensive* (Washington, DC, 1973)

Macmillan, Harold, *The Blast of War* (London, Macmillan, 1967)

Macmillan, Harold, *War Diaries* (London, Macmillan, 1984)

Malinski, M., *Pope John Paul II* (London, Burns & Oates, 1979)

Mantle, Jonathan, *Archbishop* (London, Sinclair-Stevenson, 1991)

Manvell, Roger and Heinrich Fränkel, *Heinrich Himmler* (London, Heinemann, 1965)

Manvell, Roger and Heinrich Fränkel, *Hermann Göring* (London, Heinemann, 1962)

Martin, Sir John, *Downing Street* (London, Bloomsbury, 1991)

Maurel, Micheline, *Ravensbrück* (London, Anthony Blond, 1959)

Maychick, Diana, *Audrey* (London, Sidgwick & Jackson, 1993)

McCullough, David, *Truman* (New York, Simon & Schuster, 1992)

McGovern, James, *Martin Bormann* (London, Arthur Barker, 1968)

Messenger, Charles, *The Last Prussian* (London, Brassey's, 1991)

Miller, Donald, *Eighth Air Force* (London, Aurum Press, 2007)

Miller, Lee, *Lee Miller's War* (Boston, Bulfinch Press, *c*.1992)

Milligan, Spike, *Milligan's War* (London, Michael Joseph, 1988)

Milligan, Spike, *Mussolini* (London, Michael Joseph, 1978)

Monelli, Paolo, *Mussolini* (London, Thames and Hudson, 1953)

Montgomery, Bernard, *The Memoirs of Field-Marshal Montgomery* (London, Collins, 1958)

Moorehead, Alan, *Eclipse* (London, Hamish Hamilton, 1945)

Moran, Lord, *Winston Churchill* (London, Constable, 1966)

Mosley, Leonard, *Report from Germany* (London, Victor Gollancz, 1945)

Mussolini, Rachele, *My Life with Mussolini* (London, Robert Hale, 1959)

Nicolson, Harold, *Diaries and Letters 1939–1945* (London, Collins, 1967)

O'Brien, Michael, *John F. Kennedy* (New York, Thomas Dunne Books, 2005)

O'Donnell, James, *The Berlin Bunker* (London, J. M. Dent, 1979)

Padfield, Peter, *Dönitz* (London, Victor Gollancz, 1984)

Panter-Downes, Mollie, *London War Notes* (London, Longman, 1973)

Paris, Barry, *Audrey Hepburn* (London, Orion, 1998)

Parmet, Herbert, *Jack* (New York, Dial Press, 1982)

Patton, George, *War as I Knew it* (London, W. H. Allen, 1949)

Payne, Robert, *Stalin* (London, W. H. Allen, 1966)

Payne Best, Sigismund, *The Venlo Incident* (London, Hutchinson, 1950)

Pearlman, Moshe, *The Capture of Adolf Eichmann* (London, Weidenfeld and Nicolson, 1961)

Peck, John, *Dublin from Downing Street* (Dublin, Gill and Macmillan, 1986)

Perret, Geoffrey, *Jack* (New York, Random House, 2002)

Polanski, Roman, *Roman* (London, Heinemann, 1984)

Poltawska, Wanda, *And I am afraid of my Dreams* (London, Hodder & Stoughton, 1987)

Prieberg, Fred, *Trial of Strength* (London, Quartet, 1991)

Ratzinger, Josef, *Milestones* (San Francisco, Ignatius Press, 2001)

Reilly, Jo, *Belsen in History and Memory* (Portland, Or, Frank Cass, 1997)

Reitsch, Hanna, *The Sky My Kingdom* (London, Bodley Head, 1955)

Reshetovskaya, Natalya, *Sanya* (London, Hart-Davis, MacGibbon, 1977)

Riefenstahl, Leni, *The Sieve of Time* (London, Quartet, 1992)

Riess, Curt, *Wilhelm Furtwangler* (London, Frederick Muller, 1955)

Riva, Maria, *Marlene Dietrich* (London, Bloomsbury, 1993)

Ruderman, Judith, *Joseph Heller* (New York, Continuum, 1994)

Scammell, Michael, *Solzhenitsyn* (London, Hutchinson, 1984)

Schellenberg, Walter, *The Schellenberg Memoirs* (London, Andre Deutsch, 1957)

Schmidt, Matthias, *Albert Speer* (London, Harrap, 1985)

Schuschnigg, Kurt von, *Austrian Requiem* (London, Victor Gollancz, 1947)

Schuschnigg, Kurt von, *The Brutal Takeover* (London, Weidenfeld and Nicolson, 1971)

Sebag Montefiore, Simon, *Stalin* (London, Phoenix, 2004)

Seed, David, *The Fiction of Joseph Heller* (London, Macmillan, 1989)

Selwyn, Francis, *Hitler's Englishman* (London, Routledge & Kegan Paul, 1987)

Sereny, Gitta, *Albert Speer* (London, Macmillan, 1995)

Shephard, Ben, *After Daybreak* (London, Pimlico, 2006)

Shirakawa, Sam, *The Devil's Music Master* (New York, Oxford University Press, 1992)

Shirer, William, *The Rise and Fall of the Third Reich* (London, Arrow, 1998)

Sington, Derrick, *Belsen Uncovered* (London, Duckworth, 1947)

Smith, Bradley and Elena Agarossi, *Operation Sunrise* (London, Andre Deutsch, 1979)

Smuts, J. C., *Jan Christian Smuts* (London, Cassell, 1952)

Soames, Mary, *Clementine Churchill* (London, Doubleday, 2002)

Speer, Albert, *Inside the Third Reich* (London, Weidenfeld and Nicolson, 1970)

Spoto, Donald, *Enchantment* (London, Hutchinson, 2006)

Stafford, David, *Endgame* (London, Abacus, 2007)

Stalin, Joseph, *War Speeches* (London, Hutchinson, 1946)

Steinert, Marlis, *Capitulation 1945* (London, Constable, 1969)

Stock, Noel, *The Life of Ezra Pound* (London, Routledge & Kegan Paul, 1970)

Szulc, Tad, *Pope John Paul II* (New York, Scribner, 1995)

Thompson, W. H., *I was Churchill's Shadow* (London, Christopher Johnson, 1952)

Thorwald, Jürgen, *Flight in the Winter* (London, Hutchinson, 1953)

Tickell, Jerrard, *Odette* (London, Chapman & Hall, 1949)

Trevor-Roper, H. R, *The Last Days of Hitler* (London, Macmillan, 1978)

Truman, Harry, *Year of Decisions* (London, Hodder and Stoughton, 1955)

Trythall, J. W. D., *Franco* (London, Rupert Hart-Davis, 1970)

Turner, Barry, *Countdown to Victory* (London, Hodder & Stoughton, 2004)

Van der Vat, Dan, *The Good Nazi* (London, Weidenfeld and Nicolson, 1997)

Van der Zee, Henri, *The Hunger Winter* (London, Jill Norman & Hobhouse, 1982)

Vaughan, Roger, *Herbert von Karajan* (London, Weidenfeld and Nicolson, 1986)

Walker, Alexander, *Dietrich* (London, Thames and Hudson, 1984)

Walsh, Michael, *John Paul II* (London, HarperCollins, 1994)

Warner, Geoffrey, *Pierre Laval* (London, Eyre & Spottiswoode, 1968)

Weitz, John, *Hitler's Diplomat* (London, Weidenfeld and Nicolson, 1997)

Whitelaw, William, *The Whitelaw Memoirs* (London, Headline, 1990)

Whiting, Charles, *Patton's Last Battle* (Staplehurst, Spellmount, 2003)

Whiting, Charles, *The Hunt for Martin Bormann* (London, Leo Cooper, 1996)

Whitlock, Flint, *The Rock of Anzio* (Boulder, Colorado, Westview Press, 1998)

Whittle, Peter, *One Afternoon at Mezzegra* (London, W. H. Allen, 1969)

Wiesenthal, Simon, *The Murderers Among Us* (London, Heinemann, 1967)

Wighton, Charles, *Eichmann* (London, Odhams Press, 1961)

Wilhelmina, Princess, *Lonely but not Alone* (London, Hutchinson, c.1960)

Wulff, Wilhelm, *Zodiac and Swastika* (London, Arthur Barker, 1973)

Zec, Donald, *Sophia* (London, W. H. Allen, 1975)

Zhukov, Marshal, *The Memoirs of Marshal Zhukov* (London, Jonathan Cape, 1971)

Radio

BBC War Report, April–May 1945

Journals

War, Literature & the Arts. US Air Force Academy, Colorado Springs

Stars and Stripes, 29 April 1945

Time Magazine, May 7, 1945

Irish Studies in International Affairs, Vol. 3, No. 1, 1989

Spiegelonline International, 29 April 2005

Archives

Churchill Archives Centre, Churchill College, Cambridge
RAF Museum, Hendon
University of Pennsylvania Library
Imperial War Museum, London, Department of Documents:
  Bar-Chaim, R. (02/27/1)
  Blackman, Miss M. J. (01/19/1)
  Blackman, W. A. (99/85/1)
  Garbasz-Zimet, Mrs S. (97/28/1)
  Gonin, Lt-Colonel M. W. (85/38/1)
  Gow, Sir Michael (Con Shelf)
  Grunfeld, B. (99/3/1)
  Hargrave, Dr M. J. (76/74/1)
  Herzberg, A. J. (95/35/1)
  Horwell, A. R. (91/21/1)
  Kidd, H. B. (94/26/1)
  McFarlane, Miss J. (99/86/1)
  Stern, P. G. (85/29/1)
  Walker, George (84/2/1)

INDEX